"The old world is coll⸻ ⸻ ⸻ ⸻ communism is in the air. *Organizing for Autonomy* asks us to breathe deeply of that air, to stand shoulder-to-shoulder with our comrades, and to plot the way forward together. Its cohesive analysis and ambitious vision point toward the North Star and offer a militant strategy for how to get going. It is not a roadmap to the new world, but no matter. After all, communism is not the destination, it is the path itself." —Geo Maher (George Ciccariello-Maher), author of *Spirals of Revolt* and *Decolonizing Dialectics*

"CounterPower offers a deeply thoughtful analysis that is rooted in people's everyday struggles to end oppression. At a time when the criminal failures of capitalism endanger the entire planet, *Organizing for Autonomy* is rich with revolutionary possibility." —Barbara Smith, cofounder of the Combahee River Collective and Kitchen Table: Women of Color Press

"Capitalism got us into this mess. *Organizing for Autonomy* advances the conversation about how we can achieve a different—and better—way of living, in a world without bosses." —Steve Wright, author of *Storming Heaven: Class Composition and Struggle in Italian Autonomist Marxism*

"In the new phase of history, and of struggles, which is opening up now, it's essential to keep alive the link with the history of the Left, and to sum this up critically as a guide to future practice. *Organizing for Autonomy* is a great contribution to that task. That the capitalist system and its political apparatus are degenerate and parasitic, founded on a racist-imperialist infrastructure, has been true for a long time. But now, suddenly the COVID-19 crisis and racist killings have exposed these realities in exceptional and unprecedented ways. It's clear that the people's only means of survival is to generate new structures of militance and of care, emerging from within communities themselves, which can become modules of a just social order. The tools proposed in these pages—notably social investigations—are exactly the methods which can be explored in this historic cause. CounterPower offer us an important and extremely topical publication to further our struggle." —Robert Biel, author of *The New Imperialism* and *The Entropy of Capitalism*

Organizing for Autonomy

History, Theory, and Strategy for Collective Liberation

CounterPower

To the communards: past, present, future.

Acknowledgements

This book is the collective product of the cognitive, emotional, and communicative labor of many comrades, spanning nearly a decade of political praxis.

CONTENTS

Introduction

The Specter That Haunts Us

How can we get free? How can we free ourselves, our communities, our environments, our societies? And what will this freedom look like? While the present moment holds incredible possibilities to organize for our collective liberation, there are powerful forces readily willing and able to summon all available weapons of repression to contain and suppress revolutionary movements. Our present civilization, argued Herbert Marcuse, always must defend itself "against the specter of a world which could be free."[1] It is our task to give this specter an earthly form.

The question of freedom is central to all revolutionary movements. It is at the root of everyday struggles against white supremacist colonialism, heteropatriarchy, capitalism, the authoritarian state, and every other form of systemic oppression. But we have to ask, again, what will freedom look like? Often, the realities we each face constrain the ways we can answer this question, so we ask it in pieces: How do we provide for each other? How do we protect, nurture, care, love, and create? How do we liberate ourselves from the hardships of enclosure, exploitation, and dependency that are imposed on our minds, bodies, communities, and environments? How do we free our sense of freedom, so that it is not a set of individual and extractive privileges, but is instead the grounding for a communal form of abundance?

1. Herbert Marcuse, *Eros and Civilization: A Philosophical Inquiry into Freud* (New York: Vintage Books, 1962), 85.

Where we stand today is the result of centuries of struggle between forces of liberation and forces of domination. Governments and corporations pour toxins into bodies, minds, and environments, creating an unsustainable world of individualism, disposability, and extraction that festers with antiblack, heteropatriarchal, and settler-colonial violence. The powers that structure our "civilization" have brought the entire planetary system to the precipice of ecological collapse, while at the same time preparing the ground for resurgent forms of fascism that exploit ordinary people's frustrations by fragmenting the oppressed with xenophobic and antiblack sentiments. Imperialism—justified under the guise of multiculturalism and sustainable development—now increasingly must contend with forms of right-wing nationalism and white supremacy promoting a vision of the future in which outsiders of any sort are walled off by frightened and insecure attempts to recreate a mythic past of white, heteropatriarchal bliss.

As an individual, it can seem almost impossible to confront such massive forces of global devastation and reactionary violence. In isolation from one another, as individualized consumers, workers, voters, and families, it is easy for avoidance and apathy to close in and keep us from seeing that, together, side-by-side, we can turn our faces toward the storm.

"Revolutions are made not to get more (or, of course, less) of what we already have," André Gorz reminds us, "but to get something altogether different which will put an end to conditions that are felt to be unbearable."[2] The aim of social revolution is to succeed in creating *a different way of life*, one that can liberate the immense creative potential of a humanity united in its diversity. Social revolution aims to nurture new sensibilities about how life can and should be lived, and to establish the conditions for their flourishing. Social revolution is not just seizing power or tearing down

2. André Gorz, *Socialism and Revolution* (London: Allen Lane, 1975), 11.

the system, it is a passage between worlds.[3] We need analyses, visions, and strategies to guide us from this world to the next, based on an honest assessment of the material realities we face. Our values—freedom, equality, autonomy, solidarity—and the histories of struggle past and present, can help us chart a path toward liberation.

Guerrilla Theory

This book is for those interested in building a movement for social revolution. The aim of this book is to outline a theoretical system that can guide revolutionary action today and tomorrow. Past and present revolutionary struggles have overthrown oppressive states, elevated living standards, built the power of the people, and gifted the world hope and inspiration. However, these struggles have faced immense opposition in their attempts to overthrow and abolish an oppressive social system. Whatever their shortcomings, there remain many important lessons to learn from our movement ancestors to broaden our visions and strategies of liberation and to develop a revolutionary practice capable of liberating all oppressed people, from the workplace to the household.

In this book, we explore ways to ground revolutionary practice in diverse and intra-connected bodies of knowledge that cross disciplinary boundaries. We seek to learn from expertise that emerges from a wide range of standpoints, practices, and everyday struggles. We engage in what the intersectional feminist tradition has termed *guerrilla readings* of revolutionary theories and histories, "mining them for strategic openings of thought and action."[4] The novelty of this project is not in the originality of our claims, but our attempt to assemble together and put into productive dialogue materials that too often remain disconnected. According to the Russian revolutionary Alexander Bogdanov, bourgeois

3. Georges Fontenis, "Manifesto of Libertarian Communism (1953)," The Anarchist Library, https://theanarchistlibrary.org/library/georges-fontenis-manifesto-of-libertarian-communism.pdf/.

4. Ashley J. Bohrer, *Marxism and Intersectionality: Race, Gender, Class and Sexuality under Contemporary Capitalism* (New York: Columbia University Press, 2020), 13.

society divides learning "into separate specializations, each one weighted down by a mass of trivialities and subtleties, which require nearly a whole human lifetime to comprehend. Scholars themselves poorly understand each other, as each one does not see beyond their own specialization."[5] Bogdanov recognized that the revolutionary left of his day had a tendency to reproduce this disciplinary specialization in its own praxis.

We have written this book against the grain of the disciplinary and theoretical specialization that Bogdanov critiques. Too often in our own time, we maintain rigid divisions based on theoretical tradition or sector of struggle that can lead to mutual incomprehension between comrades. Our theoretical project is an attempt to produce what Bogdanov termed *tektology*: a general organizational science aiming to systematize living experience.[6] For Bogdanov, the proletariat required scientific theories to inform its revolutionary practice, and knowledge of historical practice to inform its revolutionary theories. This demanded more than just producing accessible expositions of scientific knowledge that ultimately reproduced disciplinary separations. Rather, the proletarian revolution was tasked with "systematizing afresh the content of various fields of acquired scientific experience and overcoming not only the specific terminology of the specialized fields, but also the division into disciplines itself, in order to present the available scientific knowledge in an integrated and systematic form."[7]

In this text, we attempt to reassemble Marxist critiques of capitalist political economy, anarchist critiques of authoritarianism, Indigenous and decolonial critiques of race and nation, queer, trans, and feminist critiques of gendered social reproduction, and ecological critiques of human/nature dualism, each conceived as a complementary

5. Alexander Bogdanov, "Socialism in the Present Day (1911)," Libcom (June 4, 2015), https://libcom.org/library/socialism-present-day-alexander-bogdanov/.

6. The word "tektology" is taken from the Greek word *tekton* meaning "builder."

7. James D. White, *Red Hamlet: The Life and Ideas of Alexander Bogdanov* (Leiden: Brill, 2019), 271–272.

element of an integral whole we refer to as the imperialist world-system.

In the spirit of Bogdanov's tektology, we are less concerned with writing "new" communist theory than we are with *hacking* and *repurposing* accumulated historical experiences and inherited theoretical concepts in order to furnish new tools and weapons adequate to tackling the contradictions of our time.[8] We hope this project can open a generous and generative dialogue among revolutionaries that can break down disciplinary barriers currently reproduced within our diverse ranks, contributing to a collective reimagining of self-emancipation in the twenty-first century by grounding communist praxis on a more holistic basis.

From Counterpower to Communism

This book is the product of years of collective labor by the members of CounterPower, a communist political organization based in the United States. It reflects theories that have emerged from synthesizing different revolutionary perspectives and lessons learned through direct participation in grassroots social struggles. It has been a challenging process to develop a political document that synthesizes the multiplicity of experiences of several generations of militants. Massimiliano Tomba captures this challenge well:

> As any activist well knows, writing a manifesto, declaration, or political document is always a collective endeavor. There are different drafts, sentences cut out and paragraphs added. A declaration is a battlefield on which different positions temporarily converge. For each of them, there correspond not only proper names of people but also, and above all, social forces. The author of a declaration, if and when one can speak of a single author, is only the pen in which tensions, conflicts, agreements, and disagreements converge.[9]

8. McKenzie Wark, *Molecular Red: Theory for the Anthropocene* (London: Verso, 2016), 13.
9. Massimiliano Tomba, *Insurgent Universality: An Alternative Legacy of Modernity* (New York: Oxford University Press, 2019), 1–2.

Our group came together around a politics of collective liberation that aims to unite the best of various traditions of revolutionary struggle, encompassing Marxism, queer and trans feminism, Indigenous and decolonial liberation, social ecology, and social anarchism. We use the terms "socialism" and "communism" interchangeably to describe our vision of a free society. The social revolution is most certainly a complex and protracted *process,* but not one that can be conceptualized as a rigid progression through stages, such as imagined by twentieth-century revolutionaries who adopted a two-stage conception of communist social revolution—in which "socialism" is a lower, state-centric stage characterized by the persistence of classes and "communism" is a higher, stateless stage characterized by full and free development. Here we agree with Karl Korsch, who argued that this formulation tended to overestimate the role of the state as an instrument of revolution and mystified revolutionary struggle by identifying "the development of the capitalist economy with the social revolution of the working class."[10] In other words, the pursuit of socialism as an intermediary stage allowed revolutionaries to focus their efforts on seizing control over the prevailing system, while often leaving efforts to imagine and realize a thoroughgoing transformation of social life and the institutions supporting it to an indefinitely postponed communism that might never actually arrive.[11] To avoid confusion in this text, we primarily use the word "communism" to describe our emancipatory vision, emphasizing the centrality of communality, the formation of a commune of communes, and practices of communization, or the active construction of communal relations of free association within the revolutionary struggle itself.

That said, there are many other terms that capture

---

10. Karl Korsch, "Ten Theses on Marxism Today (1950)," Marxists Internet Archive, https://www.marxists.org/archive/korsch/1950/ten-theses.htm/.

11. Bue Rübner Hansen, "Surplus Population, Social Reproduction, and the Problem of Class Formation," *Viewpoint Magazine,* October 31, 2015, https://www.viewpointmag.com/2015/10/31/surplus-population-social-reproduction-and-the-problem-of-class-formation/.

elements of our vision—words like decolonial, indigenist, queer, feminist, anti-authoritarian, ecological, democratic, and internationalist. Depending upon context, either "socialism" or "communism" conjoined with any one or more of these adjectives describes our vision of a free society. In the end, we see "communism without adjectives" as a vision predicated upon an *insurgent universality*, described by Asad Haider as "a maxim that calls unconditionally for the freedom of those who are not like us."[12] The classic Marxist mantra, that the condition for the free development of each is the free development of all, can only be realized as autonomy within solidarity.

Outline of the Book

In Chapter 1: The Weapon of Theory, we explore the question of a collective revolutionary subject formed on the basis of unity in diversity; provide some methodological tools for conducting militant social investigations to assist the formation of this subject; outline the partisan social science that guides our project; and elaborate a synthesis of Marxism, systems theory, and new materialism in order to arrive at a conceptual framework for conducting partisan social science. This conceptual framework integrates the scientific concepts of "complementarity" and "holism," recognizing the dynamic entanglement of kinship, economics, politics, communities, technics, and ecologies in the historical development of social systems. Armed with this conceptual framework, we elaborate a method of "militant social investigation" as a mode of scientific praxis for communist partisans.

In Chapter 2: Imperialism and Revolution, we provide a macro-analysis of "imperialism," which we understand as a "world-system" built upon the interlocking and intra-acting subsystems of heteropatriarchy, capitalism, colonialism, and

12. Asad Haider, *Mistaken Identity: Race and Class in the Age of Trump* (New York: Verso, 2018), 109.

the state, and the prospects for the emergence of a revolutionary movement capable of overthrowing and abolishing this system.

Chapter 3: Envisioning the Commune outlines a communist alternative grounded in the themes of "abolition," "communism at point zero," "commons," and "communal administration and coordination." It details some potential features of the "territorial commune," or the envisioned social formation we identify as the historical objective of revolutionary movements past and present in transition to a classless, stateless society, or "world commune."

In Chapter 4: Building the Commune, we explore the organizational forms that are likely to emerge in the course of a protracted revolutionary struggle, and a possible strategic trajectory for the communist movement. In particular, we explore the forms of "organized autonomy" likely to emerge from a revolutionary process, including organs of counterpower (such as autonomous assemblies, councils, and action committees), people's defense organizations, and parties of autonomy, as well as how these disparate forms could come together as a united front, ultimately articulating a system of counterpower that can contend with the imperialist system for territorial sovereignty.

We use the first-person plural throughout this book. "We"—as partisans of a communist movement—are aware of the complexities of words, and how they can be weaponized to exclude or simplify complex subjectivities. However, our organization believes it is important to embrace the cooperative practice of "being with," as opposed to "othering" through conceptual and theoretical abstractions. We are not outside or above the various social relations we critique: *we* are within them, and our language is an attempt to reflect this immanence. It is our hope that someday soon, "we" will refer to the unity in diversity of our movement and point to new worlds that embody autonomy within solidarity. For now, however, it refers to *the we that strive to be.*

1

The Weapon of Theory

1.1: Power to the People

Our communist politics is grounded by a process of militant research, whose goal is to assist in the formation of a collective revolutionary subject. To be revolutionary, this subject must have the capacity to overthrow and abolish all forms of oppression and be capable of constructing a communal social system. The communist movement has historically identified the global working class, or *proletariat,* as the subject capable of accomplishing this task. Capitalism creates this class by dispossessing masses of people of all independent means of existence. This class owns nothing but its capacity to work (or its labor-power). From the standpoint of the proletariat, we are compelled to sell our labor-power to the capitalist class in exchange for a wage in order to survive.

The worker occupies a uniquely strategic position within the capitalist world-economy: capital depends upon the exploitation of labor-power and the indirect social cooperation of our class in order to produce and circulate commodities. Organized autonomously at the point of production, the worker can break the power of capital and the state, seize the means of social (re)production, and reorganize society to meet human needs directly. The victory of the world proletariat can herald our self-abolition as a class and indeed the end of all class hierarchies.

However, the proletariat is internally stratified into several modes of life, each with their own distinct standpoint.[1] Workers, the unemployed and those rendered unemployable, people dependent upon wage-earners, people only partially dependent upon wages for their survival, people earning wages in illicit and unsanctioned markets, people working for themselves but beholden to a capitalist market that offers only exploitatively low prices; there are many different ways that actual people entangled within the capitalist world-economy might still bring them into the general orbit of what we consider to be the proletariat. In order to bring these various social groups together as a collective revolutionary subject, processes of political recomposition are required which recognize, for example, the racialized and gendered character of class exploitation.

Yet even the unification of the many proletarian standpoints into an autonomous social class—no small accomplishment!—does not address the multiple struggles for liberation emanating from indigenist, decolonial, antiracist, feminist, democratic, and ecological movements. This is why we need a holistic materialist framework for militant research: by recognizing the complex intra-actions among multiple spheres of social activity, we not only deepen our understanding of the racialized and gendered character of class exploitation, but also the autonomy of subjectivities emanating from non-economic forms of social activity. The system we face is a system not only of class exploitation, but also heteropatriarchal, colonial, and authoritarian oppression, and the intra-action of these component parts constitutes a complex whole that we call the imperialist world-system. In order to overthrow and abolish this world-system, our movement must fight for the liberation of *all* oppressed people. We need to build a communist movement of movements, capable of overcoming

1. Bue Rübner Hansen, "Surplus Population, Social Reproduction, and the Problem of Class Formation," *Viewpoint Magazine*, October 31, 2015, https://www. viewpointmag.com/2015/10/31/surplus-population-social-reproduction-and-the-problem-of-class-formation/.

fragmentation by unifying multiple fronts of struggle on the basis of autonomy within solidarity.[2]

The communist movement faces a condition of fragmentation. There exists a multitude of revolutionary subjectivities whose forms of struggle confront imperialism from different standpoints, but often in isolation. This "multitude" can be defined as "a *plurality which persists as such.*"[3] This plurality consists of the global working class in all its diversity. However, it exceeds the proletarian class struggle, as it also includes what we term the *popular social groups.* These social groups are "popular" in the sense that they form an integral part of an emergent revolutionary people. Emerging from hundreds of microrevolutions, the popular social groups include the autonomous liberation struggles waged by Black, Indigenous, Latinx, and Asian peoples and nations, migrants, prisoners, queer people, trans people, women, disabled people, elders, youth, and students.[4] While overwhelmingly proletarian in their class composition, the popular social groups exercise forms of subjectivity challenging one or more of the central organizing principles of the imperialist world-system from their particular standpoints.

Through the successful articulation of common interests and a common world-making project, *a revolutionary people* emerges from this multitude of proletarian and popular social groups. Marta Harnecker emphasizes that a revolutionary people "includes not only those who could be called impoverished from a socioeconomic point of view, but also those who are impoverished in their subjectivity."[5] It is the solidarity of this multitude of autonomous liberation struggles—from Indigenous self-determination to Black liberation, transfeminism to proletarian autonomy—that defines a revolutionary people. Thus, the people form a collective revolutionary subject when it achieves explicit

2. J. Moufawad-Paul, *Continuity and Rupture: Philosophy in the Maoist Terrain* (Winchester, UK: Zero Books, 2016), 210–211.

3. Paolo Virno, *A Grammar of the Multitude* (Los Angeles: Semiotext(e), 2004), 21.

4. Dario Azzellini, *Communes and Workers' Control in Venezuela: Building 21st Century Socialism from Below* (Leiden: Brill, 2017), 27.

5. Marta Harnecker, *Rebuilding the Left* (London: Zed Books, 2007), 31.

consciousness of itself as a "social bloc of the oppressed," having internalized and synthesized demands arising from all proletarian and popular fronts of struggle.[6] The category of "social bloc" is central, for it embodies a whole in which contradictions and struggles persist among its parts.

As a collective revolutionary subject, the people *exceeds* the class category of the proletariat, linking itself to indigenist, decolonial, antiracist, feminist, democratic, and ecological struggles. Yet to make systemic change, these struggles need to connect with the liberation struggle of the proletariat. The development of a collective revolutionary subject from a multitude of revolutionary subjectivities is a dialectical process. When the autonomous liberation struggles of the popular social groups successfully converge with the autonomous liberation struggle of the proletariat in an alternative world-making project, then we can say with confidence that a revolutionary people has emerged.

Juan Barreto defines a revolutionary people as "a multitude in movement."[7] Far from homogenizing this multitude, the unity of a revolutionary people is fundamentally heterogeneous and constituted through struggle.[8] According to George Ciccariello-Maher, this heterogeneous subject is united "through dialogue and translation" as it envisions a world beyond the existing imperialist world-system and "towards a deferred universal whose only parameters are to be glimpsed in the demands of the oppressed and excluded."[9] It is in this sense that we raise the slogan: "power to the people!"

1.2: Partisan Social Science

The word "radical" comes from the Latin word *radix,* meaning "root." According to Karl Marx, "to be radical is to grasp

6. Enrique Dussel, *Twenty Theses on Politics* (Durham, NC: Duke University Press, 2008), 75.

7. Juan Barreto, "Multitud en movimiento," *Aporrea*, October 30, 2014, https://www.aporrea.org/actualidad/a197491.html/.

8. Azzellini, *Communes and Workers' Control in Venezuela*, 29.

9. George Ciccariello-Maher, *Decolonizing Dialectics* (Durham: Duke University Press, 2017), 132.

the root of the matter."[10] Social science can help us identify, understand, and transform the root causes of oppression. One way to enter into communist politics is by using social investigation to identify alternative modes of world-making, and to assess strategic locations within the dominant social system where proletarian and popular struggles can resist oppression, build counterpower, and win collective liberation. In fact, the research process itself can play an integral part in building these forms of organized autonomy. Our approach to the study and transformation of society looks to numerous traditions of militant social investigations into material realities that are conducted through direct participation in social struggles. We hope to avoid falling into cold and detached forms of academic observation, as well as the optimistic but at times just as detached wishful thinking of unsubstantiated idealism. Instead, we make every effort to engage with the world as it is and as we experience it, in order to transform it into what it can and should become: "a world in which many worlds fit."[11]

Marx advised revolutionaries to commit to a scientific understanding of the systemic causes of oppression. However, to claim the mantle of science need not require one to be rigid and mechanistic, nor to provide "the one true account" or an "absolute truth" that lies beyond the realm of questioning. We understand science through the lens of feminist thinkers such as Sandra Harding, as a method of inquiry that is always self-reflexively grounded both historically and geographically, and that enables the production of tentative conclusions reached through collaborative processes of knowledge co-production that always remain open to future developments. We embrace "a world of sciences" that recognizes the unique standpoints of diverse peoples and movements in shaping our collective understandings of

10. Karl Marx, *A Contribution to the Critique of Hegel's Philosophy of Right* (1843), Marxists Internet Archive, https://www.marxists.org/archive/marx/works/1843/critique-hpr/intro.htm/.
11. Subcomandante Insurgente Marcos, "Fourth Declaration of the Lacandon Jungle," in Juana Ponce de León (ed.), *Our Word is Our Weapon: Selected Writings* (New York: Seven Stories Press, 2002), 80.

social systems.[12] For our purposes, radical social science is a continuous process of inquiry, exploration, experimentation, theorization, and communication that requires accessibility so as to always remain open to popular review and critique by non-specialists. To achieve this goal, radical social science must be applicable to everyday situations, and it must pay attention to complex social dynamics including gender, sexuality, race, nationality, ethnicity, language, religion, spirituality, class, ability, health, age, governance, citizenship, territory, art, culture, technology, science, ecology, and so on.[13]

As revolutionaries who fight for a communist social system, we need a *partisan science* that is transformative of our lived social relations, and oriented towards overcoming internalized oppression and actualizing liberation through the construction of autonomous social movements. We stand against the idea that scientific theory and practice is neutral and disembodied.[14] Which side are we on? With whom do we think? We concur with Marta Malo de Molina's answer: "With workers' struggles, with dynamics of social conflict and cooperation, with women, with 'crazy people,' with children, with local communities, with subjugated groups, with initiatives of self-organization."[15] Our task is to liberate science for the people by integrating proletarian and popular social groups into the making of theory, organizing social investigations where we can learn with and from the direct participation of diverse communities in understanding and transforming material reality.

12. Sandra Harding, *Objectivity and Diversity: Another Logic of Scientific Research* (Chicago: University of Chicago Press, 2015), 120–121.

13. Arturo Escobar, *Designs for the Pluriverse: Radical Interdependence, Autonomy, and the Making of Worlds* (Durham, NC: Duke University Press, 2017), 134; Michael Albert et al., Liberating Theory (Boston: South End Press, 1986), 5.

14. Marta Malo de Molina, "Common Notions, Part 2: Institutional Analysis, Participatory Action-Research, Militant Research," European Institute for Progressive Cultural Policies (2004), http://eipcp.net/transversal/0707/malo/en.

15. Malo de Molina, "Common Notions, Part 2," 2004.

1.3: Social Investigation

By conducting *social investigations*, revolutionaries can reveal forms of everyday resistance and alternative modes of world-making. Through militant research we situate ourselves within the material relations of the present, connect different sectors of struggle, and help articulate a collective revolutionary subject from a multitude of revolutionary subjectivities.[16] The aim of the militant researcher conducting a social investigation is that of a catalyst: to establish themselves within a sector of struggle, draw out latent revolutionary aspirations, encourage their expression, synthesize them, and concentrate them in the form of political programs.[17]

Social investigation has been a part of the communist tradition from the beginning. In *The Condition of the Working Class in England* (1845), Frederick Engels analyzes the lives and struggles of predominantly Irish women and children toiling in the factories of Manchester, England.[18] In "A Worker's Inquiry" (1880), Karl Marx proposed 101 questions to inform "a serious inquiry into the position of the French working class."[19] In the *Report on an Investigation of the Peasant Movement in Hunan* (1927), Mao Zedong revealed that the class struggle waged by poor peasants in the countryside would prove integral to the Chinese Revolution, in contrast to the prevailing centering of the subjectivity of urban industrial workers.[20] In Italy during the 1960s and 1970s, radicals such as Mario Tronti, Romano Alquati, Raniero Panzieri, Sergio Bologna, and Antonio Negri—the so-called "anarcho-sociologists"—made this praxis explicit in the form of class composition analysis

16. Marcelo Hoffman, *Militant Acts: The Role of Investigations in Radical Political Struggles* (Albany: State University of New York Press, 2019), 16.

17. Kristin Ross, *May '68 and its Afterlives* (Chicago: University of Chicago Press, 2002), 110.

18. Frederick Engels, *The Condition of the Working Class in England* (Chicago: Academy Chicago Publishers, 1994).

19. Karl Marx, "A Worker's Inquiry (1880)," Marxists Internet Archive, https://www.marxists.org/archive/marx/works/1880/04/20.htm/.

20. Mao Zedong, *Report on an Investigation of the Peasant Movement in Hunan* (1927), Marxists Internet Archive, https://www.marxists.org/reference/archive/mao/selected-works/volume-1/mswv1_2.htm/.

through workers' inquiries conducted in the factories of FIAT, Olivetti, and Mirafiori.[21] Through these inquiries, the centrality of the class struggle waged by migrant workers from southern Italy became obvious to the communist movement.[22] In 1970s France, *Groupe d'information sur les prisons* (Prisons Information Group, GIP), cofounded by Michel Foucault, sought to use social investigations to solicit the self-expression, self-organization, and self-activity of prisoners against the prison system.[23] Feminist struggles historically formed consciousness-raising circles with the aim of deepening resistance to patriarchy through a process of investigation "aimed to focus on the self-awareness that women have about their own oppression, in order to promote a political reinterpretation of their own life and establish bases for its transformation."[24]

In 1996, the Bus Riders Union (BRU) in Los Angeles, California organized a campaign against transit racism as manifested by the Metropolitan Transportation Authority's (MTA) refusal to reduce overcrowding among its primarily low-income Black, Latinx, and Asian ridership. The BRU's "No Seat, No Fare" campaign called for a fare strike by bus riders. In order for the campaign to succeed, they first had to answer some questions: "Were bus riders angry about the overcrowded conditions on the buses? Were they willing to take action to remedy the problem by refusing to pay their bus fare if they didn't have a seat?"[25] Fifteen BRU organizers went out to survey approximately 850 bus riders. The results of this inquiry proved to be complex:

21. Gigi Roggero, "Notes on Framing and Re-inventing Co-research," *Ephemera* 14, no. 3 (2014): 515.

22. Steve Wright, *Storming Heaven: Class Composition and Struggle in Italian Autonomist Marxism* (London: Pluto Press, 2002).

23. Hoffman, *Militant Acts*, 103.

24. Marta Malo de Molina, "Common Notions, Part 1: Workers' Inquiry, Co-research, Consciousness-Raising," European Institute for Progressive Cultural Policies (2004), http://eipcp.net/transversal/0406/malo/en/.

25. Eric Mann, *Playbook for Progressives: 16 Qualities of the Successful Organizer* (Boston: Beacon Press, 2011), 105.

Of the approximately 850 people we spoke with, a hundred said they would refuse to pay the fare to stop the overcrowding. Two hundred said they thought the conditions on the bus were unbearable, but about half said it was immoral not to pay the fare even if they had to stand. Another hundred were ambivalent but leaning towards refusing to pay. Another hundred did not focus on the campaign but on the Bus Riders Union itself; they did not know enough about the BRU and had questions about whether they could trust our leadership. Another hundred said they supported the moral issues of the strike but were undocumented and feared retaliation and deportation. Another fifty were young people with 'strikes,' prior offenses due to California's 'Three-Strikes Law,' and were afraid of being arrested and sent back to prison for parole violation. And the remaining few hundred had no opinion.[26]

This social investigation led organizers to make a few important tactical decisions, such as making the campaign public ninety days before launching it. The decision was risky because it alerted the MTA, but the BRU's investigation indicated that there was potential support for the strike if they gave bus riders and BRU organizers sufficient time to prepare for action. This created a situation where the pressure was on the organizers to deepen their relations with bus riders and build trust in the BRU, using hundreds of one-on-one conversations to make the case for the fare strike. These efforts generated mass support, with hundreds of bus riders and bus drivers participating. The campaign ultimately won its objectives, with the MTA agreeing to purchase 2,500 new buses to reduce overcrowding.

Social investigation makes no claim to pure objectivity: the research aim is political, consciously situated within the contradictions that permeate our society. The militant researcher seeks to identify, organize, and deepen counter-systemic antagonisms to the point of revolutionary rupture. It is a form

26. Mann, *Playbook for Progressives*, 105–106.

of "hot investigation" in contrast to the forms of passive and detached "cold investigations" conducted by professional academics.[27] Social investigation takes as its starting point the assertion that the multitude of proletarian and popular social groups has the power to revolutionize society, though not under the historical-geographical conditions of our choosing. More concretely, this means "that a revolution must be made by a revolutionary people, that a revolutionary people must develop from a non-revolutionary people, and that the people change from the one to the other through their own revolutionizing practice."[28] Instead of placing itself outside a cycle of struggle, social investigation establishes itself as a catalyzing agent acting from within the struggle.

Decoding the Hidden Transcript

Every struggle has a story. Social investigation can reveal underground networks of what James C. Scott terms "infrapolitics," encompassing "a wide variety of low-profile forms of resistance that dare not speak in their own name."[29] This "hidden transcript" can serve as the basis for elaborating a counter-hegemonic narrative of oppression, resistance, and liberation.[30] Communist partisans can decode these hidden transcripts through social investigations, fostering encounters between the everyday infrapolitics of oppression and resistance and the emancipatory project of communism. In what follows, we adapt the methods of Brazilian educator Paulo Freire to the task of social investigation.

As our consciousness is often fragmented and contradictory, the goal of social investigation is to assist the formation of a more coherent revolutionary consciousness that exceeds the limits imposed by one's isolated standpoint and limited

27. Yann Moulier, "Introduction," in Antonio Negri, *The Politics of Subversion: A Manifesto for the Twenty-First Century* (Cambridge: Polity Press, 1989), 14.

28. Scott Harrison, *The Mass Line and the American Revolutionary Movement*, The Mass Line, 2018, http://massline.info/mlms/mlms.htm/.

29. James C. Scott, *Domination and the Arts of Resistance: Hidden Transcripts* (New Haven: Yale University Press, 1990), 19.

30. Scott, *Domination and the Arts of Resistance*, 14.

experiences as an individual. This can only be overcome through *collective* experiences of inquiry and struggle. The fusion of communist analysis, vision, and strategy with the everyday life of the proletarian and popular social groups is thus a *dialogic process*—a social conversation—among complementary social forces, each with diverse subjective experiences, needs, and potentials. A social investigation is not a prelude to the organization of struggle, but rather an active part and catalyst in processes of organization.[31] In other words, the formation of a program of revolutionary struggle is a collective and generative process, engaged in horizontal dialogue and informed by partisan social science. The process of social investigation has three main components, which will each be discussed in turn: initial survey, synthesis, and problematization.

The militant research collective must first determine the parameters of their research area through an *initial survey*, learning the terrain through secondary sources, excursions, and preliminary fieldwork. The research collective aims to cultivate a network of contacts who are open to participating in the social investigation and agreeable to the revolutionary process implicated within it. From this informal network emerges another tier of active participants in the research process. These participants begin to collect data about everyday life—tensions, contradictions, problems, hopes, fears, struggles, possibilities—as directly experienced by the community in question, though this data is secondary to the active participation of community members in the process of investigation itself. The area of research thus constitutes a hidden transcript or "living code" that can be effectively deciphered through the social investigation process. This coded data is collected via direct participation in the everyday life of the people through observation, conversation, attending meetings and events, frequenting key hangouts, working the same jobs, playing games and sports, and so on.[32]

31. L'Union des communistes de France marxiste-léniniste, *Le livre des paysans pauvres: 5 annés de travail maoïste dans une campagne française* (Paris: François Maspero, 1976), 92.
32. Paulo Freire, *Pedagogy of the Oppressed* (New York: Continuum, 2000), 112.

As the process proceeds beyond the initial survey, the research collective completes field reports to be aggregated, circulated, and discussed internally. The research collective should convene regular *evaluation meetings* with all participants in the social investigation at or near the area of investigation itself. Through these evaluation meetings, the research collective can present and review the findings of the initial survey—including not only historical and empirical data, but also feelings, affects, and emotions associated with various shared experiences—which constitutes a process of verification. The research collective then engages in critical assessment and summation through dialogue, integrating their research into an increasingly comprehensive picture. This prompts the next iteration of the social investigation process, *synthesis*, through which the research collective maps the core contradictions of everyday life in the research zone.

The research collective now selects one or more of these core contradictions to assemble alternative codifications that embody lived experience. These are used as tools in the consciousness-raising process of *popular decoding dialogues.* The codifications used should be familiar to the community with whom the social investigation is unfolding: *the task is for participants to analyze their own reality by decoding the hidden transcript.* By presenting a familiar scenario, the research collective facilitates a process in which individuals begin to identify with a counter-hegemonic narrative they have co-produced. Through this process, participants come to recognize the dynamics of oppression, resistance, and liberation at work in everyday life and begin—*from direct experience*—to identify constitutive elements of a revolutionary program. The research collective should record these popular decoding dialogues for later critical assessment and summation.

Now, the research collective reviews the recorded results of the popular decoding session(s) to identify and organize thematics generated by these core contradictions. These consolidated thematics form the basis upon which a program of revolutionary struggle can be synthesized with the community in question. The core contradictions and emergent program identified by the research collective should be put to use informing the ongoing work of political agitation, education, and organization conducted by communist partisans. During this time, the research collective may also take note of important thematics not addressed through the popular decoding dialogues. In line with the dialogic principle, research militants also have the right to participate in social conversations by adding additional thematics.

Rather than returning to the community with a finished program, the results of the process are presented in the form of a *problem to be solved*. Through participatory assemblies, the people participate directly in the co-production of solutions. In other words, social investigation becomes immanent to the cycle of struggle itself.[33] In this sense, we conceive of the revolutionary program as generative and immanent to the direct experience of an emergent revolutionary people. Through militant social investigation, communists embed themselves within a rising cycle of struggle, engaging in research with the multitude of proletarian and popular social groups. Social investigation aims to articulate a revolutionary people and co-produce a system of counterpower.

Social revolutions—like the system of counterpower we envision and work to build—alter a society's organizational patterns, structures, and processes, thus creating new core characteristics radically different from those of the past. What distinguishes a communist social revolution is its transformation of the core characteristics of almost every aspect of society, from what it means to be human to the institutions that structure social life.

1.4: A World of Sciences

For partisan social science, research is grounded in situations arising from multiple social locations: the household, workplace, school, prison, or neighborhood. Our investigations

33. Freire, *Pedagogy of the Oppressed*, 123.

are meant to identify general trends, tendencies, tensions, and contradictions present in the development of a social system so that we can formulate programs of action. While social science cannot make predictions in the manner of chemistry, biology, or physics, it can help us explain relationships, envision possibilities, delineate trends, and identify potential trajectories, all in ways that broaden our perspective and counteract internalized biases that might otherwise limit our scope of action.[34] The goal is to build towards what Sandra Harding calls *strong objectivity*, where research is not based on detached observation, but is instead conducted by active participants embedded in a vibrant world.[35] By embracing "a world of sciences," diverse conceptual frameworks and research methodologies can be united in the service of communist social revolution, leaving us with the task of "strategizing how to maximize and harmonize the scientific and political benefits of multiple scientific questions, conceptualized from multiple social perspectives, with a multiplicity of useful methods."[36]

For us, this leads to the crucially important concept of *intra-action*. As theoretical physicist and feminist theorist Karen Barad explains, "We are not outside observers of the world. Neither are we simply located at particular places *in* the world; rather, we are part *of* the world in its ongoing intra-activity."[37] In contrast with the concept of inter-action, Barad insists that "intra-action recognizes that distinct agencies do not precede, but rather emerge through, their intra-action . . . *agencies are only distinct in relation to their mutual entanglement; they don't exist as individual elements.*"[38] For example, race and class do not inter-act as two distinct and separable forms of oppression, they intra-act as mutually constitutive forms of oppression that can only be understood

34. Albert et al., *Liberating Theory*, 5.
35. Harding, *Objectivity and Diversity*, 31–39.
36. Harding, *Objectivity and Diversity*, 50.
37. Karen Barad, *Meeting the Universe Halfway: Quantum Physics and the Entanglement of Matter and Meaning* (Durham, NC: Duke University Press, 2007), 184.
38. Barad, *Meeting the Universe Halfway*, 33.

through, not despite, their historical-geographical entanglement. Here we see our efforts aligned with attempts to synthesize revolutionary Marxism with intersectional social theory.[39] We choose instead the concept of intra-action to emphasize that we do not see isolated and distinct phenomena (such as race and class) intersecting with one another while still maintaining their separate coherence. Instead, approaching partisan social science through the lens of intra-action requires us to remain attentive to the complexity of social systems, to the entangled and co-constituting spheres of social activity that shape relations of oppression and resistance and which can never actually or fully be pried apart from one another. It follows for us that politically, a collective revolutionary subject will similarly have to emerge from the mutual entanglement of multiple social antagonisms and liberation struggles. Communist theory and practice must account for this complexity.

Against Reductionism

We approach partisan social science through the lens of intra-action and the construction of a world of sciences as a rejection of otherwise prevalent tendencies toward reductionism in both social scientific and revolutionary thought. It is common to find thinkers who confidently assert that one sphere of social activity plays a primary role in the understanding of historical causality. Such conceptual frameworks reduce the complexity of the world to a single dimension, often to the exclusion of many other social forces that are deemed less essential. It becomes impossible to assess the intra-action of various constituent forces, because within a reductionist framework, all things must ultimately be explained via reference to one singular aspect of social life. Bogdanov argued that reductionist conceptual frameworks are themselves reflections of a society fragmented by hierarchical divisions of labor; just as each worker must

39. See: Bohrer, *Marxism and Intersectionality.*

only concern themselves with one isolated task, each thinker within what we now might call the "edu-factory" is similarly only concerned with one theoretical or disciplinary set of explanatory tools.[40] When all you have is a hammer, the whole world starts to look like a bunch of nails. The danger here is that through such specialization, potential comrades become mutually incomprehensible to one another and even pitted against one another in competition to demonstrate that *their* conceptual framework is the most accurate or effective.[41] Knowledge systems become fragmented by an internally competitive field (a war of sciences), as opposed to united through a collective liberation struggle (a world of sciences).

Throughout the history of radical social science, and still today, *economic reductionism* is an important example of such a paradigm, basing itself upon a very narrow reading and interpretation of Karl Marx and Frederick Engels.[42] This mode of radical analysis views every aspect of contemporary social life as ultimately reducible to the struggle between labor and capital, understood as a struggle taking place on the factory floor—or wherever workers are being exploited as wage labor. It reduces the complex social conditions of the proletariat to a generic abstraction of the industrial worker, excluding the informal, unpaid, and often still exploitative forms of work and care that make the formal waged sector possible in the first place. Spaces of social reproduction, settler-colonial oppression beyond wage labor (including the dispossession of Indigenous communities, historic and ongoing forms of enslavement, and virulent forms of anti-blacknesss), the partitioning of the world into metropolitan centers and impoverished peripheries, and other forms of violence—including ecological devastation—are all reduced to a less-essential "level" of analysis. As David Harvey

40. Edu-Factory Collective (ed.), *Toward a Global Autonomous University: Cognitive Labor, The Production of Knowledge, and Exodus from the Education Factory* (New York: Autonomedia, 2009).

41. White, *Red Hamlet*, 287.

42. Tatiana Cozzarelli, "Class Reductionism is Real, and It's Coming from the Jacobin Wing of the DSA," *Left Voices*, June 16, 2020, https://www.leftvoice.org/class-reductionism-is-real-and-its-coming-from-the-jacobin-wing-of-the-dsa/.

observes, this approach fails to develop an adequate praxis of liberation, produces rigid and monotonous institutional arrangements, and "[freezes] the possibility to explore new social relations and mental conceptions."[43] Not only does this mode of analysis obstruct broader systemic understanding, it also obscures its analytical target: class composition and class struggle. Instead of clarifying material reality, reductionist conceptual frameworks actually mystify things, denying the complexity of social, psychological, and ecological relations within which politics happen and people make their world.

Reductionist conceptual frameworks generally share a tendency to dissect complex systems into discrete pieces, examining fragments instead of the intra-activity of the whole.[44] Though reductionist paradigms are distinguished from each other by the selection of different defining or driving features of society, their basic conceptual framework is generally the same. Each typically exaggerates the influence of its favored sphere of social activity as a motor force in historical causality, underestimates the influence of other spheres, and largely ignores the material reality that every sphere of social activity is itself critically influenced by multiple sources of social definition.

Instead, to co-produce concrete knowledge of our material reality that can lend itself to revolutionary transformation, we look to feminist, decolonial, and Marxist traditions which explicitly break with these forms of reductionism. Only then can we begin to envision and create "a world in which many worlds fit."[45]

Matter in Motion

Our approach to radical social science recognizes *unity in diversity* as a complement to a communist politics of *autonomy within solidarity*. In order to assemble a partisan social science that militates against reductionist fragmentation, we

43. David Harvey, *The Enigma of Capital and the Crises of Capitalism* (Oxford: Oxford University Press, 2011), 136.
44. Albert et al., *Liberating Theory*, 8.
45. Subcomandante Insurgente Marcos, "Fourth Declaration of the Lacandon Jungle," 80.

turn to thinkers such as Karen Barad, who help us apply the lessons of new materialism to a renewed conception of Marxism as historical-geographical materialism. For Marx and Engels, materialism begins with the premise that *social being* precedes *social consciousness*.[46] Matter conditions thought, thought shapes social activity, and social activity transforms matter, in a spiral process of continuous feedback.

Matter refers to the materiality of the world, but Barad asks us to consider this materiality in its most expansive and dynamic sense. Matter is never static, she argues. It is "substance in its intra-active becoming—not a thing, but a doing, a congealing of agency."[47] For Barad, this intra-activity of substance encompasses the organic and inorganic, the human and nonhuman. Matter is therefore "a dynamic and shifting entanglement of relations, rather than a property of things."[48] Human agency—our capacity to act—is situated within a particular material context. One's conceptual framework is an apparatus for making a "cut" in this material fabric. If the framework is changed, so too is the "cut," and thus the identification of causal logics, patterns of organization, structures, processes, and prospective agents of change.[49]

Proceeding from this basis, we see social formations as complex, open systems entangled with technological infrastructures and in metabolic relation with our planetary geosphere and biosphere.[50] Partisan social science must account for: (a) humans as fundamentally social beings, existing within specific historical and geographical social systems, and (b) social systems as inseparable from broader ecological systems in which they are embedded in complex metabolic relations with the more-than-human world and its expansive web of life. Social systems generate a series of

46. Karl Marx and Frederick Engels, *The German Ideology* (New York: International Publishers, 2007), 51.

47. Barad, *Meeting the Universe Halfway*, 210.

48. Barad, *Meeting the Universe Halfway*, 224.

49. Barad, *Meeting the Universe Halfway*, 175.

50. Albert et al., *Liberating Theory*; Robin Hahnel, *The ABCs of Political Economy: A Modern Approach* (London: Pluto Press, 2002).

integrated circuits of complex relational networks, structures, and processes, in which various social determinations, categories, and role requirements constitute elements of a unified whole (even if this whole is in a constant state of flux). These constituent parts intra-act to produce a web of mutual entanglements that can be understood as "a multilayered structure of living systems nesting within other systems—networks within networks."[51]

Historical-geographical materialism looks to the world as a complex entanglement of relations, between people, between people and other living beings, between other living things and non-living things. Everything only exists in relation to all that it intra-acts with; you are as much a being-in-relation to your ancestors as you are to your boss or your lover. You are as much in relation to your coffee mug as you are to whatever liquid you are drinking out of the mug as you are to the trillions of microorganisms living in and on your body. As Erik Swyngedouw writes, behind the flat world of everyday "things" and their appearances is a complex world of material processes and living experience:

> The coffee I sip in the morning reflects and embodies relations between peasants and landowners, between merchants and producers, shippers and bankers, wholesalers and retailers, etc. These relations and processes are more important in terms of understanding the objects/phenomena than the characteristics of things/phenomena themselves. 'Coffee' is then no longer just coffee, but also a whole host of other things that are part and parcel of what constitutes 'coffee' as coffee. The characteristics of coffee as a thing can only give me clues to what is hidden underneath. The excavation of these relational processes is at the heart of historical-geographical materialist inquiry. If I were to reconstruct the myriad social relations through which coffee becomes the liquid I drink, I would uncover a historical geography of the world that would simultaneously provide powerful insights into the many

51. Fritjof Capra and Pier Luigi Luisi, *The Systems View of Life: A Unifying Vision* (Cambridge: Cambridge University Press, 2018), 306.

mechanisms of economic exploitation, social domination, profit-making, uneven development, ecological transformation, and the like.[52]

To know the world is to be of the world and its processes of intra-active becoming.

The framework of *complementary holism,* developed by Michael Albert and Robin Hahnel, offers another way to articulate this approach.[53] In its most basic articulation, complementary holism recognizes that social systems have multiple spheres of activity (encompassing kinship, community, economy, polity, technics, and ecology), which are necessary for the ongoing reproduction of human social life. Approaching this complex whole from the materialist perspective outlined above, we can analyze it as an assemblage of intra-acting parts. Each part actively constitutes the broader system through "reciprocally conditioning relationships between part and part and between part and whole."[54] The constitutive parts of this dynamic whole intra-actively co-define one another, "even though each appears often to have an independent and even contrary existence."[55]

While in theory our material realities are knowable, they may have aspects that are irreducible to one another, requiring a multiplicity of diverse approaches for a maximally grounded materialist understanding. Such a recognition places a strong emphasis on *standpoint,* or the perspective that those with direct experiences internal to particular social relations have insights that any one scientific researcher may not (i.e., local knowledge). Standpoints are not to be misunderstood

52. Erik Swyngedouw, "The Marxian Alternative: Historical-Geographical Materialism and the Political Economy of Capitalism," in Eric Sheppard and Trevor J. Barnes (eds.), *A Companion to Economic Geography* (Malden, MA: Blackwell Publishing, 2000), 45.

53. Michael Albert and Robin Hahnel, *Unorthodox Marxism* (Boston: South End Press, 1978); *Marxism and Socialist Theory* (Boston: South End Press, 1981); Michael Albert, Holly Sklar, Leslie Cagan, Noam Chomsky, Robin Hahnel, Mel King, and Lydia Sargent, *Liberating Theory* (Boston: South End Press, 1986).

54. David Baronov, "The Analytical-Holistic Divide Within World-System Analysis," in Roberto Patricio Korzeniewicz ed., *The World-System as Unit of Analysis: Past Contributions and Future Advances* (New York: Routledge, 2017), 8.

55. Albert et al., *Liberating Theory,* 12.

as fragmented or isolated perspectives to choose between, but as myriad "cuts" into the relational fabric of the world, which can themselves be woven into a complex whole. For example, the critique of capitalism could take the standpoint of capital, with the aim of developing a critique of how capitalism works to justify its expansionary logic, or how the logic of profit maximization and worker exploitation is logically coherent within and through capital's law of value. Even here, the standpoint of financial capital (investment bankers) might be different than the standpoint of real estate capital (landlords) or innovation capital (tech entrepreneurs). Alternatively, this critique could take any number of proletarian standpoints, for example: of the wage worker, the indebted student, the informal worker, the care-giver, the prisoner, the migrant, the unfree worker, etc., and it could then articulate an equally extensive repertoire of relational experiences leading towards various interlinked-yet-distinct forms of revolutionary praxis. This could perhaps encompass the direct socialization of the commons, abolitionist reimagining of social institutions, and governance by federated people's assemblies. All of these standpoints are equally material, even if they are not all revolutionary. Each is loaded with divergent political content, informed by the social antagonisms from which it arises, and understanding as many of these cuts into the social fabric as possible is necessary for communist politics to operate strategically.

In other words, we can only know together. The key to partisan social science then is to avoid any temptation to reduce science to the standpoint of a single scientist, and to recognize, integrate, and defer to insights produced from otherwise marginalized standpoints. Together, as a unity in diversity, a science of many sciences, we can develop a praxis of liberation suitable to our shared revolutionary project. In this way, partisan social science is an important tool in building "solidarity in the house of difference," and a weapon in the struggle to overthrow and abolish all forms of oppression.[56]

56. Bohrer, *Marxism and Intersectionality*, 254.

Only then can we begin to ask whether it is possible to work towards articulating the standpoint of humanity in general, developing an insurgent universality that doesn't exclude the dehumanized or collapse irrevocably diverse and divergent forces into an undifferentiated container of "inclusivity." Only then can we approach the question of what Marx called *collective labor,* in the broadest possible sense, as a world of many worlds united through creative social activity and the web of intra-actions of which we cannot but be a part. This is how we work towards a voice that can speak as a collective agent of history: "no people, no labor; no labor, no society; no society, no people."[57]

Being Human as Praxis

What does it mean to be human? Against imperialism's conception of the monohumanist Man, Jamaican novelist and social theorist Sylvia Wynter asserts that "being human is a praxis."[58] In contrast to reductionist paradigms, our conceptual framework must account for the category of "the human" as not reducible to mere biological explanation. Rather, the very category of humanity is a social construct, co-produced through histories of violence and oppression— as well as resistance and liberation—making the human as much a cut through the biological fabric of reality as it is a cut through viciously murderous efforts to establish the category of Man as an exclusionary justification for imperialist domination, particularly settler-colonial expansion and antiblack violence. We must liberate ourselves from systems of knowledge that obscure the narrative co-production of what it means to be human.

Any human social system incorporates an assemblage of people with distinct needs and desires, potentials and

57. Paul Paolucci, *Marx's Scientific Dialectics: A Methodological Treatise for a New Century* (Chicago: Haymarket Books, 2009), 85.

58. Sylvia Wynter and Katherine McKittrick, "Unparalleled Catastrophe for Our Species? Or, to Give Humanness a Different Future: Conversations," in Katherine McKittrick (ed.), *Sylvia Wynter: On Being Human as Praxis* (Durham, NC: Duke University Press, 2015), 23.

powers, personalities and behaviors.[59] People have the power to transform our social systems through collective labor in accordance with the material possibilities of a particular conjuncture. However, at present we are trapped inside a world-system that not only fails to meet basic human needs and limits human potential, but limits the potential for human agency and indeed partitions the world into the human and non-human or sub-human, the wretched of the earth. We cannot simply accept any universal sense that humanity exists independent of the history of imperialist violence that has offered some the dignity of being human even while strategically denying this same dignity to so many others. The human is itself a contested terrain, which is why Wynter asks us to consider the very act of being human as itself a form of praxis; a message we see resonant with current antiracist rebellions demanding that a white supremacist society stop allowing its racist cops and fascist vigilantes to murder Black, Indigenous, and other people of color with impunity. This most recent iteration of the Black liberation struggle asks us all to begin with a most basic and fundamental revolutionary principle: Black Lives Matter.

Humans, like all living organisms, must be analyzed within an environmental context. This context encompasses a complex entanglement of social and ecological systems. According to biologists Humberto R. Maturana and Francisco J. Varela, all living beings are characterized by the continuous process of self-production.[60] We can thus understand the category of the human as an open-ended project of co-producing bodies which are malleable in various ways, mutually entangled within material and semiotic boundaries, and ultimately inseparable from the more-than-human web of life of which we will always be a

59. Hahnel, *The ABCs of Political Economy*, 2–10.
60. Humberto R. Maturana and Francisco J. Varela, *The Tree of Knowledge: The Biological Roots of Human Understanding* (Boston: New Science Library, 1988), 43.

part.[61] This relational view of being human as praxis conceives of the body as "internally contradictory by virtue of the multiple socioecological processes that converge upon it."[62] Humans are *of* the world, "intra-actively (re)constituted as part of the world's becoming. Which is not to say that humans are the mere effect, but neither are they/we the sole cause, of the world's becoming."[63]

From here, we can approach three distinct aspects of human praxis.[64] First, humans are *social*, which means we identify and realize our needs and potentials in cooperation with others. Second, humans manifest *consciousness*, understood not as a function performed by a specific part of the brain or special neural structures, but as "an emergent property of a particular cognitive process."[65] This cognitive process is itself embedded within the web of life, co-emerging from the intra-action of an autopoietic unit (in this case, the social individual) and the socioecological environment. To be conscious is to be self-aware. Revolutionary consciousness requires a systemic understanding of one's standpoint within a social system as it relates to the many other standpoints that together shape the variegated social conditions of oppressed people. The development of such a consciousness is essential to our revolutionary project. Finally, humans manifest *creativity*, which means that in seeking to identify and realize needs and potentials today, we choose to act in ways that can change our social characteristics tomorrow. Creativity exists in many forms, from birthing, caring for, and raising a child, to planting a garden, to admiring the complex intra-actions of a forest ecosystem. It can mean painting a picture, developing a new technology, planning a rebellion, or envisioning new worlds worth living in.

---

61. Donna Haraway, *Simians, Cyborgs, and Women: The Reinvention of Nature* (New York: Routledge, 1991), 200–201; David Harvey, *Spaces of Hope* (Berkeley: University of California Press, 2000), 98.

62. Harvey, *Spaces of Hope*, 98.

63. Barad, *Meeting the Universe Halfway*, 206.

64. Hahnel, *The ABCs of Political Economy*, 1–2.

65. Capra and Luisi, *The Systems View of Life*, 265.

The actual praxis of being human is shaped by particular personality traits, skills, ideas, and attitudes that combine to form a character structure.[66] Not only are these delimited by the role requirements and expectations of prevailing social institutions, but they are also constrained at any moment by the personalities, skills, knowledge, and values that people have internalized. While character structures can be lasting, they are not permanent. Changes in social organization and structure can lead to changes in human behaviors, as well as the ways people express and orient their creativity. Domination by an oppressive social system can cultivate character structures detrimental to the realization of certain needs and potentials at both the individual and collective levels. For example, we can fail to recognize the consequences of activities chosen to fulfill immediate needs, as in the case of certain technological systems that have produced unintended path dependencies that lead towards ecological devastation and/or mass unemployment. Alienated social relations (such as those produced by heteropatriarchy, capitalism, colonialism, or the state) distort autonomous decision-making power and obscure the intrinsic collectivity of social (re)production. This is how people become estranged from the land, the products of collective labor, and the patterns of social activity co-produced by members of a society.

Oppression becomes internalized as a result of these institutional factors, enabling an attachment to oppressive social systems that forms the basis for various reactionary social phenomena, such as male chauvinism, white chauvinism, national chauvinism, settler-colonialism, consumerism, and fascism. For example, Wilhelm Reich explored these factors when researching the social function of the authoritarian family in the production of reactionary character structures appropriate for fascism.[67] He argued that the authoritarian family's rigid social conditioning and use of sexual repression socializes young people to be "good" and "adjusted" to

66. Hahnel, *The ABCs of Political Economy*, 7–9.
67. Wilhelm Reich, *The Mass Psychology of Fascism* (New York: Orgone Institute Press, 1946).

authoritarian social systems. This conditioning and repression then contains and suppresses rebellious impulses within young people so that they acclimate to what Reich refers to as "the authoritarian miniature state, the family."[68] This acclimation then conditions people to accept subsequent subordination to capital and the state later in life.

Institutional Boundary and Spheres of Social Activity

All social systems are bound by a particular set of social institutions, or complex assemblages created to meet needs and organize creative social activity in metabolic relation with complex environments. Each social institution structures a conglomeration of interconnected roles and common expectations for behavioral patterns.[69] We refer to this as an "institutional boundary" to emphasize the ways that we are "bound" by certain role requirements and behavioral expectations.[70] People express their creative autonomy within defined institutional settings that place important limitations on their options and establish patterns of expectations within which social activity occurs. Institutions are a necessary component of any social system, ensuring continuity of effort and the transmission of knowledge derived from experience.

Any social system's institutional boundary makes some individual choices easier and others harder, and therefore shapes the relative autonomy of individuals. The relevant question about social institutions is not whether we "need" them to exist, but whether a particular institution poses unnecessarily oppressive limitations. So for instance, it may be clear (to many of us at least) that society has no need for a racist and authoritarian institution such as the police, but that does not mean that we may not need other institutional forms to fulfill roles of public safety and conflict resolution through affirmative and caring approaches to community wellness, accountability,

68. Reich, The Mass Psychology of Fascism, 24.
69. Albert and Hahnel, *Marxism and Socialist Theory*, 74–75.
70. Hahnel, *The ABCs of Political Economy*, 10–13.

and de-escalation. Part of our work as partisan social scientists is to help imagine how specific institutional forms can promote the free and integral development of social individuals to the greatest extent possible, maximizing the potential for autonomy within solidarity, comradely cooperation, and a sustainable socioecological metabolism.

In addition to thinking about institutions, we must also consider distinct spheres of social activity that dynamically intra-act with each other and with institutions to organize social life.[71] We begin by identifying spheres of kinship, economy, polity, community, technics, and ecology.[72] Each of these spheres calls forth complex forms of social intra-action that lead to the development of elaborate institutional networks, structures, and processes that shape how we think, what we feel, and what we are capable of doing. Traversing the spectrum of race, class, gender, sexuality, and authority, social activity spheres generate important categories of differentiation that are critical to understanding processes of social reproduction and prospects for revolutionary social transformation. Each social activity sphere is a complementary aspect of a unified social, technological, and ecological whole.[73]

Kinship

Kinship consists of intra-actions among bodies, partners, parents, children, youth, adults, elders, and various nonhuman companion species through affective codes or norms of behavior.[74] Kinship activity revolves around sexuality, procreation, childrearing, affection, socialization, carework, education, maturation, aging, the organization of home life, and multispecies relations—all activities mediated by various forms of emotional and affective labor. The kinship sphere sets role requirements for participation

71. Harvey, *The Enigma of Capital*, 121–124.
72. Hahnel, *The ABCs of Political Economy*, 13–15; Harvey, *The Enigma of Capital*, 121–123.
73. Albert et al., *Liberating Theory*, 72–77.
74. Albert et al., *Liberating Theory*, 33; Donna Haraway, *Manifestly Haraway* (Minneapolis: University of Minnesota Press, 2016), 186–187.

in gendered and sexualized social relations and socialization processes, and it is the source of hierarchical social groups formed on the basis of gender, sexuality, age, ability, and health. Within the context of the imperialist world-system, heteropatriarchal kinship relations largely define gender and sexual norms.

Kinship encompasses *the relations of social reproduction,* without which all other spheres of social life would be impossible. Within the imperialist world-system, this includes reproduction of the labor-power of the working class through affective labor, which is often performed by women and includes housework, carework, and sex work. Kinship relations encompass all of the many activities required for the regeneration of human life and participation in society, whether that is the gendered housework necessary to reproduce labor-power for the capitalist world-economy, or the collectivized affective labor of a commune to provide the support, tools, and experiences necessary for full participation in a communist social system.

Economy

The economic sphere encompasses the social activities of production, allocation, consumption, and waste management.[75] Production includes the collective labor and means of production (land, resources, agriculture, industry, technology, scientific knowledge, etc.) that enable the creation and circulation of goods and services. It also includes *productive relations,* which govern the use of society's productive assets and the organization of the production process. Whether production is structured by global capitalist relations or by a world commune, there will be some institutional form determining how and why certain things get produced, and in what quantities. Allocation encompasses the distribution and exchange of intermediary and final goods and services that society produces, and consumption refers to the use of

75. Albert et al., *Liberating Theory,* 47–61.

these goods and services. Finally, waste management encompasses the reuse or disposal of consumed goods.

Economic activity has historically been seen as the sphere of class formation, struggle, and recomposition. Class hierarchies separate populations into antagonistic socioeconomic groups formed on the basis of a common relationship within the processes of production and the allocation and consumption of the social product. While class antagonisms between capitalists and workers remain constant in late capitalism, the structures of exploitation are constantly changing and unstable, subject to rearrangement to suit the rapidly changing needs of capital accumulation.

Polity

The polity consists of a social system's institutions of legislation, implementation, adjudication, security, and defense.[76] It is the sphere of public deliberation and decision making, encompassing constituent and constituted forms of political power, jurisprudence, and territorial sovereignty. Via the polity, territorial borders, boundaries, and frontiers are established or dissolved, and social priorities, policies, laws, and regulations are determined. In general terms, the polity functions as the regulatory framework for a social system. For bourgeois liberal polities, this often covers the official world of juridical politics, including laws and other aspects of administration and governance. The sphere of the polity encompasses *geopolitics*, the territorial borders of social formations, interstate and international relations, global resource usage and environmental protections, and the political parameters of the world-economy, as well as *biopolitics*, the disciplinary ordering, control, and regulation of the human body.

For social systems based on institutionalized hierarchies between oppressor and oppressed, the dominant social groups create and exercise *state power* to consolidate and

76. Albert et al., *Liberating Theory*, 63–64.

coordinate their hegemony on the basis of shared collective interests. This necessitates the formation of *state apparatuses*, legitimized on the basis of *state ideology*, to contain and suppress oppositional struggles emerging from the proletarian and popular social groups, redirect massive resources to ensure the material reproduction of the social system as a whole, and manufacture consent to domination.[77] The state is a necessary regulatory mechanism for imposing a social system that would otherwise collapse from the weight of its own contradictions—specifically the revolt of those who do not benefit from relations of enclosure, exploitation, and dependency. It is in the polity that the categories of state and non-state, citizen and non-citizen, public and private, have historically been formed, and it is through state bureaucracies that social groups are classified, formalized, and legitimized.

Community

The community sphere consists of groups of people who share a common historical identity and heritage.[78] This shared identity is typically derived from a common culture, which includes but is not limited to forms of language, ritual, storytelling, spirituality, art, philosophy, science, design, recreation, fashion, and cuisine. Historically, this shared identity develops among members of a community living in close geographical proximity. Today, the formation of communities also occurs with the transmission and circulation of various cultural affinities and artifacts through networks established by communication and transportation technologies. High-speed transportation grids and the Internet have both contributed to the formation of communities across great geographical distances and enable rapid translation of communications between peoples of different languages.

77. Louis Althusser, *On the Reproduction of Capitalism: Ideology and Ideological State Apparatuses* (London: Verso, 2014), 92–93.
78. Albert et al., *Liberating Theory*, 23.

Identification with one or more communities has important social implications for people's needs, desires, responsibilities, forms of ritual and celebration, and methods of accommodating to diverse institutional requirements. We do not develop community identifications *biologically*, but by adopting particular sociocultural beliefs and behaviors; communities evolve through recombinant social relations.

Technics

Technics refers to a broad sphere of technology, craft, and human know-how. It is not just instruments and devices, but the intergenerational forms of knowledge production and transmission that make the creation of any specific technologies possible in the first place. Technics must always be understood within a broader matrix of social and ecological relations. This "technosphere" encompasses the various tools, devices, machines, infrastructures, and systems of knowledge that enable humans to appropriate and alter our environments. Complex technological assemblages reflect the specific institutional structures of the social system from which they emerge, embedded within intra-acting spheres of social activity.

We can analyze how the adoption of particular technologies propels the development of systemic path dependencies, "meaning historical implementation strongly influences future development, precluding or making difficult many configurations we may find desirable."[79] Within capitalism, a classic example of a technology manifesting a systemic path dependency is the adoption of fossil fuels as an energy source, and with it the technological infrastructures that ensure collective dependency on this particular system of energy production, storage, and transmission. Such path dependencies hold populations hostage to a particular social system and its attendant hierarchies.

---

79. Jasper Bernes, "The Belly of the Revolution: Agriculture, Energy, and the Future of Communism," in Brent Ryan Bellamy and Jeff Diamanti (eds.), *Materialism and the Critique of Energy* (Chicago: MCM Publishing, 2018), 334.

Ecology

All social systems are situated within the Earth's geosphere and biosphere, which provided the initial bio-geochemical conditions for the emergence and development of life, and which are co-produced and co-evolve with the creative social activities of humans.[80] The *geosphere* consists of the lithosphere (Earth's outermost shell), hydrosphere (Earth's combined water mass), cryosphere (areas of the Earth where water is in solid form), and atmosphere (the layer of gas surrounding the Earth, held in place by high gravity and low temperature). The *biosphere* is a global ecological system—the zone of life on Earth—integrating all living beings and our mutual entanglements, including our intra-actions with non-living elements of the geosphere.[81] The preservation of the geosphere and biosphere, collective stewardship of the planet as an environmental commons, and maintenance of a sustainable socioecological metabolism are imperatives for the survival of the human species and all living matter, and are central to the ongoing stability of any human social system.

In addition to the geosphere and biosphere, it is possible to add a third ecological layer to the Earth system: the *noösphere,* encompassing the physical transformation of the geosphere and biosphere by human social activity.[82] Derived from the Greek word *nous,* meaning "mind" or "intellect," the mid-twentieth century Russian geologist and geochemist Vladimir Vernadsky postulated the emergence of human social activity as a geological force in its own right. Anticipating the more recent conceptualization of the Anthropocene, Vernadsky recognized that humanity's task was to consciously reorganize our social systems in order to establish a sustainable socioecological metabolism. In an era of anthropogenic

80. Vladimir I. Vernadsky, *The Biosphere* (New York: Copernicus Books, 1998).

81. Vladimir I. Vernadsky, "The Biosphere and the Noösphere," *American Scientist* 33, no. 1 (January 1945).

82. Ian Angus, "Vladimir Vernadsky and the Disruption of the Biosphere," *Climate and Capitalism,* June 5, 2018, https://climateandcapitalism.com/2018/06/05/vladimir-vernadsky-and-the-disruption-of-the-biosphere.

climate change, thinking through the idea of what liberation within the noösphere might entail is of strategic importance in the struggle for survival and liberation.

Intra-actions among spheres of social activity

Our goal is not to simply place concrete phenomena into one sphere or another, but to use these spheres as different ways to make analytical cuts in a complex material whole. As you might imagine, almost any concrete social phenomenon can be traced through most, if not all of these spheres. Take farming for instance. It is easy to see how farming operates in the economic sphere, as a form of production and distribution, as well in the ecological sphere as a nature-making practice. Farming also operates in the kinship and community spheres, both in terms of various agriculture-based households and communities, as well as the ways in which industrial farming corporations seek to promote a mythology of small and natural farming practices in order to conceal their otherwise dehumanizing and ecologically devastating practices. Reliance on low-paid migrant labor to serve the needs of the corporate agricultural sector fundamentally reshapes the household configurations and relations of the laborers and their families. Battles over the technics of farming put these industrial producers at odds with far less industrially-mediated agroecological practices, many of which are passed through intergenerational webs of peasant and Indigenous knowledge systems (as opposed to the patent office). And of course in terms of polity, we see how the very existence of this massive industrial agricultural sector is predicated upon non-market forms of governmental support and the lobbying required to preserve these subsidies, which in turn creates massive surpluses of staple foods that can then be mobilized as food aid towards imperialist ends.

Seeing a single aspect of social life in this way, we can appreciate the complex intra-actions and layered dynamics that will factor into the various standpoints on farming and agriculture that we may encounter: urban rebellions may focus on food deserts and access to affordable and healthy food, whereas land-based peasant and Indigenous struggles may focus on defending agroecological practices, controlling land and technics, and challenging the imperialist state's policies that threaten enclosure and dispossession at every corner. Meanwhile environmentalists in the metropole might focus on the ecological devastation wrought by the mass slaughter of factory-farmed animals and want to see community relations push towards foodways that are less reliant on meat consumption. Economic, kinship, political, communal, technical, and ecological relations will always exist, though their particular configurations may vary greatly according to time and location. While we could categorize farming as "economic activity," conflict resolution as "political activity," spiritual rituals as "communal activity," and childrearing as "kinship activity," each of these abstractions risks limiting our understanding of how the actual processes involved manifest in all of these spheres simultaneously. As radical social scientists, our goal is to interpret each unique sphere of social activity as interconnected, intra-acting, and multidimensional to avoid falling into a reductionist trap.

If we study the characteristics of each sphere in isolation, we may misidentify the dynamics at play because we are not considering how they are influenced by, and intra-act with, the social activity of other spheres. We may overlook the immense historical-geographical complexity that led to a specific form's emergence in the first place. As David Harvey has emphasized, these seemingly distinct fields of force share a common time-space, as "the complex flows of influence that move between the spheres are perpetually reshaping all of them."[83] Every social activity has aspects that can be effectively understood from the standpoint of a different sphere.[84]

In relatively stable social systems, there is a constant intra-action of mechanisms to reconcile or adapt to contradictory dynamics before they generate lasting instability,

83. Harvey, *The Enigma of Capital*, 123–124.
84. Albert et al., *Liberating Theory*, 73–76.

disequilibrium, crisis, and collapse. Antagonistic contradictions that cannot be resolved within the framework of the prevailing social institutions—such as the class struggle between the proletariat and bourgeoisie in late capitalism—characterize unstable social systems ripe for revolution. As partisan social scientists, it is our job to help identify these contradictions, and work towards their resolution in ways that contribute to the communist social revolution.[85]

For example, with no intra-action among spheres, kinship activities might socialize us to become non-acquisitive and cooperative, while economic activities might demand that we be possessive and competitive.[86] Community activities might co-produce mutual respect for different cultures and worldviews, while political activities might require instrumentalist, elitist, and authoritarian traits. If one sphere of society says that we should have a particular quality, and another sphere says that we should have the opposite quality—and the quality in question is one that will help define our character structure and shape our individual life prospects—tensions arise that can lead to social instability, antagonistic social contradictions, and thus openings for revolutionary social transformation.[87] Linking our theoretical knowledge of the complex intra-actions among multiple spheres of social activity and their fields of force with militant social investigation can help us anticipate how instabilities and contradictions arising from particular organizational patterns, structures, and processes are likely to co-produce revolutionary situations.

The important point in outlining multiple spheres of social activity and their dynamics of intra-action is that antagonisms emerging from any one sphere can generate revolutionary change, so long as this change is in productive intra-action with transformations in other spheres as well.

---

85. Mao Zedong, "On Contradiction (1937)," Marxists Internet Archive, https://www.marxists.org/reference/archive/mao/selected-works/volume-1/mswv1_17.htm.

86. Albert et al., *Liberating Theory*, 76–77.

87. Albert et al., *Liberating Theory*, 76–77.

Meanwhile, there are forces emanating from and between each of these spheres that are intent to maintain stability and avoid revolutionary transformation, or at least accommodate and co-define any transformations in ways that re-channel transformative energies back into a reproduction of the imperialist world-system. Bogdanov termed this "substitution," whereby "the formal properties of any given activity can become the experimental template for any other."[88]

So for instance, when labor militancy in the early twentieth century US threatened to fundamentally transform the economic sphere, a solution emanating from the polity—which became known as the New Deal—found a way to bureaucratize labor organizations and incorporate them into a "compromise" that afforded relatively high wages to a white, male labor aristocracy while excluding vast sectors of workers of color and women workers. These solutions were buttressed by programs aimed at helping (white and male) workers and soldiers purchase suburban homes, while deploying tactics such as redlining to exclude Black, Indigenous, and most people of color from the same opportunities. Further, we could see this push towards suburban home and automobile ownership as an accommodation of technological changes—specifically the emergence of a petroleum and petrochemical industry that needed ready markets for its goods. Efforts were made in the community sphere to promote mass consumption of petroleum-based goods and suburban living as constitutive of the US way of life, which the polity also mobilized in its ideological war against the Soviet Union. This led to such absurdities as the "kitchen debate" between Nixon and Krushchev, each determined to portray an idealized version of their standard of living as socially and technologically superior to the other.

We could go on and on. But the point we hope to make is that it is impossible to imagine a revolutionary challenge to this complex system as a whole without waging a struggle on multiple fronts. This is due to the degree to which

88. Wark, *Molecular Red*, 27.

different core characteristics emanating from different spheres intra-act within the overall historical-geographical development of this particular social system. For example, a workers' movement that ignores the gendered and racialized division of labor will reproduce heteropatriarchal and colonial social dynamics while also proving ineffective at liberating the working class. Similarly, any movement that doesn't acknowledge the devastating consequences of continuing with a petrochemical mode of life will prove ineffective.

Alternatively, we can envision a revolutionary process whereby communal kinship forms may initiate dynamics of co-reproduction in the economy, through which affective forms of care become inseparable from the social organization of the workplace. For a revolution to be successful in any one sphere, it would likely have to be accompanied by *a total social revolution*—effectively altering all spheres of social activity and all core characteristics. We agree with David Harvey: "The revolution has to be a *movement* in every sense of the word. If it cannot move within, across, and through the different spheres then it will ultimately go nowhere at all."[89]

89. Harvey, *The Enigma of Capital*, 138.

2

Imperialism and Revolution

2.1: The Imperialist World-System

Empire as a World-Producing Force

The word "imperialism" comes from the Latin *imperium*, meaning "power to command." In this chapter, we outline a macro-analysis of what we call the imperialist world-system. A *world-system* can be understood as "an integrated zone of activity and institutions which obey certain systemic rules."[1] It is comprised of interdependent and hyper-complex social, technical, and ecological subsystems. The reproduction of each of these subsystems depends upon indirect forms of cooperation in all spheres of social activity. However, these indirectly cooperative subsystems are characterized by hierarchization, differentiation, and separation. Our lives are entangled within, and co-produced through, these contradictory relationships and the institutions working to maintain them. And yet, within the cracks and fissures of this contradictory *unity in division* emerge a multiplicity of forms of resistance—sometimes open, sometimes hidden—that perpetually drive the development, reconfiguration, and restructuring of this world-system. It is at these sites of struggle that we can identify communism as *a real tendency* immanent to our lived social realities, and it is from the unification, consolidation, and generalization of diverse points

---

1. Immanuel Wallerstein, *World-Systems Analysis: An Introduction* (Durham, NC: Duke University Press, 2004), 17.

of struggle that the possibility of a communist social revolution on a world scale, capable of rupturing this oppressive system of command and control, might be realized. In this way, the unity in division of imperialism gives way to the *unity in diversity* of communism.

We define *imperialism* as a totalizing system of command and control based on the historical-geographical enmeshing of heteropatriarchy, capitalism, colonialism, and the state, whereby bodies, social relations, and natures are constantly made and unmade by the domination of abstract social forces moving within and through the web of life. This is not to suggest that imperialism is *the world*, but that imperialism, as a social system, *articulates and produces a world* within which our bodies, creative social activities, and a multiplicity of natures are subordinated to certain systemic logics and path dependencies.[2] We refer here to the web of life to make clear that every world-system is simultaneously a *world-ecology*, as "the earth is an environment for humans, and humans are environments (and environment-makers) for the rest of life on planet earth."[3] Viewed from this perspective, human social activity simultaneously *enfolds* and *unfolds* within and through the web of life as humanity-in-nature/nature-in-humanity.

By combining multiple nodes of analysis into a rudimentary macro-analysis or "big picture," our aim is to provide an analytical framework to inform and complement a communist praxis of militant social investigation and revolutionary organizing. The difficulties of such a macro-analysis should be obvious: as all human social systems are defined by hyper-complexity (and hence unknowable in a comprehensive fashion), we can only produce a fragmentary analysis based on partial information compiled from our specific standpoints, with the hope that, when combined with other analyses, these fragments will

---

2. Wallerstein, *World-Systems Analysis*, 16–17; Jason W. Moore, *Capitalism in the Web of Life: Ecology and the Accumulation of Capital* (London: Verso, 2015), 45.
3. Moore, *Capitalism in the Web of Life*, 46.

prove useful to the protracted revolutionary struggle. We are aware that our analysis is being assembled by a particular community drawing from a range of limited sources. This analysis remains immanent to our present reality and has been conducted within the actual time-space of our organized political activities. Such immanence necessarily restricts the quantity and quality of information available, as well as the analytical tools and weapons of struggle at our disposal.

We define *empire* unconventionally, referring to both the metropolitan social formations of the imperialist world-system (e.g. the US empire) and the aggregate of world-producing social forces that drive imperialism as a world-system to expand through time-space and, when necessary, compel it to scorch the earth to prevent alternative systems from arising. As the *telos* [sense of direction] and *conatus* [tendency of self-preservation] of imperialism, the vortex of empire can be conceptualized as the convergence and fusion of several complementary social forces—heteropatriarchy, capitalism, colonialism, and the state—that coalesce into the totalizing world-system of the imperialist singularity. Empire is a world-producing force concretely manifest in the apparatus of imperialist command and control through the simultaneous inclusion, affirmation, and hierarchical management of difference.[4] A central paradox of empire is the expansionary drive to increase the unification and interdependence of social, technological, and ecological activity through circuits of social (re)production while simultaneously intensifying hierarchical separation and management maintained through the multiplication of difference. That is, while imperialism exhibits tendencies towards the construction of a unitary system of authoritarian governance and the homogenization of class antagonisms, it can also produce a multiplication and hierarchical ordering of disparate social groups, partitioning the world into specialized zones of activity and maintaining a

4. Michael Hardt and Antonio Negri, *Empire*, (Cambridge, MA: Harvard University Press, 2000), 198–199.

limited sphere of experimentation for creative social activity in order to later parasitize it.

As a complex of world-producing social forces, empire propels the spatial expansion of the imperialist world-system. In this sense, imperialism's constitutive spheres of social activity have mutually accommodated, co-defined, and co-reproduced through dynamic intra-action. Imperialism has evolved through the dispossession of the global peasantry and repression of heretics; centuries of genocidal wars waged against Indigenous communities; the kidnapping, enslavement, and super-exploitation of African peoples; witch hunts waged for the domination and control of women's bodies; massive, bloody inter-imperialist world wars; and the systematic destruction of the biosphere and geosphere. Most national social formations, regardless of their present social position within the imperialist hierarchy (i.e., center, periphery, semi-periphery), are entangled within these histories and geographies of oppression, governed by institutions driven by the world-producing social force of empire and, therefore, typically containing the potential—however limited—to become imperialist powers themselves.

The world-producing social force of empire drives the imperialist world-system to subsume the totality of historical-geographical time-space to itself, creating "a world after its own image."[5] Empire consistently forms and reforms marginalized peripheries as sites of domination populated by those who have "been robbed of all their own means of production, and all the guarantees of existence" that were previously in place.[6] Imperialism itself is a composite reflection of the accumulated social struggles between center and periphery, inscribed upon peripheral bodies, spheres of social activity, and natures "with letters of blood and fire."[7]

5. Karl Marx and Frederick Engels, *The Communist Manifesto* (New York: International Publishers, 1948), 13.

6. Karl Marx, *Capital: A Critique of Political Economy, Volume I* (New York: Vintage Books, 1977), 875.

7. Marx, *Capital*, Vol. I, 875.

Heteropatriarchy and feminist struggle

There are several distinct analytical standpoints from which we might study these antagonisms that co-define and co-reproduce the imperialist world-system, and from which communist counter-tendencies emerge. The critical study of heteropatriarchy and feminist struggle recognizes the emergence of a world-producing social force driving the creation of institutions of heterosexual, cisgender male dominance through the biopolitical control of sexed, gendered, and sexualized bodies. This control entails: invisibilization, naturalization, and devaluation of non-remunerated forms of reproductive labor; the social construction of masculine/feminine and man/woman binaries; the creation of the cisgender heteronormative nuclear family as a site of biological and social reproduction; and a socioecological rupture premised upon the "man against nature" binary, male control of population growth, and the exhaustion of environmental resources.[8]

Maria Mies has suggested that women were constituted as "the first colony," upon which all subsequent colonialisms and denials of autonomy are based. Building upon this, we know that patriarchy is more accurately understood as *heteropatriarchy*, hostile towards the nonbinary, nonconforming queer body and towards forms of gender and sexuality that challenge heteropatriarchal binaries and their institutional manifestations. Whenever queer feminist subjectivities and subjects sabotage heteropatriarchal domination, the reaction of the world-system is to deepen its authoritarian character through the disciplinary violence of the state, family, school, and cultures of misogyny, queerphobia, and transphobia. Indeed, "the fact that patriarchy is today an almost universal system which has affected and transformed most pre-patriarchal societies has to be explained by the main

8. Maria Mies, *Patriarchy and Accumulation on a World Scale: Women in the International Division of Labour* (London: Zed Books, 1998); Silvia Federici, *Caliban and the Witch: Women, the Body and Primitive Accumulation* (Brooklyn: Autonomedia, 2004); Françoise d'Eaubonne, "What Could an Ecofeminist Society Be?," *Ethics and the Environment* 4, no. 2 (2000): 180–181.

mechanisms which are used to expand this system, namely robbery, warfare, and conquest."[9] Here we find a mechanism integral to imperialism's continuing domination of social relations outside itself, as well as forms of feminist resistance prefiguring communism.

Capital, capitalism, and proletarian class struggle
The critical study of capital, capitalism, and proletarian class struggle aims to grasp our subordination to the law of value, with value understood in this context as "an abstract general form of wealth in terms of which all forms of material wealth can be quantified."[10] The world-producing social force of capital refers to the drive to accumulate self-expanding value through production, circulation, and financialization.[11] On the one hand, capital only exists within a concrete historical-geographical matrix, necessarily implying heteropatriarchal capitalism, racial capitalism, state capitalism, and a distinctly capitalist ecology. On the other hand, capital in the abstract (or we might say, capital from the standpoint of capital itself) is defined by "its absence of determinations, the fact that it has no historical or cultural *content per se*."[12] Capital constitutes itself as the subject and object of history, rewriting world history as a story of the inevitable becoming-capitalist of everything. Capital only understands people as potential sources of labor, and even then only as abstract labor, not real people doing real work, but merely an abstract source of value, or in other words, a means by which to reproduce more and more of itself.[13] From our proletarian standpoint (as opposed to the stories that capital tells about itself as subject and object of history) capital only actualizes

9. Mies, *Patriarchy and Accumulation on a World Scale*, 38.

10. Moishe Postone, *Time, Labor, and Social Domination: A Reinterpretation of Marx's Critical Theory* (Cambridge: Cambridge University Press, 1996), 268.

11. Nick Dyer-Witheford, *Cyber-Proletariat: Global Labour in the Digital Vortex* (London: Pluto Press, 2015), 22.

12. Alberto Toscano, "The Open Secret of Real Abstraction," *Rethinking Marxism* 20, no. 2 (2008): 276.

13. Postone, *Time, Labor, and Social Domination*, 76.

itself by accommodating to and co-defining the patriarchal, colonial, and statist relations that precede its dominance. This dual character allows capital to integrate the wildest hypocrisies—to conceive of itself as multicultural, feminist, democratic, libertarian, post-racial, or even socialist—in its effort to subordinate the totality of society to commodification and the law of value. These contradictions require that we distinguish between *capital* as a world-producing social force and *capitalism* as a specific historical-geographical configuration of a world-economy or concrete mode of production, allocation, consumption, and waste management.

The world-producing social force of capital compels societies to organize themselves in accordance with the law of value and the logic of commodity production and circulation. This means society is organized according to the institutional basis of private property, competitive market allocation, and the state regulation and planning of markets to ensure the hegemonic dominance of particular corporations. It also entails hierarchical divisions of labor within and beyond the workplace and remunerative schemes premised upon the ownership of property and the collective bargaining power (or lack thereof) among the subordinate classes. Capital drives to maximize the productivity of mechanized, cybernetic, super-exploitative, and non-remunerated forms of labor, often through gendered and racialized processes. The relation of capital contains within it the capitalist and working classes, as well as various intermediary classes, sectors, and strata locked in an ongoing asymmetric class war. The working class organizes itself into resistance associations (such as unions, councils, defense organizations, and parties), while capital organizes itself as the state—with its powerful repressive and ideological machinery—and via a range of auxiliary forces that include employers' associations, corporate lobbies, and mercenaries to repress working-class resistance. As this capitalist vortex is driven to subsume the web of life, capital accumulation drives the "multiplication of the proletariat" who subsequently form the vast majority of the global human population.[14] Emerging from the class struggles of the proletariat, we can identify a range of political challenges to capital and capitalism that prefigure communism.

Colonialism, white supremacy, and decolonial struggle

The critical study of colonialism, white supremacy, and decolonial struggle aims to understand the world-producing social force of *colonialism* as an expansionary drive to create dependent peoples and peripheries as: (1) sites for the *extraction* of resources and labor-power by the dominant center via racialized processes of super-exploitation and underdevelopment; and (2) corporeal, social, and natural sinks into which the entropy generated by systemic crises can be *exported*. Exportation includes the biopolitical management and deportation of migrants, the containment and suppression of surplus populations through mass incarceration, physical relocation of waste production, or, in the case of modern anti-Jewish, anti-Muslim, and anti-immigrant racism, the projection of the transformations unleashed by imperialism onto a whole people.[15]

Geographically, these colonies could be *external* to a state, as in the case of historical colonies established by the Spanish, Portuguese, Dutch, or British empires or today's neocolonies in the Global South dominated by transnational corporations and financial institutions and backed by the politico-military force of metropolitan state power. Alternatively, colonies could be *internal* to a state, as in the colonial oppression of the Irish, Basque, Jewish, and Romani peoples within Europe; and the colonial oppression of Indigenous First Nations, New Afrikans, Xicanxs, Pacific Islanders, and Boricuas in the United States. The global periphery also includes traveling communities such as the Romani people,

14. Marx, *Capital*, Vol. I, 764.
15. Robert Biel, *The Entropy of Capitalism* (Chicago: Haymarket Books, 2013), 217; Moishe Postone, "Anti-Semitism and National Socialism," *New German Critique*, no. 19, special issue 1 (1980): 106–107.

nations occupied or subdivided by imperialism such as Palestine and Kurdistan, various diaspora communities, and the peoples of overseas territories dominated by the metropolitan core, such as Martinique and Puerto Rico.[16] While mass migration is transforming the social composition of the metropolitan core (and thereby opening new possibilities for revolutionary struggle by expanding the proletariat concentrated within the core itself), it seems probable that the peripheries of the Global South will continue to constitute the frontline of anti-imperialist struggle. From proletarian uprisings by factory workers in China and miners in South Africa to the reappropriation of the commons by landless people's movements in Brazil and Namibia, from the rebel barrios of Caracas, Venezuela to the red base areas in Mindanao, Philippines, anti-imperialist political prisoner David Gilbert reminds us that "the most basic divide is still between imperialism and the oppressed majority of humankind in, and from, Africa, Asia, Oceania, and Latin America. We can expect the fiercest clashes there and the most advanced politics."[17]

The particular organizational patterns taken by colonialism vary according to historical-geographical conjuncture. Due to the hegemonic role played by European empires and their settler-colonial offshoots, as well as the continuing role of US hegemony in the imperialist world-system, colonial oppression has generally evolved as Christian, Eurocentric, and white supremacist. White supremacy is one of the dominant modes for organizing the community sphere within imperialism, a key divide-and-rule strategy for the imperialist ruling class, and a mechanism for the (re)production of racial character structures that account for the ongoing dispossession and super-exploitation of Indigenous peoples and the peoples of the continents and diasporas of Africa,

---

16. Gabriel Kuhn, "Oppressor and Oppressed Nations: Sketching a Taxonomy of Imperialism," *Kersplebedeb*, June 15, 2017, https://kersplebedeb.com/posts/oppressor-and-oppressed-nations/.

17. David Gilbert, *Love and Struggle: My Life in SDS, the Weather Underground, and Beyond* (Oakland: PM Press, 2012), 324.

Asia, Oceania, and Latin America. The resistance waged by decolonial liberation struggles under the banners of communal self-determination and territorial sovereignty constitutes a frontline in the anti-imperialist struggle and a visionary anticipation of a communist alternative.

State power, state apparatuses, and anti-authoritarian struggle

The critical study of state power, state apparatuses, and anti-authoritarian struggle aims to understand the means through which the hegemonic power of imperialism is maintained and reproduced, and the social force that drives the containment and suppression of non-state alternatives. This drive to constitute and maintain state power results in the formation of state apparatuses that function as "containers" for the contradictions produced by the center/periphery hierarchies of imperialism that ultimately surround, reshape, and enmesh everyday life.

All state apparatuses build bureaucracies in accordance with a particular state ideology. Today, such bureaucracies are generalized throughout all spheres of social activity, encompassing the *repressive state apparatus* of "the government, administration, army, police, courts, and prisons," the *ideological state apparatus* of educational, familial, religious, political, associative, informational, communicative, and cultural institutions, and the *economic state apparatus* of regulatory, productive, and infrastructural institutions responsible for monetary policy, planning, technical training, scientific research and development, and other functions critical to articulating the framework through which the capitalist world-economy operates within a national territory.[18] The unity of the repressive, ideological, and economic state apparatuses constitutes *an integral state*, which reproduces the hegemony of the ruling class.

The imperialist *power elite*—the "center of the center" of this integral state—is concentrated in the metropolitan core

18. Althusser, *On the Reproduction of Capitalism*, 75; Nikos Poulantzas, *State, Power, Socialism* (London: Verso, 2014), 166–179.

and composes a plutocratic oligarchy of warlords, the corporate rich, and the political directorate of the state.[19] At the world level, the imperial core includes the transnational ruling class, metropolitan aristocracies, and various celebrities and "powerful" people connected by corporate, financial, educational, familial, religious, political, and military ties. The core, with its privileged socialization processes and unitary coordination of its polycentric network, ensures the protection and reproduction of the world-system during times of crisis.[20] Should the imperialist ruling class be removed without abolishing the institutional basis of their power, then a new elite would be generated, and the vicious cycle of oppression and resistance will repeat itself again. Instead of specific individuals, the reproduction of alienated social relations and abstract forms of domination is the crux of the problem. Our enemy is thus a world-system "that subjects people [and natures] to impersonal structural imperatives and constraints that cannot be adequately grasped in terms of concrete domination (e.g., personal or group domination), and that generates an ongoing historical dynamic."[21]

Dominant Centers, Dominated Peripheries

As we have stressed, the basis of contemporary imperialism is the generalization or diffusion of hierarchical center/periphery relations throughout the fabric of society, encompassing both historical and geographical dimensions.[22] While there is no singular command-and-control center for the imperialist world-system, there are *parametric centers* such as nation-states, global financial institutions, and multinational corporations, that subject creative social activity to their specific institutional modalities of abstract domination.[23]

19. C. Wright Mills, *The Power Elite* (Oxford: Oxford University Press, 2000), 8–9.

20. Mills, *The Power Elite*, 19–20.

21. Postone, *Time, Labor, and Social Domination*, 3–4.

22. Federação Anarquista do Rio de Janeiro (FARJ), *Social Anarchism and Organisation* (Johannesburg: Zabalaza Books, 2012), 9.

23. Massimo De Angelis, *The Beginning of History: Value Struggles and Global Capital* (London: Pluto Press, 2007), 174.

Parametric centers articulate and reproduce the power elites who administer this polycentric network of domination; privileged social groups benefit from the reproduction of this network and can be rallied to its defense. Taken together, these centers form a network ensuring that creative social activity conforms to the institutional boundary established by the imperialist world-system. This manifests in many ways, such as particular configurations of family life, market relations, resource extraction, conflict resolution, transnational logistics, and energy systems.

As a result, the multitude of proletarian and popular social groups are cast into the peripheries of the world-system and differentially subjected to imperialism's relations of enclosure, exploitation, and dependency. Since the onset of neoliberalism, this process has been marked by the transnational diffusion of industry, high-tech computerized automation of production processes, and massive population regroupment to enable ruthless super-exploitation of the working-class peripheries. This is accomplished through systems of unequal trade regimes, unrelenting debt, and militarized occupations, all pursued under the guise of "humanitarian intervention."

Geographically, the peripheries of imperialism constitute a vast "hinterland, defined by expulsion and exclusion."[24] The peripheral hinterland "is often a heavily industrial space—a space for factory farms, for massive logistics complexes, for power generation, and for the extraction of resources from forests, deserts, and seas."[25] This encompasses hybrid urban-rural spaces dominated by the command and control systems of the integral state, which function as the key zones for the exploitation or super-exploitation of cheap labor-power, cheap energy, cheap food, and cheap environmental resources by capital.

Far beyond the increasingly gentrified and fortified

24. Phil A. Neel, *Hinterland: America's New Landscape of Class and Conflict* (London: Reaktion Books, 2018), 17.

25. Neel, *Hinterland*, 17.

central cities of the metropolitan core exist the peripheries of the *far hinterland*:

> The far hinterland is more traditionally 'rural,' though now the 'rural' is largely a space for disaster industries, government aid, and large-scale industrial extraction, production, and initial processing of primary products. Much of the far hinterland is also dominated by the informal economy, including black markets, the mass production of illegal drugs or other contraband commodities, and human trafficking—all of which is often synchronized with the formal economy. Though largely rural, the far hinterland also includes large urban zones of collapse, which exhibit almost identical characteristics.[26]

In closer geographic proximity to the central cities are the peripheries of the *near hinterland*:

> The 'near' hinterland, by contrast, encompasses the foothills descending from the summit of the megacity. It is largely 'suburban' in character, though this is something of a misnomer given the term's connotation of middle-class white prosperity. Much of the urban population in the U.S. (and in the world generally) lives in this near hinterland. In some countries, such as those in Europe, it takes the shape of towering apartment centers that ring the city, housing immigrants who staff large logistics complexes that exist beyond the urban core or who commute downtown to work in the service industry. Elsewhere, as in the cities of Africa and Latin America, the near hinterland takes the shape of the slum city, often walled off from wealthier exurbs and the downtown core.[27]

The near hinterland has become a key geographic site of resistance to the imperialist world-system, as exemplified by the uprising of Muslims and North African migrants in the

26. Neel, *Hinterland*, 18.
27. Neel, *Hinterland*, 18.

banlieues [working-class suburbs] of Paris in 2005 and the Black liberation uprisings of Ferguson and Baltimore in 2014 and throughout the US in 2020. These near-hinterland uprisings are of immense strategic importance for the communist movement, as they can blockade imperialism's global supply chain and create opportunities to build bases of counterpower at imperialism's logistical chokepoints.

The depletion of the peripheries is the "default mode" of imperialism. As capitalist value in the form of cheap resources and labor-power flows from periphery to center, hegemony and repression flow from center to periphery.[28] As systemic crises deepen, imperialist governance will likely fall back on this default mode. Beyond a spatial relationship of value flowing from peripheries to the center, and domination flowing from the core to the peripheries, the entropy generated by imperialism is exported "to the future . . . and at some point it will inevitably flood back."[29] In other words, the peripheries of the Global South are doubly oppressed. First, via the destruction produced by colonial warfare and super-exploitation that enables the Global North's growth and development, and second, through the delayed yet inevitable consequences—socially and ecologically—of this present-day extraction and violence which will accumulate in debased infrastructures of social reproduction, landscapes polluted into death-dealing toxic wastelands, and the more general devastation wreaked by climate change.[30] The constitution, generalization, and ongoing domination of peripheries by the centers of imperialism typically consist of processes of *enclosure, dependency,* and *exploitation.* These manifest with varying degrees of intensity in different historical-geographical locations. We define *enclosure* broadly, as "ending communal control of

28. Athina Karatzogianni and Andrew Robinson, *Power, Resistance and Conflict in the Contemporary World: Social Movements, Networks and Hierarchies* (London: Routledge, 2012), 70–71.

29. Biel, *The Entropy of Capitalism*, 126.

30. Biel, *The Entropy of Capitalism*, 127.

the means of subsistence,"[31] the destruction of "communal land and space that forms an energy well of proletarian power,"[32] and the planned containment and suppression of autonomous territories. The process of enclosure entails alienation from ourselves, our environments, and the various social processes that make alternative forms of life possible. The expropriation and alienation of enclosures create large populations that imperialism exploits by means of a cultivated dependency. To the degree that common forms of life persist, they are locked in a constant battle against processes of enclosure.

A relation of *dependency* is established on the basis of enclosure. When communal forms of social reproduction have been curtailed or destroyed, the dispossessed have no choice but to appeal to the imperialist centers for access to the means of reproducing life. The peripheral social formation is thereby underdeveloped or "de-developed," and its material existence is tethered to, and structured in accordance with, the perverse needs and desires of the imperialist centers.[33]

On the bases of enclosure and dependency, a relation of *exploitation* can be established whereby the peripheral social group or social formation is compelled to labor for the benefit of the center, for durations and intensities far beyond what is required to meet the collective needs and desires of the worker or their community, and the centers are able to extract, appropriate, and selectively distribute this surplus created through the proletariat's collective labor. A relation of *super-exploitation* exists when the forms of compensation provided by the center for peripheral workers are below the bare minimum of what is required to reproduce human labor-power.[34]

---

31. Midnight Notes, *Midnight Oil: Work, Energy, War, 1973–1992* (Brooklyn: Autonomedia, 1992), 321.

32. Midnight Notes, *Midnight Oil*, 327.

33. Zak Cope, *Divided World, Divided Class: Global Political Economy and the Stratification of Labour Under Capitalism* (Montreal: Kersplebedeb, 2012), 27–28.

34. Cope, *Divided World, Divided Class*, 182.

The differential integration of proletarian and popular social formations is potentially constructive to the extent that it creates the possibility of autonomous forms of social reproduction, gradually building the critical mass required to break the domination of the world-system. As with prior struggles, the peripheries of imperialism constitute important strategic sites for the communist social revolution's construction of base areas—from India's "red corridor" to the self-governing cantons of Rojava—as well as the resurgence and renaissance of long-repressed communal forms of life and knowledge co-production.[35] This suggests that the combined and uneven development of imperialism can be used to the social revolution's advantage, "because it means there are still-functioning grassroots structures in the [global periphery] which could form the basis of an alternative social system."[36]

The Ecological Rift

We are living in a new geological era marked by the anthropogenic transformation of the planetary biosphere and geosphere. Humans have always altered and co-produced our environments; but an abstract humanity—or, humanity in general—is not responsible for the present ecological devastation. Rather, it is the imperialist world-system that has initiated and continually deepened ecological rifts, crafting a fundamentally unsustainable socioecological metabolism built upon the "man against nature" binary.[37] As a result of the hierarchical power relations embedded within imperialism, the effects of the ecological crisis will be

35. Leanne Betasamosake Simpson, *Dancing On Our Turtle's Back: Stories of Nishnaabeg Re-Creation, Resurgence, and a New Emergence* (Winnipeg: Arbeiter Ring, 2011); James Yaki Sayles, *Meditations on Frantz Fanon's Wretched of the Earth: New Afrikan Revolutionary Writings* (Montreal: Kersplebedeb, 2010), 155.

36. Robert Biel, *The New Imperialism: Crisis and Contradictions in North/South Relations* (London: Zed Books, 2000), 111.

37. Jason W. Moore, "Name the System! Anthropocenes & the Capitalocene Alternative," *Jason W. Moore*, October 9, 2016, https://jasonwmoore.wordpress.com/2016/10/09/name-th e-system-anthropocenes-the-capitalocene-alternative/.

unevenly distributed: "For most people, it will mean increased hardship and a fight for survival, while for some there will be easy lifeboats."[38] While some have named this new period the Anthropocene, many others challenge the way that this term seems to suggest that all of humanity is responsible for the current ecological crisis. Marxist, feminist, and antiracist scholars have since offered alternative concepts, such as racial capitalocene or plantationocene, that more explicitly acknowledge how the imperialist mode of world-making produces ecological devastation.[39] Whichever concept is chosen, we see the utility of naming and studying this fundamental transformation in human history and geological time:

> Today's concept of the Anthropocene thus reflects, on the one hand, a growing recognition of the rapidly accelerating role of anthropogenic drivers in disrupting the biogeochemical processes and planetary boundaries of the Earth system and, on the other, a dire warning that the world, under 'business as usual,' is being catapulted into a new ecological phase—one less conducive to maintaining biological diversity and a stable human civilization.[40]

This "business as usual" is the continuation of a social system premised upon heteropatriarchy, capital, colonialism, and the state. From its inception, imperialism has cultivated a deeply imbalanced and destructive socioecological metabolism, grounded in the objectification of nature, whereby environmental resources and multi-species life are subjected to processes of commodification, enclosure, and extraction, as diverse and abundant forms of life are reduced to potential

38. Aaron Vansintjan, "The Anthropocene Debate," *Uneven Earth*, June 16, 2015, http://unevenearth.org/2015/06/the-anthropocene-debate/.

39. Françoise Vergès, "Racial Capitalocene," in Gaye Theresa Johnson and Alex Lubin (eds.), *Futures of Black Radicalism* (New York: Verso, 2017), 72–82; Donna Haraway, "Anthropocene, Capitalocene, Plantationocene, Cthulucene: Making Kin," *Environmental Humanities* 6, (2015): 159–165.

40. John Bellamy Foster, "The Anthropocene Crisis," *Monthly Review*, September 1, 2016, https://monthlyreview.org/2016/09/01/the-anthropocene-crisis/.

sources of value for capital. Coming at the expense of ecological diversity, this ruthless enclosure and extraction of nature results in widespread resource depletion and environmental destruction, ultimately undermining the reproduction of the world-system itself. Hence, imperialism as a project is co-produced by natural processes, "the unruly movements of bundled natures, through which civilizational projects discover spectacular contradictions."[41] At present, this entropic metabolism is manifest in myriad socioecological crises, including: habitat destruction, the mass extinction of numerous species, soil degradation, ocean acidification, rising sea levels, land erosion, widespread drought, water supply contamination, environmental resource depletion, and the spread of disease. So long as imperialism remains the dominant world-system, it will pursue the management of these crises in ways that inevitably deepen the systemic oppression of the proletarian and popular social groups who inhabit the peripheries, accelerating tendencies towards authoritarianism, militarism, and ultimately fascism.

The ecological rift is thus a political problem—a problem of particular forms of *environment-making*—caused by the reproduction of the imperialist world-system. This situation has been co-produced through the development of imperialism's specific socioecological metabolism through the web of life, premised upon boundless capital accumulation, endless growth, technocratic modernization, and the centralization of state and corporate power for the metropolitan core. Resource wars have already taken on great importance for the metropolitan core and its competitors, as witnessed with the proliferation of proxy wars waged throughout the Middle East and Africa. While in the global peripheries, adaptation to the Anthropocene takes on a range of forms with divergent political implications (from cooperative mutual aid and revolutionary struggle to narcotics trafficking and religious fundamentalism), in the metropolitan core, "the multilayered crisis appears as the politics of the armed lifeboat: the

41. Moore, *Capitalism in the Web of Life*, 47.

preparations for open-ended counterinsurgency, militarized borders, aggressive anti-immigrant policing, and a mainstream proliferation of right-wing xenophobia."[42]

Resurgent Fascism

In the twentieth century, fascism emerged from imperialism in decay. According to Matthew Lyons, fascism is "a revolutionary form of right-wing populism, inspired by a totalitarian vision of collective rebirth, that challenges capitalist political and cultural power while promoting economic and social hierarchy."[43] It is "revolutionary" in the sense of waging a social *counter-revolution,* seizing state power to reengineer and reorder the gender, sexual, class, racial, ethnic, national, and state hierarchies inherited from imperialism, typically in favor of an alliance of "native citizens" of middle class and declassed men forged through prolonged crisis. The social base of fascism generally feels abandoned by "their" national empires, which have been compromised by pursuing an insufficiently nationalist, racist, authoritarian, and militarist form of imperialism.[44] As a prerequisite to the stabilization of its power, fascist social engineering projects require the violent containment and suppression of all forms of left opposition, especially any form of communism. While fascism varies widely according to its specific historical-geographical location—from the Ku Klux Klan to the National-Socialist German Workers' Party to the Argentine Anticommunist Alliance—all forms of fascism share a variant of "blood and soil" ideology, or a "commitment to the regeneration and rejuvenation of their own national communities, understood

42. Christian Parenti, *Tropic of Chaos: Climate Change and the New Geography of Violence* (New York: Nation Books, 2011), 225–226.

43. Matthew Lyons, "Two Ways of Looking at Fascism," *Socialism and Democracy*, March 8, 2011, http://sdonline.org/47/two-ways-of-looking-at-fascism/.

44. J. Sakai, "The Shock of Recognition: Looking at Hamerquist's *Fascism and Anti-Fascism,*" in *Confronting Fascism: Discussion Documents for a Militant Movement* (Montreal and Chicago: Kersplebedeb, Chicago Anti-Racist Action, and Arsenal, 2002), 88–89.

as communities of people related to each other by ethnicity, culture, religion, language, and homeland."[45]

Constructing an external Other to be excluded, dominated, or exterminated, fascism relies upon variations of the organizational forms typically associated with the left, united with an ideology naturalizing hierarchy and violence:

> Fascism doesn't just terrorize and repress. It also inspires and mobilizes large masses of people around a vision of collective rebirth in a time of crisis. Building a mass movement outside traditional channels is central to fascism's bid to win state power. As a regime, fascism uses mass organizations and rituals to create a sense of participation and direct identification with the state. Fascism celebrates the nation, race, or cultural group as an organic community to which all other loyalties must be subordinated. In place of individual liberties or social justice, fascism offers its followers a culture of action, virility, heroic sacrifice, cathartic public spectacle, and being part of a vast social organism.[46]

At the present moment, the intensification of imperialism's systemic crises could create a situation where fascist movements gain mass support among certain declassed social groups. Already in 2020, during the Black liberation uprisings sparked by the public execution of George Floyd by police in Minneapolis, we see antifascist organizing being vilified by the forces of white nationalism, and the antifascist movement branded as a left-wing terrorist organization.[47] In our current conjuncture, however, these forces of white nationalism are paradoxically "antistatist," with a vision of "making America great" built upon a contradictory commitment to strong centralized and militarized policing of

45. Roderick Stackelberg, *Hitler's Germany: Origins, Interpretations, Legacies* (London: Routledge, 2009), 24.

46. Matthew Lyons, "Is the Bush Administration Fascist?," *New Politics* 11, no. 2 (Winter 2007), http://newpol.org/content/bush-administration-fascist/.

47. Annie Karni, "Facebook Removes Trump Ads Displaying Symbol Used by Nazis," *The New York Times*, June 18, 2020, https://www.nytimes.com/2020/06/18/us/politics/facebook-trump-ads-antifa-red-triangle.html.

the world's Others (be they people of color and antifa at home, migrants and asylum seekers at the borders, or potential economic, cultural, or political rivals abroad) coupled with a desire for an interior in which they can wield power and authority without the intrusions of state authority (or unwarranted taxation). The imperialist ruling class, in continuing its experiment with complexity-governance (i.e., governance through chaos), stokes these tensions in order to maintain hegemony. Such strategies encourage the proliferation of low-intensity warfare throughout society by enabling fascist forces to engage in terroristic activity against the Left, effectively "creating fear to justify repression."[48] One of the unintended consequences of such strategies is, of course, that the imperialist ruling class never fully commands and controls the forces it unleashes.

Among the immediate dangers for a resurgent revolutionary movement is that fascism will parasitize its social base, defuse social antagonisms between oppressor/oppressed, and deflect the class hatred of workers away from the imperialist ruling class by redirecting material and existential frustrations against an internal Other. The responsibility falls on communist and allied organizers to successfully assemble a social bloc of the oppressed that can defeat fascism both ideologically and in the streets, avoid traps set by the ruling class and its repressive state apparatuses, and take the initiative to seize openings created by the crises and decay of imperialism to wage a protracted revolutionary struggle to overthrow and abolish this oppressive system, build a communist alternative, and win collective liberation.

2.2: Revolutionary Situations

There are no shortcuts to the overthrow and abolition of imperialism, nor to the construction of communist alternatives. Despite a variety of possible scenarios, the only certainty is that the emergence of a new world from the ashes of the old

48. Biel, *The Entropy of Capitalism*, 186.

is a protracted process. Nonetheless, imperialism is predisposed towards certain world-systemic crises, which manifest themselves at particular historical-geographical conjunctures and territories. At such locations, a convergence of crises can operate as a catalyst for situations conducive to advancing a communist social revolution. For example, World War I created a world-systemic crisis which converged with a series of internal crises and cycles of struggle particular to Russian society, creating the conditions for the revolutionary situation that culminated in the Russian Revolution of 1917. However, the convergence of world-systemic crises with the crises of a determinate social formation is not sufficient in and of itself to produce a revolutionary situation: the decisive factor is always the existence of a revolutionary movement with the capacity to contend with the state for power.

What is a crisis? According to Antonio Gramsci: "The crisis consists precisely in the fact that the old is dying and the new cannot be born; in this interregnum a great variety of morbid symptoms appear."[49] Crises thus manifest a complex dialectical movement of revolution/counter-revolution. Whenever insurgencies waged by the proletarian and popular social groups impose crises on imperialism—through collective refusals, workers' struggles, and revolutionary countercultures—empire responds by turning these crises against the people in order to destructure its political composition and restore command and control through counter-revolution.[50] With this dialectic of crisis in mind, what makes for *revolutionary situations*?

As Lenin outlined in "Lessons of the Crisis" (1917), an important factor to consider is at what point the hegemony of the dominant social system has been breached and the wavering, contradictory middle strata swings toward the camp of the social revolution.[51] This swing propels the forces of

49. Antonio Gramsci, *Selections from the Prison Notebooks* (New York: International Publishers, 1971), 276.

50. Harry Cleaver, *Reading Capital Politically* (Oakland: AK Press, 2000), 74.

51. V.I. Lenin, "Lessons of the Crisis (1917)," Marxists Internet Archive, https://www.marxists.org/archive/lenin/works/1917/apr/22b.html/.

revolution and counter-revolution into the streets, rallying their respective bases for the coming struggle. There is an unfolding movement of *encirclement*, in which the revolutionary movement advances from its peripheral bases to the centers of reactionary power, simultaneous to an enfolding movement of *counter-encirclement*, in which the reactionary movement advances from its centers to the peripheral bases of revolutionary counterpower. The clash between the forces of revolution and counter-revolution thus begins. The only way out of the downward spiral of crisis and decay becomes social revolution, which depends upon the multitude of proletarian and popular social groups having the confidence to build a movement capable of leading the revolutionary struggle.

As Herbert Marcuse explained, the imperialist world-system has now evolved to require the permanent organization of preventative counter-revolution in its centers and peripheries. "In its extreme manifestations, it practices the horrors of the Nazi regime. Wholesale massacres in Indochina, Indonesia, the Congo, Nigeria, Pakistan, and the Sudan are unleashed against everything which is called 'communist' or which is in revolt against governments subservient to the imperialist countries."[52] Empire's river of blood flows into the present, with the imperialist ruling class waging permanent war against the peoples and nations of the global periphery under the banner of the so-called War on Terror.

Today, the imperial war machine has begun to turn its counter-revolutionary apparatus inward against the liberation struggles in the metropole. With the neo-fascist Trump regime intent on criminalizing antiracist and antifascist movements and all those who oppose the imperialist world-system, all partisans of the liberation struggle can rest assured that, regardless of where we stand politically, we are all "communists" in the eyes of the imperial ruling class. We shall either unite in the trenches of revolutionary struggle to articulate a common project of collective liberation and achieve victory, or unity shall be imposed by our enemies

52. Herbert Marcuse, *Counterrevolution and Revolt* (Boston: Beacon Press, 1972), 1.

when our backs are against the wall. We would do well to listen to the advice of Black communist revolutionary George Jackson: "Settle your quarrels, come together, understand the reality of our situation, understand that fascism is already here, that people are dying who could be saved, that generations more will die or live poor butchered half-lives if you fail to act. Do what must be done, discover your humanity and your love in revolution."[53]

The Dangers of Assimilation

Given the crisis-prone tendencies of imperialism, the metropolitan core states have constructed a loyal base of supporters at home to protect it from uprisings launched by the oppressed masses of the global peripheries, to perform domestic policing duties and serve as cannon fodder in imperialist wars, and to function as a domestic consumer market. According to Zak Cope, the ruling class of the metropolitan core attempts "to incorporate the core-nation working class into the imperialist system by means of granting it political, cultural, and material benefits. These can take the form of extensive enfranchisement, increased leisure time, higher wages, legal pay arbitration, the right to organize, public welfare services, and relative cultural esteem."[54] Historically, this process of differential integration of a gendered and racialized 'worker elite' or 'labor aristocracy' through social imperialism has entailed an active approach to cultivating loyalty via the ideological state apparatuses, especially mass media, and a proliferation of heteropatriarchal brotherhoods, pro-business associations, corporatist labor unions, and racist community associations and civic institutions.

The forces of liberal inclusion attempt to contain and suppress mass unrest through various modes of incorporation into the prevailing order, such as pulling organizers away from the people's liberation struggle into the non-profit

53. George Jackson, *Soledad Brother: The Prison Letters of George Jackson* (Chicago: Lawrence Hill Books, 1994), xxv.
54. Cope, *Divided World, Divided Class*, 94.

industrial complex. While the communist movement fights to achieve victories for *all* oppressed people, the ruling class attempts to defuse insurgent social antagonisms through *differential concessions,* which often requires the neutralization of grassroots militancy through cooptation and repression as a prerequisite for implementation. They respond to a movement such as Black Lives Matter—which calls for defunding and abolishing the police—with calls instead to spend money on "cultural sensitivity training" and other such palliatives meant to keep the underlying structures of systemic oppression intact. Imperialism makes token concessions such as these in order to disarm and defuse our movements, to shift popular support in favor of the imperialist system, and to prevent movements from gaining further ground (let alone winning collective liberation). Through the selective expansion of social welfare programs by corporations and the state, the worker elite and its professional, managerial, and small business allies are able to accumulate a degree of socioeconomic stability and status in the form of home ownership, job and income security, financial savings, healthcare, and education. "Above all else," writes Bromma, "a worker elite is defined by its preferential social contract with the bourgeoisie."[55] Thus, social imperialist welfare policies serve as the material basis of privilege and a mechanism for the containment and suppression of metropolitan class struggle, while also ensuring the internal fragmentation and disunity of the proletariat.

These policies have deepened an ideology of Social Darwinism among certain classes, sectors, and strata within the metropolitan core populations, rooted in "the Malthusian premise that you had better line up behind your own imperialist power in order to grab as much as possible of the (finite) resources, which can then be shared out within that particular national society."[56] To maintain hegemony, imperialism

55. Bromma, *The Worker Elite: Notes on the "Labor Aristocracy"* (Montreal: Kersplebedeb, 2014), 21.
56. Biel, *The Entropy of Capitalism*, 41.

alternates between assimilationist and exclusionary modes according to context, balance of forces, ideological line, and the depth of world-systemic crisis. While obscured for a time by the neoliberal ideology of "multiculturalism," ecological crises and neo-fascism have made it abundantly clear that the metropolitan core intends to reap the material benefits of cheap labor-power and cheap nature for itself, while leaving the global peripheries—both internal and external to the core—to bear the consequences. The social chauvinism produced by imperialism in its various forms emerges as a major obstacle to the development of revolutionary consciousness, self-organization, and self-activity among sections of the metropolitan population, who accrue psychological and material benefits from the ongoing super-exploitation of the global peripheries. The task of communists concentrated within the metropolitan core is to agitate, educate, and organize to break the hold of social chauvinist ideologies; to learn and build alliances *with* liberation movements emerging from the global peripheries; and to work to structurally undermine imperialism at the base through the construction of a metropolitan communist movement among the multitude of proletarian and popular social groups.

We must consciously prepare for multiple contingencies as we begin to rebuild a revolutionary communist movement and assemble the elements of a communist alternative. In the next chapter, we begin to outline the contours of a communal social system before elaborating a strategic framework for pursuing its realization.

3

Envisioning the Commune

Communism is immanent to our conjuncture, manifest in "the necessary and ongoing struggle of humanity to achieve freedom—to liberate itself from its own alienated existence."[1] We take seriously the task of envisioning the contours of communist alternatives and strategizing for their realization. Our objective in this chapter is to stimulate the radical imagination and to recover and revive a vision of the world commune as the actuality of communism. Here we attempt to put our theoretical framework from Chapter 1 to work by addressing communism in relation to the different spheres of social activity and the need for institutional forms (what we describe as various forms of commons, councils, and communes) to provide stability for a fully transformed society that strives to become a global commune.

We approach these questions in a variety of ways, from more abstract concerns regarding overarching principles and strategies to more concrete designs on the particulars of how social life can be administered otherwise. Neither of these approaches is complete without the other as complement; our aim is to demonstrate a wide variety of different—and necessary—approaches to the question of how communism can and will come to be. The first two sections address fundamental questions regarding kinship and community relations, orienting our sense of just what a complete abolition of the present state of things requires. Then we turn towards institutional forms (which we envision as commons, councils, and communes) and examples of the ways that technical

1. Unity and Struggle, "The Communist Theory of Marx," *Unity and Struggle*, November 2, 2012, http:// unityandstruggle.org/2012/11/02/the-communist-theory-of-marx/.

that communal participatory planning can establish a robust communist society that is capable of equitably producing, distributing, and maintaining abundance at a global scale.

As this chapter turns towards social administration and coordination, we hope it is apparent that our intention is not so much to demonstrate that we already know exactly what a communist society will look like or how it will operate, but that we know—today—that the possibility for such a society is imminently possible and that it will be midwifed through precisely this sort of collective labor—deliberating, describing, and defining the details of a communism we are readily able to create. Our hope is that together, we can identify the principles of communist society while determining how we might enact and reproduce these principles in institutional form.

3.1 Abolition

A social revolution is the negation of the negation: "that is, not only the destruction of the old but the creation of the new."[2] A task of communist politics is to synthesize immanent potentialities for liberation into visionary platforms, programs, and projects within grassroots social struggles. It is not just to imagine how to seize power or the means of production, but to reimagine how life can be collectively organized on the basis of autonomy within solidarity. This is how we interpret Marx and Engels, who write, "Communism is for us not a state of affairs which is to be established, an ideal to which reality [will] have to adjust itself. . . We call communism the real movement which abolishes the present state of things."[3] Whereas economic reductionists interpret Marx and Engels here to refer primarily to the abolition of capital, we begin with a more expansive understanding of abolition that includes not only the abolition of capital and wage labor, but also the abolition of the heteropatriarchal family, the

2. Peter Hudis, "Rethinking the Idea of Revolution," *Herramienta, January–February* (2003), https://www.herramienta.com.ar/articulo.php?id=78/.
3. Karl Marx and Frederick Engels, *The German Ideology* (New York: International Publishers, 2007), 56–57.

abolition of whiteness, antiblackness, and all systems of racial ordering, the abolition of colonial domination, the abolition of fossil-fueled forms of production. . . in other words, we take Marx and Engels at their word, that every dimension of the present state of things needs to be critically assessed and purged of its relations of domination, exploitation, intergenerational violence, and dehumanization.

Towards this abolitionist vision, we see decolonial liberation struggles as central aspects of the broader protracted revolutionary struggle to construct communist alternatives. Due to the specifically racialized character of the imperialist world-system—primarily in the form of white supremacist colonialism—the ongoing genocide and super-exploitation of racialized peoples and the looting and destruction of the lands they inhabit is distinct from, but entangled with, the oppressive relations of heteropatriarchy, capital, and the state. Moreover, decolonial liberation struggles for community self-determination are not struggles for equal, non-discriminatory access to the spoils of imperialist plunder (this is the neocolonial delusion propagated by the comprador elite). Rather, the aim is to construct an alternative socioecological metabolism grounded in the principle of autonomy within solidarity.

According to Michi Saagiig Nishnaabeg scholar Leanne Betasamosake Simpson, we must reject conceptions of communism as a "white" construct. To the contrary, Indigenous social systems are the negation of the imperialist world-system:

> My Ancestors didn't accumulate capital, they accumulated networks of meaningful, deep, fluid, intimate collective individual relationships of trust. In times of hardship, we did not rely to any great degree on accumulated capital or individualism but on the strength of our relationships with others. . . We have no such thing as capital. We have relatives. We have clans. We have treaty partners.[4]

4. Leanne Betasamosake Simpson, *As We Have Always Done: Indigenous Freedom Through Radical Resistance* (Minneapolis: University of Minnesota Press, 2017), 77.

Peruvian communist José Carlos Mariátegui proposed that the foundation of the territorial commune must be the complete autonomy of Indigenous communities.[5] The recognition and exercise of Indigenous land claims establishes a potential material basis as a point of leverage for the world commune to move past paradigms of endless growth, extraction, consumption, and waste, fostering the general development of convivial technics and the realization of autonomy within solidarity. Consider what was witnessed in Canada with the resurgence of the liberation movements of Indigenous First Nations within Idle No More in 2013:

> Indigenous liberation must be viewed as the sum of all the particular struggles for national self-determination of any given Indigenous people. There is not merely a generalized 'Aboriginal,' nor solely an Indigenous struggle. There is a Haudenosaunee struggle, an Algonquin struggle, an Anishinaabe struggle, a Dene struggle, a Cree struggle, an Innu struggle, a Miq'mak struggle, etc.; and all these particularities entail a resurgence and reclamation of their particular nationhoods.[6]

If decolonial liberation is the basis for the abolition of racial society, this necessarily entails coming to terms with the traumas of white supremacist colonial violence, recovering stolen and repressed histories, and reconnecting with pre-colonial, pre-racial forms of life as well as practices of previous waves of decolonial liberation struggles. However, the aim of this movement is not to look backward: "it remains open to the future in the sense that it comprises, as a fundamental part of its makeup, a critical dialogue with tradition."[7] While constituting a frontline in the anti-imperialist struggle, decolonial liberation can be seen as a point of departure for the

---

5. José Carlos Mariátegui, "Peru's Principal Problem," in Harry E. Vanden and Marc Becker (eds.), *José Carlos Mariátegui: An Anthology* (New York: Monthly Review Press, 2011), 141.

6. Amil K. "After #IdleNoMore: How Can We Unite the Struggle for Communism with the Indigenous National Liberation Struggles?," *Revolutionary Initiative*, February 28, 2013, https://revolutionary-initiative.com/2013/02/28/after-idlenomore-how-can-we-unite-the-struggle-for-communism-with-the-indigenous-national-liberation-struggles/.

7. Robert Biel, *Eurocentrism and the Communist Movement* (Montreal: Kersplebedeb, 2015), 186.

broader revolutionary struggle to create a world commune that remains open to the future, crafting areas of autonomy without succumbing to exclusionary nationalism, autarky, xenophobia, and jingoism.

The abolition of racial hierarchies and the racialized categorization of peoples on the basis of phenotype (skin color) or any other arbitrary factor (religion, ethnicity, etc.), and the ultimate abolition of all racialized forms of society, is one of the communist social revolution's primary objectives. As Malcolm X pointed out, it is unlikely that we can have various forms of intercommunal solidarity in the proletarian class struggle without first prioritizing the overthrow and abolition of white supremacist colonialism, which is achieved through decolonial liberation.[8] Far from mere changes in the social charter and constitution, "the undoing of bondage— abolition—is quite literally to change places," destroying the geographies of white supremacist colonialism (reservations, plantations, prisons, etc.) requires a fundamental transformation in how future possibility is imagined.[9]

From a sociocultural perspective, "changing places" is about allowing visions of desirable and possible futures to emerge from other standpoints (and abolishing those visions of the future that are patterned by various imperialist standpoints). But it also has a more direct, grounded meaning, requiring reparations and the rematriation of land, an actual changing over of the places within which social life occurs. The entanglement of nation, land, and ecology is central to the construction of communist social systems.[10] Hence communist futures demand the direct seizure of and sharing in common of lands that have been historically dispossessed. The abolitionist project of place-changing through participatory forms of communal labor—*minga, tequio, gauchada, guelaguetza*—"underpins the commons, and is the true material

8. Malcolm X, *Malcolm X Speaks* (New York: Grove Press, 1965), 21–22.

9. Ruth Wilson Gilmore, "Abolition Geography and the Problem of Innocence," in Gaye Theresa Johnson and Alex Lubin (eds.), *Futures of Black Radicalism* (London: Verso, 2017), 231.

10. Max Ajl, "A Socialist Southern Strategy in Jackson," *Viewpoint Magazine*, June 5, 2018, https://www.viewpointmag.com/2018/06/05/a-socialist-southern-strategy-in-jackson/.

base that produces and reproduces living communities, based on relations of reciprocity and mutual help."[11] Such forms of creative socioecological activity are "the means through which the *comuneros* and *comuneras* make a community."[12]

Out of these abolitionist and decolonial struggles, alternative forms of kinship and community generate what Frantz Fanon saw as clandestine or underground cultures that would, through victorious decolonial liberation struggles, give way to new aboveground cultures that transcend the mere preservation of tradition in resistance to colonial genocide, constituting a liberated public sphere that overcomes the old colonial culture through creative reinvention. This renaissance provides the cultural basis of a revolution that can radically reinvent language, art, aesthetics, literature, music, design, fashion, erotica, and architecture:

> The struggle itself in its development and in its internal progression sends culture along different paths and traces out entirely new ones for it. The struggle for freedom does not give back to the national culture its former value and shapes; this struggle which aims at a fundamentally different set of relations between [people] cannot leave intact either the form or the content of the people's culture.[13]

Abolitionist and decolonial struggles liberate our communist imagination, allowing us to envision a new world on entirely new ground. Fred Moten and Stefano Harney say it best: "What is, so to speak, the object of abolition? Not so much the abolition of prisons but the abolition of a society that could have prisons, that could have slavery, that could have the wage, and therefore not abolition as the elimination of anything but abolition as the founding of a new society."[14]

11. Raúl Zibechi, "Counter-power and self-defense in Latin America," *ROAR Magazine*, January 29, 2018, https://roarmag.org/essays/raul-zibechi-counterpower-self-defense/.

12. Zibechi, "Counter-power and self-defense in Latin America."

13. Frantz Fanon, *The Wretched of the Earth* (New York: Grove Weidenfeld, 1991), 245–246.

14. Stefano Harney and Fred Moten, *The Undercommons: Fugitive Planning and Black Study* (Wivenhoe/New York/Port Watson: Minor Compositions, 2013), 42.

Along these lines we must connect emergent areas of autonomy with the multiple ecologies of Indigenous world-making: "The interrelationships between our ethics, cosmologies, lifeways and the waters, lands, and life-forms that sustain us are as complex and critical to our survival as those between the rivers, lakes, and wetlands within the watershed where we reside."[15] Beyond attempts to construct a singular universal, visions of an indigenist communism posit "the universal can only be pluriversal."[16] The insurgent universality of communism must produce a pluriversality grounded in the dialogic entanglement of the multiplicity of worldviews, cosmologies, and cosmovisions of Indigenous peoples. Communist social systems must embrace indigenist pluriversality and establish the material basis for the physical reconstitution of Indigenous communities, fostering a cultural revolution that restores and builds upon Indigenous modes of world-making.[17] For instance, restitution through reparations and the exercise of self-determination, such as the proposal to form a North American Union of Indigenous Nations comprising the unceded lands stolen by the imperialist United States, could create a just basis for a commune of communes, sustainably inhabiting and thriving within various bioregional contexts, fostering voluntary interdependence, and ensuring that "each Indigenous nation will choose for itself the exact manner and extent to which it expresses its autonomy, its sovereignty."[18]

As we continue through this chapter, we will outline many ways that this fundamental reenvisioning can happen. This is not to say that we look primarily to culture as opposed to the material conditions of an actually possible world commune, but that by assessing the intra-action of multiple spheres of social life, we will be able to assess more

15. Alex Wilson and Praba Pilar, "Grounding the Currents of Indigenous Resistance," *ROAR Magazine*, January 16, 2018, https://roarmag.org/essays/indigenous-peoples-resistance-americas/.
16. Walter Mignolo, "On Pluriversality" (2013), http://waltermignolo.com/on-pluriversality/.
17. Ward Churchill, *Struggle for the Land: Indigenous Resistance to Genocide, Ecocide and Expropriation in Contemporary North America* (Monroe: Common Courage Press, 1993), 403.
18. Churchill, *Struggle for the Land*, 432–433.

clearly the social building blocks that we have to work with. Do we need, for instance, to think about simply providing better forms of housing to nuclear families, or do we first need to consider—as we will below—whether the heteropatriarchal family-form itself needs to be abolished? Similarly, advanced capitalist economies have produced immensely powerful technologies capable of almost unimaginable feats. We must be able to assess which of these technological infrastructures are sedimentations of imperialist domination, and run the risk, were they to be simply "seized" by a territorial commune, of reproducing imperialist forms of extractive violence or authoritarian forms of coordination.

Based on such assessments, our revolutionary agency will often have to manifest negatively, through the blockade and sabotage of strategic chokepoints (such as pipelines, borders, and cages) that render the system inoperable, effectively rupturing with the path dependencies of imperialism and liberating the time, space, and resources for communist experiments to flourish. Given the massive dispersal of imperialism's technological infrastructure across the globe, the construction of communism is faced with a situation that makes it difficult to actualize the traditional conception of "seizing the means of production." We may need to find new ways to meet our collective needs and desires through *bricolage*, the art of "improvising something new from the materials at hand."[19] The delinking of territorial communes from the global flows of imperialism and their subsequent networking as a world commune is a matter of planetary survival:

> How to ensure that there is water and that the sewers function? How to avoid meltdowns of nuclear reactors? What does local food production look like? What types of manufacture happen nearby, and what kinds of things can be done with its productive machinery? This would be a process of

19. Out of the Woods Collective, *Hope Against Hope: Writings on Ecological Crisis* (Brooklyn: Common Notions, 2020), 181.

inventory, taking stock of things we encounter in our immediate environs, that does not imagine mastery from the standpoint of the global totality, but rather a process of *bricolage* from the standpoint of partisan fractions who know they will have to fight from particular, embattled locations, and win their battles successively rather than all at once.[20]

Prior to a revolutionary situation, militant social investigation could be used to map the flows and linkages of the territories we inhabit, such that there is shared knowledge within the communist movement of "which technologies and productive means would be orphaned by a partial or total delinking from planetary flows, which ones might alternately be conserved or converted, and what the major practical and technical questions facing a revolutionary situation might look like."[21] And of equal or greater importance for the construction of communism will be the technological and ecological transformations unleashed from below by the revolutionary struggle of the proletarian and popular social groups, emerging from diverse forms of direct social cooperation, communal life, and vibrant cultural creativity.

The Abolition of Class Society

We begin with abolition, not to deny the central importance of ending capitalist social relations, but to put this project into its proper context. There is no question that communization entails the formation of direct social relations, creating a free association of producers and consumers. A communist economy is a mode of social production, allocation, consumption, and waste management that creates a diverse range of useful goods and services to meet collective needs and desires through communal participatory planning. It aims to achieve the abolition of capital, capitalism, the law of value, and all forms of class division, including

20. Jasper Bernes, "Logistics, Counterlogistics and the Communist Prospect," *Endnotes #3: Gender, Race, Class and Other Misfortunes* (London: Endnotes, 2013), 201.
21. Bernes, "Logistics, Counterlogistics and the Communist Prospect," 201.

hierarchies formed on the basis of property ownership, divisions of labor, market competition, wages, and rent.

Communism aims for the liberation of free time for all and the creation of a free association of social individuals—a commune of communes—administering our mutually interrelated productive activities in ways that maximize autonomy within solidarity. As Marx explains: "Freedom, in [the sphere of economy], can consist only in this, that socialized [humanity], the associated producers, govern the human metabolism with nature in a rational way."[22] This is complementary to the realization of freedom in other spheres of social activity, and a requirement in order to make the ethical leap to communal abundance. Such an arrangement establishes "the predominance, in a society without classes and liberated of capitalist alienation, of 'being' over 'having,' i.e., of *free time* for the personal accomplishment by cultural, sportive, playful, scientific, erotic, artistic, and political activities, rather than the desire for an infinite possession of products."[23]

Rupturing with the class divisions of the imperialist world-system, communist social revolution expropriates capitalist property and abolishes capitalists as a class. It aims to absorb the former capitalist and coordinator classes under the counter-hegemonic communal governance of the proletariat and to construct a classless society. Communism abolishes unemployment, underemployment, and overemployment through relations of collective labor grounded in care and creativity, accounting for the labors of social reproduction that remain hidden and unpaid under capitalism. Within this context, economic activity is re-embedded within a broader social matrix wherein "labor is no longer just a means of keeping alive but has itself become a vital need."[24] The abolition of abstract la-

22. Karl Marx, *Capital: A Critique of Political Economy, Volume III* (New York: Penguin Books, 1991), 959.

23. Michael Löwy, *Ecosocialism: A Radical Alternative to Capitalist Catastrophe* (Chicago: Haymarket Books, 2015), 35.

24. Karl Marx, *The First International and After* (London: Verso, 2010), 347.

bor inherited from capital requires the development of a rational system of communal participatory planning, in which the free association of social individuals cooperatively determines the amount and characteristics of the concrete activities necessary to reproduce the conditions of our existence, advancing from social subsistence to communal abundance.

The goal, as we will now explore, is not the expansion of abstract "leisure time" (the complementary opposite of labor under capital or, socially necessary abstract labor time). Rather, the aim is to establish conditions for all to enjoy spontaneous free time, afforded by living within a free community. Our goal should be nothing less than a radical redefinition of labor, and even time itself, by creating new forms of creative production. When a material foundation to ensure collective survival and abundance is established in which basic needs are more than sufficiently met, then "the true value of human labor is not measured in the amount of material goods produced but in the level of creativity expressed, the degree of human fulfillment, and the overall extent of both spiritual and material satisfaction that is achieved."[25] We envision all types of "wildcat production"[26] and the proliferation of diverse forms of art, fashion, food, and experimental techniques emerging from commons, councils, and communes. Production can be directed to meet the needs and desires of a community that go beyond mere survival, in which "thousands of societies will spring up to gratify every taste and every possible fancy."[27]

3.2 Communism at Point Zero

Communism is a social revolution at point zero; that is, focused on "the question of reproduction, intended as the

25. Gregory Nevala Calvert, *Democracy from the Heart: Spiritual Values, Decentralism, and Democratic Idealism in the Movement of the 1960s* (Eugene, OR: Communitas Press, 1991), 222.

26. André Gorz, *Ecology as Politics* (Boston: South End Press, 1980), 42.

27. Peter Kropotkin, *The Conquest of Bread* (Oakland: AK Press, 2007), 140.

complex of activities and relations by which our life and labor are daily reconstituted."[28] Communism aims for radical transformations on the terrain of social reproduction, creating a new molecular basis for the ongoing material reproduction of everyday life rooted in the principle of autonomy within solidarity. We prefigure the relations of communism as we struggle for liberation against imperialism. This implies that communism—as a communal social system and process of collective liberation—posits *a new form of politics* that organizes itself according to the rhythms of everyday life. Politics does not exist "elsewhere," but in our everyday social intra-actions, hence the necessity of overthrowing and abolishing everyday hierarchies rooted in the binary divisions of man/woman, straight/gay, abled/disabled, young/old, manual/conceptual, rote/empowering, and public/private.

Silvia Federici has proposed that this demands feminist struggle waged by women at the level of the household:

> If the house is the *oikos* on which the economy is built, then it is women, historically the house-workers and house-prisoners, who must take the initiative to reclaim the house as a center of collective life, one traversed by multiple people and forms of cooperation, providing safety without isolation and fixation, allowing for the sharing and circulation of community possessions, and above all providing the foundation for collective forms of reproduction.[29]

We would like to queer Federici's perspective, recognizing the household as central to the processes of gender and sexual socialization in general, of which domestication of women is only one (albeit integral) aspect within heteropatriarchal imperialism. It is frequently within the household that queer and trans people are repressed, rejected, and effectively subjected to the disciplinary command and control of the

28. Silvia Federici, *Revolution at Point Zero: Housework, Reproduction, and Feminist Struggle* (Oakland: PM Press/Common Notions, 2010), 5.

29. Federici, *Revolution at Point Zero*, 147.

heteropatriarchal nuclear family. This form of family is therefore an institution for the social (re)production of gender and sexual hierarchies through disciplinary violence.

How might house-workers and house-prisoners of the world revolutionize kinship relations? One possibility is to wage feminist struggle for new kinship relations at the point of both social reproduction and production, with the formation of collective enterprises for the provisioning of tasks that remain privatized under heteropatriarchal imperialism but could otherwise be directly socialized as part of a commune. Collective enterprises such as communal kitchens, restaurants, laundromats, clothing repair centers, housekeeping collectives, and childcare are all possible grounds for the abolition of heteropatriarchal institutional boundaries.[30] New forms of communal living are also possible to envision, in which all members of a community participate in the labors of social reproduction, sharing its burdens and benefits, and abolishing gendered divisions of labor, developing queer relationalities in their place.

Given that the historical means by which heteropatriarchy attempts to usurp the autonomy of the rebel body, impose heteronormativity and compulsory heterosexuality, and subordinate the vast majority of the human species to a system of super-exploitation was through maintaining a monopoly on armed force, why not envision the formation of autonomous defense organizations led by queer people, trans people, and women? Such defense organizations could safeguard the biopolitical autonomy of all rebel bodies against residual and resurgent heteropatriarchal oppression.

Further, these queer social relations may require the support of durable social institutions. For example, the municipal commune could provision social housing, allocating space for collective dwellings; the communal polity could ensure complete freedom of movement for all peoples; and the curriculum of an autonomous education system could emphasize kin-making and comprehensive sexual

30. Sheila Rowbotham, *Women, Resistance and Revolution* (Middlesex: Penguin Books, 1974), 144.

education—spanning subjects such as active consent, sexual freedom, self-exploration, cooperative relationships, free partnerships, and the embrace of diverse sexualities and gender identities or non-identities. To this end, gender and sexual liberation will become possible in ways previously considered impossible. Queer, lesbian, gay, bisexual, transgender, intersex, two-spirit, gender nonconforming, asexual, straight, and cisgender peoples will be liberated from the burden of image, appearance, size, and performance, creating a new sensorium in which liberated human desire, sensuality, play, pleasure, curiosity, and self-exploration can flourish in a non-repressive environment based on the self-regulating and self-governing potential of human character structures. "Today's rebels want to see, hear, feel new things in a new way: they link liberation with the dissolution of ordinary and orderly perception."[31] Such a new sensorium is linked to the communist conception of being human as praxis, to "the autonomous human production of subjectivity, the human production of humanity—a new seeing, a new hearing, a new thinking, a new loving."[32]

Free Love and Free Partnerships

Communist kinship relations break with past histories of partnerships as a means of obtaining economic benefits, or as transmitters of oppressive hierarchies based on privilege and exploitation. By delinking partnerships from economic entitlement, communism ends the dominance of the traditional heterosexual partnership between men and women as the only acceptable form of intimate relationship, historically an involuntary and socially imposed relationship based on unremunerated labor, sexual exploitation, and compulsory monogamy in which women are confined to the home, responsible for giving birth and raising children, and providing uncompensated support for men's labor-power. In contrast,

31. Herbert Marcuse, *An Essay on Liberation* (Boston: Beacon Press, 1969), 37.
32. Michael Hardt, "The Common in Communism," in Costas Douzinas and Slavoj Žižek (eds.), *The Idea of Communism* (New York: Verso, 2010), 141.

communism upholds the feminist goal of the free partnership, in which all partners share equitably in the everyday responsibilities and joys of intimate relationships. Partners may choose whatever form of union they wish, and no benefits shall be accrued from a voluntary union between consenting partners other than those decided autonomously by the partners themselves.

Communist social systems unleash what Alexandra Kollontai referred to as the "winged eros" of "love-comradeship" experienced by people rooted in cultures of "sensitivity, responsiveness, and the desire to help others."[33] Communism envisions opening spaces for such experiences with all members of a community. Indeed, such love-comradeship is autonomy within solidarity, reinforced through practices of mutual aid, responsiveness to the needs and desires of others, and sensitivity through active listening.

In a communist social system, the accepted norms of sensuous, sexual, and erotic relations will be based on free association. Free time, conceived as the temporality of autonomy and measure of real wealth, is a necessary precondition for the meaningful generalization of free love. The spatio-temporalities established in communist society will create the conditions for new forms of sensuous, sexual, and erotic experience.[34] Within this context, an "expanding realm of freedom becomes truly a realm of play—of the free play of individual faculties."[35]

A Psychedelic Transformation of Everyday Life

"Without a reworking of the psyche and reinvigoration of the spirit, can there even be talk of revolution?"[36] An integral

33. Alexandra Kollontai, *Selected Writings of Alexandra Kollontai* (New York: W. W. Norton & Company, 1977), 289.

34. Jose Rosales, "What Would it Mean to Love as a Communist? To Love as a Comrade?" *The Tragic Community*, October 6, 2017, https://thetragiccommunity.wordpress.com/2017/10/06/what-would- it-mean-to-love-as-a-communist-to-love-as-a-comrade/.

35. Marcuse, *Eros and Civilization*, 204.

36. Georgy Katsiaficas, *The Subversion of Politics: European Autonomous Social Movements and the Decolonization of Everyday Life* (Oakland: AK Press, 2006), 221.

aspect of constructing communist alternatives must be the playful subversion of everyday life towards the maximization of freedom. We imagine a psychedelic or "mind-manifesting" cultural revolution, utilizing a diverse range of subversive techniques "useful for opening individuals to potentials for spiritual growth."[37] These "technologies of the non-self"— such as collective meditation, somatics, bioenergetics, yoga, dance, athletics, aimless wandering, artistic creation, and psychedelic experiences—have subversive potential to transcend the artificial constructs of bourgeois individualism in favor of collective subjectivity.[38]

Communist social systems can foster spaces for communal healing and a holistic psycho-physical reenergizing of mind, body, and spirit.[39] For example, the Workers' League for Sport and Body Culture in Austria, founded in 1924, created sporting communities to practice gymnastics, cycling, hiking, swimming, skiing, football, handball, martial arts, and tennis. The general aims of the workers' sport movement were revolutionizing consciousness, building community, and prefiguring communist social relations:

> At the heart of the workers' sport movement stood the fight against individualism, competitiveness, and commercialism. The values promoted were community, sportsmanship, and health. Running competitions were replaced by walking tours of the countryside; swimming races by life-saving courses; duels in wrestling by collective workouts; 'tournaments' by 'sports festivals'; 'national teams' by 'federations'; 'performance mania' by 'physical exercise.'[40]

---

37. Calvert, *Democracy from the Heart*, 224.

38. Jeremy Gilbert, "Psychedelic Socialism: The Politics of Consciousness, the Legacy of the Counterculture and the Future of the Left," *jeremygilbertwriting*, September 2017, https://jeremygilbertwrit- ing.files.wordpress.com/2017/09/psychedelic-socialism2.pdf; Guy Debord, "Definitions," *Internationale Situationniste*, no. 1 (1958), Ken Knabb (trans.), https://www.cddc.vt.edu/sionline/si/definitions.html.

39. George Katsiaficas, *The Subversion of Politics: European Autonomous Social Movements and the Decolonization of Everyday Life* (Oakland: AK Press, 2006), 221.

40. Gabriel Kuhn, *Antifascism, Sports, Sobriety: Forging a Militant Working-Class Culture, Selected Writings by Julius Deutsch* (Oakland: PM Press, 2017), 27.

Perhaps it is our task to create decommodified, non-alienated sporting cultures that display the pluripotentials and achievements of diverse bodies that are not rooted in competitive egoism, individualism, or the endless sale of sporting goods.[41] Such sporting cultures could function as an outlet for social tensions and a means of fostering social cooperation.

Historically, the surrealist movement offered another approach towards the psychedelic transformation of everyday life and the deployment of technologies of the non-self. Surrealism was conceived as "a movement of the human spirit in revolt and an eminently subversive attempt to re-enchant the world: an attempt to reestablish the 'enchanted' dimensions at the core of human existence—poetry, passion, mad love, imagination, magic, myth, the marvelous, dreams, revolt, utopian ideals—which have been eradicated by [imperialist] civilization and its values."[42] We understand surrealism to be a mental location where anarchism meets communism. Indeed, it is the forging of a distinctly anti-authoritarian communism open to the permanence of revolutionary experimentation.[43] Walter Benjamin noted, "an ecstatic component lives in every revolutionary act." The aim of surrealism is "[t]o win the energies of intoxication for the revolution."[44] Benjamin called for uniting this anarchic ecstasy with "the methodical and disciplinary preparation for revolution."[45]

Surrealism aims to develop techniques to overcome the reified oppositions of bourgeois culture: "dualisms of matter and spirit, exteriority and interiority, rationality and irrationality, wakefulness and dream, past and future, sacred and profane, art and nature."[46] Found not merely in artistic and literary artifacts housed in galleries and libraries, but in games,

41. Kuhn, *Antifascism, Sports, Sobriety*, 28.
42. Michael Löwy, *Morning Star: Surrealism, Marxism, Anarchism, Situationism, Utopia* (Austin: University of Texas Press, 2009), 1.
43. Löwy, *Morning Star*, 26–27.
44. Walter Benjamin, *Reflections: Essays, Aphorisms, Autobiographical Writings* (New York: Schocken Books, 2007), 189.
45. Benjamin, *Reflections*, 189.
46. Löwy, *Morning Star*, 5.

festivals, and the aimless wandering or drifting of the *dérive*, conceived as "experimental behavior linked to the conditions of urban society: a technique of rapid passage through varied ambiances."[47] The municipal commune—with its expansive green spaces, community gardens, bicycle roadways, vibrant polycultural neighborhoods, collective enterprises, and governance by federations of autonomous councils—could be the ideal space within which to experience a dérive, with surreal environments nurturing chance encounters, spontaneous creations, more-than-human vitality, and a generalized *eros effect.*[48]

Commenting on the intergalactic themes present in the Afrofuturism of Sun Ra, George Clinton, and Lee "Scratch" Perry, historian Robin D.G. Kelley suggests that we cannot limit our assessment of the polycultual foundation of the New Afrikan community to Earth: such psychedelic surrealities are indeed products of another state of mind, if not another world or dimension altogether.[49] It is in a similar sense that the Zapatistas speak of building an *Intergaláctiko*, uniting many peoples, cultures, and movements within and across multiple territories and worlds.[50] The polycultural and intercommunal place-changing and place-making of the communist social revolution will be psychedelic and surreal, magical and marvelous, global and intergalactic.

Polyculturalism and Intercommunalism

A communist vision of community relations beyond the system of nation-states could base itself upon "polyculturalism" and "intercommunalism."[51] With the overthrow and

47. Debord, "Definitions."

48. George Katsiaficas, *The Imagination of the New Left: A Global Analysis of 1968* (Boston: South End Press, 1987), 7.

49. Robin D.G. Kelley, "The People in Me," *Utne Reader*, September–October 1999, https://www.utne.com/politics/the-people-in-me.

50. R.J. Maccani, "Enter the Intergalactic: The Zapatistas' Sixth Declaration in the U.S. and the World," *Upping the Anti #3*, October 26, 2009, http://uppingtheanti.org/journal/article/03-enter-the-intergalactic/.

51. Kelley, "The People in Me"; Huey P. Newton, "Speech Delivered at Boston College: November 18,1970," in David Hilliard and Donald Weise (eds.), *The Huey P. Newton Reader* (New York: Seven Stories Press, 2002), 170.

abolition of white supremacist colonialism and all forms of racial society, achieved through national self-determination, the restoration of Indigenous sovereignty, and communal autonomy, a foundation is laid for alternative forms of cross-cultural and inter-community relations on the basis of unity in diversity, facilitated through communicative and associative freedom, transcending the limits of both assimilationist and separatist politics.[52] Whereas "multiculturalism" tends to treat cultures as fixed in time and space, polyculturalism recognizes the multiplicity of cultural forms embodied in our everyday lives and their permanent transformation through socioecological activity. Reflecting upon the experience of the Black community in North America, Robin D.G. Kelley recognizes the dynamic hybridity of Black culture:

> Black people were polycultural from the get-go. Most of our ancestors came to these shores not as Africans, but as Ibo, Yoruba, Hausa, Kongo, Bambara, Mende, Mandingo, and so on. Some of our ancestors came as Spanish, Portuguese, French, Dutch, Irish, English, Italian. And more than a few of us, in North America as well as in the Caribbean and Latin America, have Asian and Native American roots.[53]

As all humans have multiple community affiliations and cultural identities, perhaps such hybrid cultures prefigure the polycultural forms that could flourish within the context of a communist social system.[54] We can glean anticipations of such cultural forms by viewing the global proliferation of revolutionary movements, where for instance, the Black Liberation and Irish Republican Movements are grasped in their mutual interdependence via the common cause of decolonial liberation.[55] What is to be done? How can we build a polycultural and intercommunalist social system? "We can each

---

52. Justin Podur, "Polyculturalism and Self-Determination," *Znet*, July 15, 2009, https://zcomm.org/znetarticle/polyculturalism-and-self-determination-by-justin-podur/.

53. Kelley, "The People in Me."

54. Podur, "Polyculturalism and Self-Determination."

55. Kelley, "The People in Me."

narrow the territory that our common oppressor occupies. We can liberate ourselves, learning from and teaching each other along the way. But the struggle is one; the enemy is the same."[56] Through such solidarities, communist polycultural and intercommunal forms emerge.

Intercommunalism originates in the praxis of the Black Panther Party (BPP); specifically, in their experimental construction of a rainbow coalition encompassing New Afrikans, Boricuas, and Appalachian migrants within the imperialist United States, and on a global scale spanning six continents, from Cuba to Vietnam, China to Mozambique, encompassing Palestinians and Mizrahi Israelis.[57] Intercommunalism aims to constitute an inclusive unity beyond nation-states through the free association of free communities, which calls upon us "to formulate an ethics of complementarity in which cultural differentia mutualistically serve to enhance human unity itself."[58] Huey P. Newton, cofounder of the BPP in 1966, understood that if a communist social revolution was successful on a world scale, "the Black Panther Party will no longer be the *Black* Panther Party."[59] However, through the construction of territorial communes, the historical-geographical legacies and memories of white supremacist colonialism and inter-community conflict will not instantly disappear and give way to polycultural harmony.[60] Intercommunalism is grounded in an awareness that our past, present, and potential futures, as well as our historical-geographical roots as culturally distinct peoples, will remain with us for a long time.

56. Huey P. Newton, "Uniting Against a Common Enemy: October 23, 1971," in David Hilliard and Donald Weise (eds.), *The Huey P. Newton Reader* (New York: Seven Stories Press, 2002), 239–40.

57. Delio Vasquez, "Intercommunalism: The Late Theorizations of Huey P. Newton, 'Chief Theoretician' of the Black Panther Party," *Viewpoint Magazine*, June 11, 2018, https://www.viewpointmag.com/2018/06/11/intercommunalism-the-late-theorization s-of-huey-p-newton-chief-theoretician-of-the-black-panther-party/.

58. Murray Bookchin, *The Next Revolution: Popular Assemblies and the Promise of Direct Democracy* (London: Verso, 2015), 131.

59. Huey P. Newton, "Intercommunalism (1974)," *Viewpoint Magazine*, June 11, 2018, https://www.viewpointmag.com/2018/06/11/intercommunalism-1974/.

60. Michael Albert and Robin Hahnel, *Socialism Today and Tomorrow* (Boston: South End Press, 1981), 350.

Polycultural diversity and intercommunal solidarity have the potential to strengthen the adaptive capacities of communist social systems. The mutual recognition of the historical contributions of diverse communities to the commonwealth of human culture provides the basis for a range of possible responses to various socioecological situations and crises.[61] As each culture produces and reproduces particular systems of knowledge, intercommunal cooperation among different cultures can enhance the intracommunal dynamics of each.[62] With the passage of time and the growth of polycultural and intercommunal forms of life, it is likely that the enmeshing of multiple cultures and communities will yield the freedom to autonomously choose communities on the basis of preference, superseding the inheritance of particular cultural identities and community affiliations on the basis of parentage or geographic location.

A component of intercommunalism is the active construction of mutual respect for and preservation of the diversity of cultural communities, ensuring that each community has sufficient means to reproduce itself and communicate its histories, experiences, traditions, innovations, and current events to the larger global society. While it will not always be clear what constitutes the "sufficient means" communities should be guaranteed to ensure their continued cultural reproduction, some basic criteria include:

1. For communities historically oppressed by colonialism, the exercise of national self-determination, territorial sovereignty, or communal autonomy is non-negotiable.

2. Within the context of a polycultural, intercommunal social formation, all communities should have equal political and economic freedom.

3. Historically oppressed communities must have specific legal, territorial, communicative, and associative

61. Biel, *The Entropy of Capitalism*, 30–33.
62. Albert and Hahnel, *Socialism Today and Tomorrow*, 350.

freedoms to ensure their capacity to autonomously self-define, self-determine, develop, and share their cultural praxis.[63]

The historical experiences, traditions, institutions, and ways of life of diverse communities are often connected via a specific relationship to the land, with certain locations having special importance for the cultural praxis of a community. What has given life to many villages, streets, neighborhoods, wards, cities, and even entire regions, have been the distinct cultures that emerged from diverse historical experiences within specific geographical locations, and the socioecological relations established by various communities with the land. Intercommunalism upholds the claims of historically oppressed communities to "free the land," such as the freedom to inhabit and steward certain ancestral lands, and to seek collective resolutions to disputed claims of land stewardship.[64] However, under no circumstances is the land to be enclosed, owned, and used as means of fostering exploitation and dependency. Instead, the freedom of communities—especially those formerly oppressed by white supremacist colonialism—to dwell on and steward the land in common on their own terms, must be upheld and protected by respecting communal autonomy, territorial sovereignty, and the cooperative sharing of contested spaces.

3.3 Commons

The commons refer to the cellular form or basic building block of a communist social system, including resources, physical and digital spaces, knowledge, skills, tools, technologies, sciences, services, and affective relations shared by all,

63. Albert and Hahnel, *Socialism Today and Tomorrow*, 352.

64. Dan Berger, "The Malcolm X Doctrine: The Republic of New Afrika and National Liberation on U.S. Soil," in Karen Dubinsky, Catherine Krull, Susan Lord, Sean Mills, and Scott Rutherford (eds.), *New World Coming: The Sixties and the Shaping of Global Consciousness* (Toronto: Between the Lines, 2009), 49.

upon which all members of a social community are reliant for our continuing survival, socioecological reproduction, and creative development. This could include environmental commons, technical commons, social commons; anything upon which the collective wealth and abundance of society depends, can and should be held in common.[65] The communist social revolution implies a commons that generalizes throughout the fabric of global society by "proliferating, self-strengthening, and diversifying."[66] This does not by any means need to counter polyculturalism and intercommunalism, or the central importance of reparations, restitution, and the restoration of Indigenous sovereignty as non-negotiable prerequisites for the transitioning to a world commune premised upon unity in diversity.[67]

A directly socialized commons implies the organization of society on the basis of an irreducible minimum or guaranteed global livelihood, including the universalization of free and direct access to basic necessities. The commons are required for us to autonomously grow, develop, flourish, and actualize our potential: they are a collective social, technological, and ecological inheritance to which *all* are entitled. In accordance with the communist project of establishing a sustainable socioecological metabolism, the commons must be directly linked to environmental stewardship, whereby we take collective responsibility for sustaining and preserving the biosphere and geosphere we inhabit, and from which we appropriate our means of existence. As a collective inheritance established through the creative social activities of previous generations, the commons should be preserved for the shared use of future generations to come.

Communism is concerned with several categories of common systems:

65. Nick Dyer-Witheford, "Commonism," in Turbulence Collective (eds.), *What Would it Mean to Win?* (Oakland: PM Press, 2010), 106; Federici, *Revolution at Point Zero*, 139.
66. Dyer-Witheford, "Commonism," 110.
67. Roxanne Dunbar-Ortiz, *An Indigenous Peoples' History of the United States* (Boston: Beacon Press, 2014), 230.

1. *Environmental Commons:* Scarce resources and vital sinks that are appropriated by humans from our planet's biosphere and geosphere, such as arable land, water, atmosphere, fisheries, and forests, as well as the natures, spaces, and places co-produced and co-habitated by non-human life.[68]

2. *Technical Commons:* Tools, devices, machinery, hardware, software, useful technological artifacts and found objects, built structures, media, information and communications technologies, modes of transportation, energy grids, sanitation systems, and the multiple forms of accumulated artistic, scientific, technological, engineering, and design knowledge that govern various practices of use and environmental alteration.[69]

3. *Social Commons:* Bases of social production and reproduction, such as collective enterprises (farms, factories, workshops, studios, laboratories, etc.), and forms of full social provisioning characterized by free and direct access, such as healthcare, childcare, education, recreation, transportation, libraries, theaters, cinemas, festivals, parks, gardens, cafeterias, consumer cooperatives, and autonomous social centers.[70]

Too often, revolutionary struggles have found themselves having to limit their needs and potentials to the dictates of circumstances imposed externally by or inherited from imperialism. However, by placing the commons at the disposal of a communal federation of autonomous institutions, communism creates a material foundation through which basic needs can be met while simultaneously creating new needs

68. Dyer-Witheford, "Commonism," 106.

69. Jesse Goldstein, *Planetary Improvement: Cleantech Entrepreneurship and the Contradictions of Green Capitalism* (Cambridge: MIT Press, 2018), 164–165; Elizabeth R. Johnson and Jesse Goldstein, "Biomimetic Futures: Life, Death, and the Enclosure of a More-than-Human Intellect," *Annals of the Association of American Geographers* 105, no. 2 (2015): 387–396; Murray Bookchin, Post-Scarcity Anarchism (Oakland: AK Press, 2004), 78.

70. Dyer-Witheford, "Commonism," 106; De Angelis, *The Beginning of History*, 148.

and potentials, and subsequent pathways towards their collective realization.

While direct socialization of the means of social (re)production is certainly an aspect of constructing a commons, the question of how we use technologies to transform ourselves, each other, and our environments is central. What communist logics and principles of praxis, what new sensibilities, might govern the utilization of resources held in common? One way to approach these questions is through Ivan Illich's concept of *conviviality*, which recognizes the particular ways in which tools are utilized within a given social system. Ivan Illich explains:

> Tools foster conviviality to the extent to which they can be easily used, by anybody, as often or as seldom as desired, for the accomplishment of a purpose chosen by the user. The use of such tools by one person does not restrain another from using them equally. They do not require previous certification of the user. Their existence does not impose any obligation to use them. They allow the user to express [their] meaning in action.[71]

This could provide the rudimentary basis for elaborating the invention and design criteria of a communist alter-modernity, or an alternative "understanding of modernity as a thing in becoming, its components forming a whole through ceaseless differential and synchromesh."[72] Such a convivial perspective could inform the innovation of the technical commons itself, and the corresponding social relations governing the entanglement of the technical commons with environmental and social commons.

Specific social relations are embodied within the technical commons, as a given technological system has an optimal,

71. Ivan Illich, *Tools for Conviviality* (London: Marion Boyars, 2009), 22.
72. Simon Sadler, "The Dome and the Shack: The Dialectics of Hippie Enlightenment," in Iain Boal, Janferie Stone, Michael Watts, and Cal Winslow (eds.), *West of Eden: Communes and Utopia in Northern California* (Oakland: PM Press, 2012), 79.

tolerable, and negative range.[73] This is illustrated by the tension between the values of individual velocity achieved via automobiles and the attendant highway system (a mode of transportation that demands urban social life restructure itself accordingly, fosters social atomization, and is dependent upon extractive industries of a deeply destructive character), versus the autonomy achieved via bicycles as a potentially convivial mode of transportation. A municipal commune that decides to maximize the availability and usability of bicycles through urban planning and manufacturing will likely obtain significant gains in terms of everyday face-to-face interactions, safety, urban aesthetics, and ecological sustainability.[74] This could be achieved without losing the efficient aspects of automobiles via the construction of covered bicycle roadways that connect neighborhoods, utilization of freight cycles to transport goods and services, and the strategic placement of bike repair stations along key routes.[75] Nor would such a convivial transportation system need to lose the advantages of long-distance transportation, which could be achieved through a variety of alternative modes of transportation, such as municipal light rails and high-speed trains connecting central hubs, as well as maintaining a limited and subordinate role for automobiles, as in the form of delivery trucks, buses, and transportation for emergencies and for disabled people.

Communal Habitations

To overthrow and abolish the heteropatriarchal nuclear family means envisioning alternative centers for the biological and social reproduction of human life—a new mode of habitation—and demands "the invention of new *amorous institutions*."[76] Communal habitations or *micro-communes* can be established as alternative centers of social reproduction—a

---

73. Illich, *Tools for Conviviality*, 78.
74. Illich, *Tools for Conviviality*, 81.
75. Illich, *Tools for Conviviality*, 21.
76. C17, "11 Theses on Possible Communism," *Viewpoint Magazine*, January 31, 2018, https://www.viewpointmag.com/2018/01/31/11-theses-possible-communism/.

radical reimagining of the *kibbutz, obshina,* or *grupo de affini-dad.* A feminist praxis of social reproduction—one that brings together many of the innovations developed by prior communal living experiments—would likely "need fewer durable goods and involve less waste than households composed of atomized individuals and couples." Moreover, experimentation with "communal living expands the potential for individual life choices and creates the possibility of new types of intimate relationships and new models for child rearing."[77]

The areas of autonomy created by communist social systems can open room for diverse living arrangements to accommodate parental and non-parental partnerships, transients, ramblers, and all types of gatherings of friends, lovers, and comrades; temporary residencies needed by students, researchers, artists, travelers, and seasonal workers; and special residencies for those requiring specific forms of assistance. We have seen elements of such forms in past experiments, such as the group houses created by the revolutionary movement during the 1980s and 1990s in Germany: "Big enough to include movie theaters, practice rooms for bands, bookshops, bars, women's centers, and some of the few openly gay public spaces, group houses were the basis for autonomous culture and politics."[78] These group houses were considered by many to be nuclei of a communist social system, and bases from which to launch a revolutionary counter-offensive against imperialism. To meet the diversity of human biological, social, and spatial needs and desires, our vision proposes communal homes as alternative organizational forms of everyday life and intergenerational social reproduction. Communal homes will support a cooperative division of household tasks and collective forms of childrearing, parenting, and caregiving for elders, and disabled people.

Communism upholds and defends the biopolitical autonomy of all bodies and minds, ensuring all people direct access to the means of actualizing an independent life, to

77. Katsiaficas, *The Subversion of Politics,* 176, 247.
78. Katsiaficas, 175.

the resources supplementing our collective creativity, and to participation in communities of full care. Therapies, technologies, and medical services have to be made freely available through communal healthcare clinics as well as through networks of visiting care workers. Those who are physically or mentally unable to work, or who choose not to work, should receive economic compensation according to need.

Furthermore, the built environment of the street, neighborhood, ward, and municipality will be redesigned to maximize accessibility for all types of people. Associations and assemblies of people with disabilities will be empowered to veto decisions that disproportionately affect them, and to have an autonomous role in the co-production of educational environments, curriculum, and pedagogy.

Elders should be recognized as integral members of society, possessing wisdom that can assist present and future generations, and be encouraged to share and record their stories as part of a larger project of cultivating a collective historical memory. Elders must be supported in pursuing the life of their choosing, be it living independently, collectively, or through forms of assisted living. When ready to retire from direct participation in economic life as a free producer, elders should receive compensation and assistance according to need. While life expectancy has increased in many parts of the world, under imperialism, "the positive effects of a longer lifespan have been voided or are clouded by the prospect of loneliness, social exclusion, and increased vulnerability to physical and psychological abuse."[79] This calls for a holistic praxis of mutual aid facilitated through communities of full care and supplemented by the social provisioning established by care workers operating on the basis of the commons.

In our vision of a communist social system, communal habitations consist of a single voluntary collective living unit, residing within a common dwelling, or a cluster of individual and collective living units that might aggregate to form a communal village as a network of several living units concentrated

79. Federici, *Revolution at Point Zero*, 115.

in a compact geographical area, such as a residential street. We anticipate communal habitations to be formed fluidly, through spontaneous relations formed through common projects, associations, educational pursuits, hangouts, or encounters. Various material resources—such as land and building materials drawn from an environmental commons, and architectural design and construction collectives drawing knowledge and materials from a technical commons—are to be placed at the disposal of a new communal habitation by the various council federations of the municipal commune. Members of a communal habitation would be free to come and go in accordance with their needs and desires, as all people should be free to choose and change their preferred place of residence.

Regardless of biological relationship, all members of a communal habitation can be expected to participate in various household tasks, such as cooking, cleaning, gardening, maintenance, repairs, childrearing, and caring for elders. This cooperative division of tasks and responsibilities would create considerably more free time and flexibility for all, and serve as the material basis for the multiplication of affinities among comrades, whereby tasks, worries, struggles, and experiences are collectivized so that no single person or interpersonal relationship is forced to disproportionately carry the emotional burdens of social reproduction.

Within communal habitations, biological childbearing and birthing need not imply childrearing: daycare centers, kindergartens, educational consortiums, and parenting collectives could more than compensate. Biological parents and children choosing to live in the same communal habitation, with parenting collectives to share the benefits and burdens of social reproduction, could decenter the gendered character of carework. Communal habitations could be intimately linked to the healthcare and educational institutions of the residential street, neighborhood, ward, and municipality through various associations and assemblies.[80]

80. K.D. Griffiths and J.J. Gleeson, "Kinderkommunismus: A Feminist Analysis of the Twenty-First Century Family and a Communist Proposal for its Abolition," *Ritual*, June 21, 2015, http://www.ritual-mag.com/kinderkommunismus/.

As part of this social commons, networks of people's healthcare clinics throughout a municipal commune could provide comprehensive sexual education for all, and make available upon request: all forms of contraceptives to prevent pregnancy; protection to prevent the spread of sexually transmitted infections; access to safe abortions; and the provision of synthetic biomedical technologies to enable gender self-determination and reproductive freedom. For people who choose to have children, there should be autonomous medical facilities capable of provisioning services to meet the needs of all bodies, with complete access to the means for safe and healthy pregnancies, compensation in the event of choosing to raise children alone, or the option of collective childrearing as a member of a communal habitation. Protected by the social charter and constitution of a territorial commune's polity, and supported by the local economy of the municipal commune, gender and sexual rebels could create a tapestry of autonomous social centers, associations, assemblies, publications, and media as tools for communicating, defending, and advancing the feminist revolution.

Education for Autonomy

Education is an ongoing process. Throughout life, humans are constantly learning through co-producing knowledge and transforming praxis accordingly. The educational process can be "a meaningful encounter, sustained by interest, curiosity, and personal purpose. In this sense, education is not the mere acquisition of information, but a joyful, exhilarating and enriching exploration of the world and one's intricate relationship to it."[81] Throughout the protracted revolutionary struggle, communists emphasize critical education as a general social activity rooted in everyday experience, key to the holistic development of a free people, and not merely limited to schools and libraries. From communal habitations

---

81. Ron Miller, *What Are Schools For? Holistic Education in American Culture* (Brandon, VT: Holistic Education Press, 1990), 157.

to collective enterprises, neighborhood assemblies to cultural festivals, educational processes could socialize people to become autonomous participants in the co-production of socioecological life. The autonomous social individual of communism will be, above all else, the result of a holistic education supported by the social institutions of the municipal commune. Within this context, education would not aim to "prepare" people for all the adventures and challenges of life: education *is* life, and life *is* education.[82]

As A.S. Neill emphasized, educational institutions can bestow upon humanity a legacy of freedom or oppression: "To be a free soul, happy in work, happy in friendship, and happy in love or to be a miserable bundle of conflicts, hating one's self and hating humanity—one or the other is the legacy that parents and teachers give to every child."[83] The path to freedom in education, then, is through voluntary participation in education institutions. Within communist social systems the role of educational institutions will be significantly *expanded* on the basis of free association and popular democratic control. Such institutions will be central to the processes of socioecological reconstruction, organizing and systematizing the sharing of knowledge co-produced through experience, ensuring provisions for standard education and training in fields relevant to constructing and maintaining communal infrastructure (such as engineering, healthcare, sanitation, disease control, agriculture, etc.), and assisting the formation of a free self-governing people. This is a vision of a *polytechnic education*, enabling "a continuous rotation or simultaneous exercise of manual, administrative, technical and free creative work. This interchangeability of functions is necessary in order to abolish specializations, mutilations, social stratifications, and the state, and to achieve the voluntary division of labor within society and the self-management by associated individuals of all aspects of their social activity."[84]

82. Miller, *What Are Schools For?*, 157.
83. A.S. Neill, *Summerhill: A Radical Approach to Child Rearing* (New York: Wallaby, 1977), 297.
84. Gorz, *Socialism and Revolution*, 181–182.

We envision schools and academies acting as the core polytechnic educational institutions of a communist social system, integrating various departments and institutes focused on research and development in diverse fields of academic study.[85] Within a municipal commune, educational consortiums could federate multiple schools, academies, libraries, forums, publications, and media thereby enabling the co-production of ideas among students, researchers, and practitioners across diverse fields of study. The result would be an effective end to "professionals" and "managers" as discrete social categories through the creation of a surplus of literate, highly educated, technically skilled, and autonomous people capable of performing a variety of critical roles in all spheres of socioecological life, self-governing the environmental, technical, and social commons in accordance with convivial criteria, and participating actively in the life of the federated councils that administer the institutions of the municipal commune.[86] We envision the wild multiplication and variation of educational places and spaces, not singularly limited to the physical institution of the school or academy, as well as the proliferation of institutes rooted in a diverse range of pedagogical theories and areas of focus.

Socialization processes should free people to develop creative potentials, and communist social systems could be structured to accommodate, support, and benefit from the resulting diversification of human personalities.[87] With the liberation of a general intellect by autonomous education systems, within the context of a commons open to all, we can only speculate as to the fantastic inventiveness that people would introduce into everyday life. What if, for example, young people played an autonomous role in social planning at various levels, from the household to municipality? Instead of adults planning environments for young people, perhaps

85. Michael Knapp et al., *Revolution in Rojava: Democratic Autonomy and Women's Liberation in Syrian Kurdistan* (London: Pluto Press, 2016), 181.

86. Griffiths and Gleeson, "Kinderkommunismus."

87. Albert and Hahnel, *Socialism Today and Tomorrow*, 334.

we could envision a free community of social individuals co-producing social environments across the generations in ways that remain permanently open to future reinvention?[88]

3.4 Communal Administration and Coordination

Given the combined and uneven development of the social revolution, the construction of a world commune will likely require some form of polycentric administration for the territorial commune of communes, with "territory" understood as "a shorthand for the system of relations whose continuous reenactment recreates the community in question."[89] Such an administration would function as a point of convergence for the multiple forms of communal governance emerging from below, responsible for mobilizing the necessary resources and appropriate personnel to ensure the consolidation, generalization, federation, and defense of the emergent forms of organized autonomy. The forms of organized autonomy created by the people during the course of revolutionary struggle must be immediately consolidated and generalized as the institutional basis of communal governance and the partisan core of a vibrant civil society. Communal governance, Marx explains, is "the reabsorption of the state power by society as its own living forces instead of as forces controlling and subduing it, by the popular masses themselves, forming their own force instead of the organized force of their suppression—the political form of their social emancipation."[90]

The communist alternative we fight for is a social system based on the proliferation of environmental, technical, and social commons. A convivial logic governs our sustainable stewardship and appropriation of these commons: collective participatory decision-making is rooted in federated councils and communes. This requires a common infrastructure

88. Simon Nicholson, "Children as Planners," in Beatrice Gross and Ronald Gross (eds.), *The Children's Rights Movement: Overcoming the Oppression of Young People* (Garden City, New York: Anchor Books, 1977), 291.

89. Escobar, *Designs for the Pluriverse*, 173.

90. Marx, *The First International and After*, 250.

encompassing education, transportation, communications, sanitation, healthcare, clothing, housing, agriculture, ecological restoration, and defense. For those who think that the wild creativity of a communist society is in some way juxtaposed to social stability, we should recognize Mark Fisher's observation "that a certain amount of stability is necessary for cultural vibrancy."[91]

The communal governance we envision would need the following for its realization: (1) the formulation and adoption of a social charter and constitution that ensures the protection of the people's freedom and environmental habitats, with specific regard for the autonomy of historically oppressed communities, enumerating the responsibilities and limits of communal governance at all levels; (2) the defense and security of territory through disarmament and disbandment of the state's military and police apparatuses, confiscation of all state munitions by the people's defense organizations, mobilization against external counter-revolutionary invasion, and containment and suppression of all attempts to sabotage the revolutionary process of social reconstruction by reactionary forces; (3) the establishment of procedures for disaster preparation, response, and relief; (4) the formulation of criteria for the municipal administration of communal infrastructure, such that ensuring a basic educational curriculum is made available for all inhabitants of every municipal commune; (5) the elimination of bureaucracy and its overly complex functions of social administration; and, (6) the creation of a communal governance that relies upon working committees directly accountable to, and recallable by, federations of grassroots participatory councils.

Conviviality militates against tendencies towards authoritarian centralization, as its polytechnic character necessarily demands the sovereignty of the institutions at the base of a communal social system, such as autonomous neighborhood and workplace councils. For example, solar and wind energy

---

91. Mark Fisher, *Capitalist Realism: Is There No Alternative?* (Winchester, UK: Zero Books, 2009), 77.

could power a municipal commune engaged in economic production to directly satisfy collective needs and desires, scaled to meet the criteria of a sustainable socioecological metabolism. However, as Murray Bookchin emphasized, it is unlikely that such forms of energy production could meet the needs of the imperialist megacity and its attendant sprawling suburban hinterland, thereby demanding radical transformations in urban design and construction:

> To bring the sun, the wind, the earth, indeed the world of life, back into technology, into the means of human survival, would be a revolutionary renewal of [humanity's] ties to nature. To restore this dependence in a way that evoked a sense of regional uniqueness in each community—a sense not only of generalized dependence but of a dependence on a specific region with distinct qualities of its own—would give this renewal a truly ecological character. A real ecological system would emerge, a delicately interlaced pattern of local resources, honored by continual study and artful modification. With the growth of a true sense of regionalism every resource would find its place in a natural, stable balance, an organic unity of social, technological and natural elements. Art would assimilate technology by becoming social art, the art of the community as a whole. The free community would be able to rescale the tempo of life, the work patterns of [humanity], its own architecture and its systems of transportation and communication to human dimensions.[92]

The development of federations of municipal communes synchronized with bioregions and territories, each with their own unique cultures, governed by autonomous institutions, with convivial ethics guiding the (re)production of a technical commons, must always maintain the principle that "*the most critical function of modern technology must be to keep the doors of the revolution open forever.*"[93]

92. Bookchin, *Post-Scarcity Anarchism*, 76.
93. Bookchin, *Post-Scarcity Anarchism*, 77–78.

Councils

Councils are administrative collectivities involving autonomous participatory assemblies and their networks of committees, collectives, clubs, and associations. Councils can be central units of the communal polity—as with neighborhood, ward, municipal, regional, and territorial councils—or units of communal economic administration formed within collective enterprises. To coordinate across large geographic distances and to maintain intercommunal relations based on the inclusive unity of diverse peoples living in sustainable metabolic relation with the biosphere and geosphere, councils could form *federations*, or the free association of council organizations achieved via a system of nested and immediately recallable delegates, to network interconnected activities across various scales and levels of complexity.

The power of the councils is based on the direct participation of the masses. However, this power is diminished when political interest groups come to dominate them.[94] While we desire a multiplicity of revolutionary party organizations to proliferate and participate within a communist social system at all levels, such organizations must be prohibited from centralizing power on their own behalf within the councils. The autonomy of councils at the grassroots level must be defended, as these freedoms should remain permanent features of the people's participation in social administration, for "there can be no separation of the revolutionary process from the revolutionary goal. *A society based on self-administration must be achieved by means of self-administration.*"[95] In contrast to forms of society that "do not possess mechanisms for the self-questioning of the inherited world of meaning," councils constitute an ontological form of self-government, in which all spheres of social activity remain permanently open to critical questioning and the social system itself is continuously

---

94. Gabriel Kuhn, "Don't Mourn, Organize! Is Communism a Pipe Dream—or a Viable Future?," *Brooklyn Rail*, March 2018, https://brooklynrail.org/2018/03/field-notes/Dont-Morn-Organize-Is-Communism-a-Pipe-Dreamor-a-Viable-Future/.
95. Bookchin, *Post-Scarcity Anarchism*, 104.

reconstituted and regenerated by the autonomous participation of its members.[96]

While we aspire to create autonomous forms of participatory self-government as the foundation of a communist social system, we must remain aware that, prior to the insurrectionary establishment of a territorial commune, the council has a contradictory existence as both a prefiguration of the social system to come and a vehicle of the protracted revolutionary struggle's initiation and generalization of insurrection.[97] Herbert Marcuse reminds us: "The immediate expression of the opinion and will of the workers, farmers, neighbors—in brief, of the people—is not, per se, progressive and a force of social change: it may be the opposite. The councils will be organs of revolution only to the degree to which they represent the people *in revolt*."[98] Hence the necessity of building communism from below, in which a shared political platform and program informs and guides a revolutionary people in the process of social reconstruction, in contrast to fetishizing an abstract democracy from below divorced from the concrete particularities of the contradictions produced by the imperialist world-system.

Communes

As we have indicated, the social revolution aims to overthrow and abolish the imperialist world-system, and to replace it with a world commune. This process will not be instantaneous; it will instead consist of a protracted process through which networks of territorial communes encompassing large geographic regions are gradually consolidated. According to Raúl Zibechi, "territory is the space in which to build a new social organization collectively, where new subjects

96. Christopher Holman, "The Councils as Ontological Form: Cornelius Castoriadis and the Autonomous Potential of Council Democracy," in James Muldoon (ed.), *Council Democracy: Towards a Democratic Socialist Politics* (New York: Routledge, 2018), 140.

97. Antonio Negri, *Factory of Strategy: 33 Lessons on Lenin* (New York: Columbia University Press, 2014), 114–115.

98. Marcuse, *Counterrevolution and Revolt*, 45.

take shape and materially and symbolically appropriate their space."[99] Autonomous control of territory—conceived in the broadest possible sense—is the basis of a revolutionary people's sovereignty, as "the land is not only our source of nourishment, but it is from the land that bodies gather meaning, sensations, collective imagination."[100] As Malcolm X emphasized: "Revolution is based on land. Land is the basis of all independence. Land is the basis of freedom, justice, and equality."[101] While always present in the revolutionary struggles of the past, the increasing centrality of territory is reflective of both the present ecological crisis caused by imperialism's destruction of the earth's regenerative capacities, and "the crisis of the old territoriality of the factory and farm."[102]

In our vision of a communist alternative, each territorial commune consists of federated municipal communes as the basic units of urban and rural social (re)production. Marta Harnecker explains:

> The commune is a populated territory within which exists a number of communities that share common historical-cultural traditions, problems, aspirations, and economic vocations and use of the same services; they have the conditions to be self-sustaining and self-governing; and are willing to come together behind a common project that has been elaborated in a participatory manner and is constantly being evaluated and adjusted for new circumstances as they emerge.[103]

Municipal communes could federate to form bioregional communes, which in turn would federate to form a territorial

99. Raúl Zibechi, *Territories in Resistance: A Cartography of Latin American Social Movements* (Oakland: AK Press, 2012), 19.

100. Mariarosa Dalla Costa, "The Door to the Flower and the Vegetable Garden (2002)," *Viewpoint Magazine*, June 20, 2017, https://www.viewpointmag.com/2017/06/20/the-door-to-the-flower-and-the-vegetable-garden-2002/.

101. Malcolm X, *Malcolm X Speaks*, 9.

102. Zibechi, *Territories in Resistance*, 14.

103. Marta Harnecker, *A World to Build: New Paths Toward Twenty-First Century Socialism* (New York: Monthly Review Press, 2015), 134.

commune. In contrast to the indefinite urban expansion of imperialism, communism could foster social, technological, and ecological dynamism through programs for urban agriculture; sustainable economies of scale geared towards communal resilience, durability, reuse, and repurposing; and self-managed forms of urban planning, design, and civic life through federations of autonomous participatory councils.

Stewardship of the Commons and Collective Enterprises

Convivial stewardship of environmental, technical, and social commons by a free people creates the conditions where "property in the form of means of production becomes a non-thing."[104] One of the first steps taken towards a communist reorganization of economic life will be the radical transformation of agriculture and industry in accordance with alternative criteria established by the municipal communes. Conceived as an extension of the commons, collective enterprises in the form of farms, workshops, laboratories, factories, studios, and service providers will constitute the key units of economic production. In many cases, instead of forming an enterprise with a singular function, polytechnic and multivalent enterprises could be formed, integrating directly into the broader socioecological fabric of everyday life, further dissolving the distinction between work and non-work. These enterprises could be self-managed through federations of workers' councils—the autonomous participatory assemblies of producers—whereby workers have a direct say in decisions, in proportion to the degree that they are affected. A communist society should aim to maximize a sphere of production in which goods and services are provided freely and directly for all. However, goods and services contingent upon scarce intermediary inputs, or whose production, allocation, and consumption are associated with particularly negative socioecological impacts, would require rationing or even prohibition.

104. Michael Albert, *Parecon: Life After Capitalism* (London: Verso, 2003), 90.

With this in mind, it may be useful to distinguish between two types of collective enterprises: (1) *limited production enterprises*, in which goods and services are produced in finite quantities and redeemed for vouchers or otherwise distributed due to scarcity, labor-intensive production methods, or negative socioecological effects; and, (2) *general social-use enterprises*, or simply public collectives.[105] Limited production enterprises produce goods and services that rely upon certain inputs characterized by scarcity or negative socioecological costs, yet are deemed necessary or desirable through the planning process, as with necessary intermediary products derived from extractive mining processes or products whose consumption entails one-time use with little in the way of long-term socioecological benefit. In contrast, general social-use enterprises provide open access for all, with free and direct provisioning of goods and services. These include collective enterprises responsible for the administration of municipal and bioregional infrastructure, encompassing healthcare, energy, transportation, education, and various amenities such as cafeterias, parks, recreational facilities, and so on.

Within the context of the convivial stewardship and use of the commons, we can anticipate the transformation of farms, workshops, laboratories, factories, studios, service providers, and other productive facilities into multivalent and polytechnic enterprises producing not only tangible goods and services but also serving a multiplicity of useful socioecological functions. As producers of useful articles, stewards of the environmental commons, and sites of artistic expression and techno-scientific research, these collective enterprises could be integrated into the spatial fabric or territorial environment of a given neighborhood, ward, municipality, or bioregion. This seems increasingly feasible as advancements in micro-industrial technologies enable greater diversification of productive operations at the local level.

---

105. Gruppe Internationaler Kommunisten (GIK), "Fundamental Principles of Communist Production and Distribution (1930)," Libcom (July 25, 2005), https://libcom.org/library/fundamental-principles-communist-production-gik/.

Federated Councils of Workers and Consumers

Within every collective enterprise, large or small, for general social use or limited production, producers form *workers' councils* in which each worker has proportionate decision-making input. Everyone is free to apply for membership to the workers' council of their choice or apply to the appropriate industrial federation to form a new workers' council when starting a new collective enterprise to obtain start-up resources.

Organized in accordance with the demands of functionality and synchronized with the economic priorities of a particular social formation, smaller councils could be organized on the basis of teams, units, and small divisions within a collective enterprise, whereas larger councils could be formed on the basis of larger divisions within a collective enterprise, whole enterprises, and industries.[106] Each council could function autonomously, self-managing the projects of a team, unit, division, or the enterprise as a whole, with participants deciding upon appropriate decision-making standards for their own council.

At the level of municipal commune, bioregion, or territory, production could be organized through nested federations of workers' councils, whereby each division within a collective enterprise is self-organized into a council, itself belonging to a workers' council for the collective enterprise, which would belong to a federation of workers' councils encompassing multiple collective enterprises within that particular industry, which would belong to an even larger federation of workers' councils for the economy as a whole and organized simultaneously at municipal, bioregional, territorial, and interterritorial levels.[107]

Consumption could likewise be organized through nested federations of *consumers' councils*, overlapping with the councils of the polity. Each individual living unit would belong to a consumers' council at the neighborhood level (consisting of

106. Albert, *Parecon*, 92.
107. Albert, *Parecon*, 92.

multiple households), which could belong to a federation of neighborhood councils for the ward, belonging to a federation of ward councils for the municipal commune as a whole, and so on, up to the levels of bioregion, territory, and beyond.[108] It is through consumers' councils that personal and collective consumption are accounted for and consumption requests are aggregated and then placed in dialogue with the factors of production. Requests are then accounted for via a communal participatory planning process.

Councils could be nested in multiple federations, because at each level different decisions pertaining to production, consumption, allocation, or waste management affect people in different ways, depending on the context.[109] Far from being mechanical conveyor belts for static information, the councils are spaces of dynamic communal deliberation and debate, "carrying and interchanging the opinions, the intentions, the will of the groups of workers [and consumers]."[110] Delegates elected to different council levels are not professional bureaucrats but the workers and consumers who directly participate in collective labors of social (re)production. They always directly accountable to, and recallable by, the voting power of their constituency. This council system "weaves a variegated net of collaborating bodies through society, regulating its life and progress according to their own free initiative. And all that in the councils is discussed and decided draws its actual power from the understanding, the will, the action of working [humanity] itself."[111]

At the neighborhood-level, a consumers' council might form a consumer cooperative or general store, allocating physical space for a warehouse and distribution center where members of the neighborhood consumer cooperative could pick up various items or receive items at their place of residence from the cooperative's delivery service. If feasible, the space of

108. Robin Hahnel, *Of The People, By The People: The Case for a Participatory Economy* (London: Soapbox Press, 2012), 79.

109. Albert, *Parecon*, 93.

110. Anton Pannekoek, *Workers' Council* (Oakland: AK Press, 2003), 45.

111. Pannekoek, *Workers' Council*, 50.

the cooperative could be physically linked to the assembly hall of the residential street or neighborhood councils of the polity to ensure seamless integration of various social institutions into a functioning communal system without bureaucracy.

Communal Participatory Planning

In accordance with the principle of unity in diversity, we want an economic system that makes possible multiple plans corresponding to the diverse range of needs and desires that exist at different spatiotemporal scales, not merely at the level of a particular collective enterprise. In other words, "the plan concerns the main economic options," in contrast to the particularities of administration within a collective enterprise which, as already established, autonomously administers its internal affairs via self-managed workers' councils.[112]

Participants in a communal participatory planning process at the territorial level include: (1) federations of workers' councils organized on the basis of collective enterprise, industry, geography, and bioregion, with each council proposing the goods and services they have the capacity and desire to produce; (2) federations of consumers' councils organized on the basis of neighborhood, ward, municipality, and bioregion, with each council proposing the goods and services they would like to consume; and, (3) facilitation boards to process (a) information relevant to workers' and consumers' councils assessing the feasibility of various production and consumption proposals and long-run investment decisions throughout the multiple iterations of the planning process, (b) requests for individuals seeking new work assignments, and (c) requests for individuals and groups seeking new housing options.[113] At all levels, facilitation boards could "help units revise proposals and search out the least disruptive ways of modifying plans in response to unforeseen circumstances."[114] Operating like

112. Löwy, *Ecosocialism*, 26.
113. Michael Albert and Robin Hahnel, *The Political Economy of Participatory Economics* (Princeton: Princeton University Press, 1991), 62.
114. Albert, *Parecon*, 128.

any other collective enterprise within the communist economy, facilitation boards would be administered by a workers'
council with equitable work assignments and remunerated in
accordance with actual concrete labor time with consideration
for effort and sacrifice.

Communal participatory planning is conceived as a
social, iterative process of coordinating economic activity
via federations of councils. The planning procedure follows
three steps:

1. At the beginning of each round of planning, a facilitation board announces current estimates of positive
   and negative socioecological effects taking into account
   both current information and last year's plan, in the
   form of quantitative indicators for all production
   inputs, including: resources appropriated from the
   commons; categories of labor; and anticipated ramifications for producing and consuming various final
   goods and services.

2. Consumers' councils and federations respond to the
   facilitation board's announcement with consumption
   proposals for personal and collective consumption,
   using the quantitative indicators as a guide. Workers'
   councils and federations respond with production
   proposals, including qualitative information regarding
   the production processes involved in making various
   goods and services. Each collective enterprise enumer-
   ates the outputs they want to make available, as well
   as the inputs required to make them. Federations of
   workers' and consumers' councils aggregate proposals
   and monitor excess supply and demand.

3. The facilitation board processes all requests and
   agreements to utilize various resources drawn from
   and returned to the environmental, technical and
   social commons, including anticipated raw materials,
   categories of labor, pollutants, and waste. Estimated

quantitative indicators are subsequently adjusted in accordance with excess supply or demand.[115]

These steps are repeated in subsequent iterations until there remains no excess demand for any final or intermediate goods and services, common resources, categories of labor, or permissions to emit pollutants, increase waste production, or sacrifice certain biophysical zones to damaging forms of economic activity.[116] As workers and consumers negotiate supply and demand, "they alter their proposals to accord with the messages they receive, and the process converges."[117] The aim of multiple planning iterations is to eventually converge upon a final comprehensive plan for the year, with each round of planning beginning with more accurate assessments of costs and benefits, followed by federated councils revising their proposals in light of new information about how their projected economic activities affect others.

To autonomously coordinate and synchronize production and consumption while maintaining a sustainable socioecological metabolism, councils must have direct access to certain informational and communicative tools required to make the following decisions:

1. Assess different courses of action, such as the relative socioecological gains derived from using more or less efficient production techniques measured against the relative increase or decrease of consumer welfare; or, assessment of the projected effects of certain consumption requests measured against the total actual labor time, effort, and sacrifice required to produce the goods and services in question.

2. Assess and distinguish between average and non-average workloads and consumption requests; workers must be able to determine what constitutes an equitable

115. Hahnel, *Of the People, By the People*, 91–92.
116. Hahnel, *Of the People, By the People*, 91–92.
117. Albert, *Parecon*, 128.

workload and consumers must be able to determine what constitutes a reasonable consumption request.

3. Determine the cumulative socioecological impact of specific production and consumption choices, including an assessment of quantifiable and non-quantifiable ramifications of specific courses of action.[118]

Towards these ends, we envision three core informational and communicative devices that could assist the communal planning process: (1) quantitative indicators, (2) measures of work, and (3) qualitative activity assessments.

Quantitative indicators are a tool used by producers and consumers to discern the relative effects of economic choices. Therefore, quantitative indicators must accurately estimate full socioecological costs and benefits of various economic activities in order to effectively guide the formulation and evaluation of proposals throughout the planning process.[119] These indicators "are not binding but flexible."[120] In this respect, quantitative indicators are completely different from the monetary prices determined by the markets of a capitalist economy, which are reflective of the dynamics of class struggle, encapsulating either the degree to which capital is able to exploit workers and consumers or the extent to which workers and consumers can impose price reductions. In contrast, the quantitative indicators used by communal participatory planning "represent the best current estimates of final relative valuations. As the [planning] process unfolds these estimates become steadily more accurate."[121] Furthermore, these quantitative indicators are flexible as "qualitative information about the actual conditions of labor and implications of consuming items provides important additional guidance," and are directly controlled by workers and consumers through deliberative decision-making within the councils.

118. Albert, *Parecon*, 123.
119. Albert, *Parecon*, 124.
120. Albert and Hahnel, *The Political Economy of Participatory Economics*, 60.
121. Albert, *Parecon*, 125.

In collective enterprises with better-than-average conditions, workers could divide their time across a spectrum of useful economic activities in multiple enterprises, perhaps characterized by necessary but less-desirable tasks or tasks with highly variable desirability. With this balancing of work assignments within and across collective enterprises, we could envision that labor time plus consideration for work intensity (i.e., effort and sacrifice) to be a relatively accurate reflection of an individual worker's contribution to the macro-social product.[122] These measures of work could serve as guidelines for consumers' councils to issue consumption vouchers or allowances for scarce goods and services and, if desired, exercise their autonomy to override this social norm and grant exceptions for individual and group consumption requests according to circumstance.

Each person and council will have "access to a list of all direct and indirect factors that go into producing goods [and services], along with a description of what will be gained from consuming those goods [and services]."[123] These qualitative activity assessments will enable workers and consumers to "accurately assess the full effects of others' [production and consumption] requests and even their broad collective motives in a way that enhances solidarity."[124] We envision a central database that aggregates reports, analyses, data visualizations, ethnographies, and multimedia examples showcasing the various missions, internal operations, everyday life, and ecological impacts of industrial federations and their constituent collective enterprises. This database could be complemented by spaces of public discourse facilitated through broadcast, print, and online media that provide platforms for consumers from various locations, and workers of various industries and enterprises, to share their perspectives and experiences. When the planning procedure yields a change in quantitative indicators, qualitative data will be

122. Albert, *Parecon*, 126.
123. Albert, *Parecon*, 127.
124. Albert, *Parecon*, 127.

available for workers and consumers to access, review, and identify the sources of this change, and make decisions accordingly. Over time, we imagine people will become familiar with the aspects of the commons that go into the production and consumption of various goods and services, which enables a more accurate assessment of the effects of various proposals on the overall socioecological metabolism.

Made available to the public via the social commons, this data could be easily accessed by councils and facilitation boards to inform self-activity proposals for the annual planning process. To prepare a self-activity proposal, a base council would follow several steps:

1. Relevant data from previous annual plans are accessed by workers' and consumers' councils.

2. Information is received from facilitation boards estimating probable changes to quantitative indicators in light of projected effects, anticipated social contributions from workers required to fulfill previously agreed upon investment decisions, and changes in the workforce.

3. Information is received from higher-level workers' and consumers' councils regarding the status of long-term investment projects and collective consumption proposals agreed to in previous plans that imply continuing commitments from workers and consumers for the coming year.

4. Changes made in their own self-activity proposals during last year's planning procedure are reviewed to estimate the necessary adjustments to be made in the coming year, and compare projected changes to socioecological welfare between the coming year and the last.

5. Finally, using the previous year's final quantitative indicators as a guide, councils develop a self-activity proposal for the coming year, enumerating what they

want to produce or consume, and the qualitative data that informs their reasoning. These individual proposals are then aggregated by the facilitation board yielding an estimated total social product. This aggregated proposal is returned to the base-level councils for deliberation, feedback is shared among councils, and revisions are made in subsequent planning iterations, until final self-activity proposals are formulated for the coming year and a final plan is converged upon.[125]

In conclusion, a communist economy could integrate the convivial stewardship of the commons; administration of production, allocation, consumption, and waste management by federations of autonomous workers' and consumers' councils; organization of everyday work assignments in accordance with polytechnic and multivalent divisions of labor; social provisioning by collective enterprises organized on the basis of production for general social use or production for limited consumption; compensation for work in accordance actual labor time with consideration for effort and sacrifice; and long-term economic investment decisions facilitated through a communal participatory planning procedure whereby workers' and consumers' cooperatively negotiate, converge upon, and implement a comprehensive economic plan or series of plans.

Liberating Collective Labor

Under the rule of capital, "most jobs contain a number of similar, relatively undesirable, and relatively unempowering tasks, while a few jobs contain a number of relatively desirable and empowering tasks."[126] Liberating collective labor as the self-determination of sensuous creative activity need not "return" to artisanal craft production nor retain its character as the sale of one's labor-power relative to abstract socially

---

125. Albert and Hahnel, *The Political Economy of Participatory Economics*, 63–64.
126. Hahnel, *Of the People, By the People*, 55.

necessary labor time. A communist conception of labor bases itself upon our free participation in creative social activity—processes synchronized with the cycles of natures, the spontaneity of our communities, and the commitments we make to various projects and initiatives determined through a macroeconomic planning process. However, as not all work assignments and tasks are equally desirable or empowering, and even within the context of formally autonomous workers' councils, if some workers perform only rote tasks destructive of mind and body while other workers perform empowering tasks that bolster knowledge and capacities, then the result will likely be the rule of the latter over the former: the production of a new class hierarchy.

Polytechnic education and government by autonomous councils can help create conditions for effective participation and give workers and consumers appropriate decision-making input regarding economic affairs. Labor itself should be organized into a complex of productive activities within and across collective enterprises to overcome the reified divisions between manual and intellectual tasks. Our goal is the holistic development of social individuals, based on free association, engaged in creative activities of social production and reproduction, whereby "the labor of each person is full and positively self-constituting in ways that correspond to the general richness, varigatedness, power, and knowledge of society as a whole; individual labor would no longer be the fragmented basis for the richness of society."[127]

Each workers' council could create a committee—composed of workers, not bureaucrats—to organize work assignments with the aim of distributing and combining tasks in ways that maximize desirability and empowerment for all.[128] This is not an argument against training and expertise, as it seems probable that workers in various collective enterprises would still perform a limited range of specialized tasks, as diverse fields of social production and reproduction

127. Postone, *Time, Labor, and Social Domination*, 32.
128. Hahnel, *Of the People, By the People*, 55–56.

will continue to require particular forms of knowledge and technique from participants in a socialized work process. Within a context of polytechnic education and economic planning coordinated through federations of workers' and consumers' councils, collective labor processes could liberate the general intellect to serve the "free development of individualities," encompassing multivalent intellects that immunize against the reemergence of toxic class hierarchies, and pluripotent intellects that produce vibrant and versatile forms of life.[129]

The aim is not to eliminate divisions of labor altogether but to ensure that workers share responsibilities for a diversified sequence of tasks for which we are adequately trained, and arranged into work assignments such that no one accrues consistent advantages that could produce new class hierarchies. The project of achieving a polytechnic balance in collective labor should be a holistic process that takes environmental, technical, social, and psychological factors into account. The commune balances work assignments for desirability and empowerment within each and every collective enterprise and guarantees that workers have a combination of tasks that balance across enterprises. Balancing work assignments for a general empowerment effect could establish forms of economic organization that dissolve the binary divisions between manual and intellectual, conceptual and executive, or rote and empowering tasks, and militate against the production of permanent class hierarchies between order-givers and order-takers. Let us envision a complex of productive activities no longer subordinated to the singularity of linear time and the ongoing production of constant energy, but instead, integrated into the rhythms of cyclical time and the spontaneity of phase time.

For example, we envision comrades from a municipal commune converging upon farms in harvest season, transforming arduous work into a joyous occasion. This requires

129. Karl Marx, *Grundrisse: Foundations of the Critique of Political Economy* (London: Penguin Books, 2005), 706.

radical transformations in lifestyles and will continue to require a selective *rhythmatization* of linear time and usage of continuous energy, for "communism will prove itself much better able to adapt to the rhythms of flow energy, turning machines off and encouraging afternoon naps, perhaps, when the clouds cover the sun or the wind dies."[130]

Social Provisioning, Remunerative Justice, and Factors of Consumption

Within a context of communal stewardship of the commons by participatory councils, wherein workers and consumers cooperatively negotiate the interrelation of economic activities, the precise organization of social provisioning, the criteria for remunerative justice, and accountancy for factors of consumption remains to be determined. A communist economy abolishes the law of value (and with it property, markets, money, prices, wages, and rent), and provides all people with direct access to full social provisioning, provided for by collective enterprises producing for general social use, encompassing productive activities in agriculture, healthcare, transportation, sanitation, housing, education, environmental stewardship, and so on.

However, certain criteria for remunerative justice and accounting for factors of consumption may be required to equitably provision those limited articles of consumption that, due to real scarcity, labor-intensive production methods, or the socioecological effects associated with their production or consumption are not made available via collective enterprises producing for general social use. Within this context, a system of consumption vouchers or allowances, issued directly to workers by their respective workers' council (or consumers' council), is one possible tool for rationing such goods and services. These limited articles of consumption would be provided by limited production enterprises, with the socioecological effects associated with production and

130. Bernes, "The Belly of the Revolution," 369.

consumption processes accessed and accounted for through the communal planning process.

Communism overthrows and abolishes *abstract universal labor time*—"the time that has been separated from the subjective sensations, feelings, and experiences of working individuals"[131]—and in its place establishes *actual labor time* as "the sensuous activity of individuals mediating their relations with nature."[132] Within capitalism, workers are rented by capital "for a precisely defined time-period, in which they have to produce a maximal output of commodities or services. Each minute that they do not expend for this purpose is, from the standpoint of the purchaser of the commodity labor-power, a waste. Each and every minute is valuable, insofar as it, in the literal sense, presents potential value."[133] In contrast, the labor time of communism is autonomous time, whereby working individuals and collectives voluntarily engage in forms of sensuous creative activity of their own choosing, in accordance with a social plan of their own making, and synchronized with the rhythms of socioecological life.

Within this context, remuneration in accordance with concrete labor time in the form of consumption vouchers permits direct access to forms of social provisioning in addition to the multitude of free goods and services provided by collective enterprises producing for general social use. These vouchers or allowances "would not circulate like money, nor would they be used in relations between productive enterprises."[134] Indeed, "the social control and accounting undertaken by the associated producers in a communist society abolishes the value-relation, and for this reason abolishes money."[135]

131. Norbert Trenkle, "Value and Crisis: Basic Questions," in Neil Larsen, Mathias Nilges, Josh Robinson, and Nicholas Brown (eds.), *Marxism and the Critique of Value* (Chicago: MCM Publishing, 2014), 5.

132. Peter Hudis, "The Vision of the New Society in Marx's *Capital*," *Logos Journal* (2018), http://logosjournal.com/2018/the-vision-of-the-new-society-in-marxs-capital/.

133. Trenkle, "Value and Crisis," 5.

134. David Adam, "Marx's Critique of Socialist Labor-Money Schemes and the Myth of Council Communism's Proudhonism," *With Sober Senses*, January 21, 2013, https://www.marxisthumanistinitiative.org/alternatives-to-capital/marxs-critique-of-socialist-labor-money-schemes-and-the-myth-of-council-communisms-proudhonism.html.

135. Adam, "Marx's Critique of Socialist Labor-Money Schemes."

The function of consumption vouchers or allowances is "that of facilitating a conscious allocation of goods [and services]" in accordance with a definite social plan.[136]

To the extent that liberated work is generalized throughout society, whereby each individual performs a complex of productive tasks and hence, "labor is no longer just a means of keeping alive but has itself become a vital need," this is less of an issue.[137] However, it is probable that there will remain distinct categories of work—even within the context of a polytechnic and multivalent reorganization of economic life—that are boring, dirty, or dangerous and require additional effort and sacrifice from workers.[138] With the persistence of such situations, remunerative justice might entail compensation for effort and sacrifice in addition to the measure of actual actual labor time. This would entail the provision of additional consumption vouchers or allowances for those who exert greater effort or make greater sacrifices in socially useful productive activities.

Such qualitative accounting of differential categories of work performed is important information for a communist approach to economic planning. The transparency of such factors enables participants in the planning process to make informed decisions regarding the environmental, human, and more-than-human effects of various forms of economic activity. To implement this norm for remunerative justice, the members of a workers' council could provide fellow workers with an effort and sacrifice assessment, recognizing the differential contributions to economic life that workers make. With the disbursement of consumption vouchers or allowances, personal access to limited consumption could be extended accordingly. All workers' councils need not go about assessing fellow workers in the same way—any more than they would need to combine polytechnic and multivalent productive tasks in the same way—as this would violate the communist principle of self-management.

136. Adam, "Marx's Critique of Socialist Labor-Money Schemes."
137. Marx, *The First International and After*, 347.
138. Albert, *Parecon*, 114.

Communism aims to construct an economic praxis based on meeting human needs and desires while maintaining a balanced socioecological metabolism. A scarcity of inputs in the form of resources extracted from the environmental commons, labor-intensive production methods or negative socioecological effects implies the necessity and desirability for the real scarcity of certain goods and services available for consumption, in contrast to the boundless stream of commodities produced by capital. Once again, we must emphasize that incentivizing certain categories of work takes place within a context of relative communal abundance achieved through general social provisioning, the institutional prohibition on private accumulation—the commons are for collective social use and not for sale—and the liberation of labor by combining tasks into a complex of multivalent activities, as well as selectively automating certain processes to minimize drudgery and the necessity of exposing oneself to danger.

Within this vision, any quantitative indicators attached to scarce goods and services are set not by a market, but with socioecological accounting tools determined through participatory planning. Even if such a system of remuneration is ultimately discarded, we retain the utility of theorizing such a system, given past experiences when this aspect of a communist economic vision was overlooked. This myopia created situations of crisis lending themselves to the reintroduction of money, markets, prices, wages, rent, and, of course, the law of value, commodity production, and capital accumulation.

Negate the State

The state is a historically specific form of polity that is peculiar to hierarchical social systems, and is the central institution in the regulation and defense of the imperialist world-system. Hence the communist social revolution aims to overthrow and abolish the state. According to Marx, the Paris Commune of 1871 "was a revolution against the *state* itself," as it was "a resumption by the people for the people of its own social life."[139] Similarly, Engels argued that the Commune "had ceased to be a state in the true sense of the term," and that revolutionaries should replace the use of the term "state" when referring to the forms of communal governance established by the social revolution with words such as *Gemeinwesen* [community].[140] However, as Gustav Landauer made clear: "The state is a social relationship; a certain way of people relating to one another. It can be destroyed by creating new social relationships; i.e., by people relating to one another differently."[141] As an alternative way of people relating to one another politically, beyond the rule of the state, a communist polity includes autonomous participatory councils self-organized at the local level and combining into larger federations. Attached to each council are various working committees, such as peace and justice committees constituting the basis of a restorative justice system, intercommunal solidarity committees to foster dialogue among diverse cultures, or security and defense committees to protect the commune from counter-revolutionary forces.

Even with the overthrow and abolition of imperialism and the construction of a stateless communism, political life will not come to an end. On the contrary, for the vast majority of humanity, *real political life will begin.* Many everyday decisions will need to be made, disagreements will need to be settled among communities, and divergent viewpoints will continue to arise as people work to identify the best course of action at various conjunctures. Crises will still occur, given the damage inherited from the ecological rift opened by imperialism, and we will need to work hard to establish a sustainable socioecological metabolism for the foreseeable future. Furthermore, many controversial issues (such as animal liberation, youth autonomy, recreational drugs,

139. Marx, *The First International and After*, 249.

140. Frederick Engels, "Engels to August Bebel in Zwickau (1875)," Marxists Internet Archive, https://www.marxists.org/archive/marx/works/1875/letters/75_03_18.htm/.

141. Gustav Landauer, "Weak Statesmen, Weaker People!," in Gabriel Kuhn (ed.,) *Revolution and Other Writings: A Political Reader* (Oakland: PM Press, 2010), 214.

resource scarcity, artificial intelligence, cloning, bioengineering, deep ecology, and religion) will continue to pose challenging ethical questions for communist social systems, requiring political resolutions. As unity in diversity is a goal of communism, an experimental approach should permeate all aspects of political life. However, while competing ideas should be simultaneously implemented whenever possible, it will often be the case that only one political project, policy, or program will be implemented in a given situation. The problems of political experimentation and socioecological choice will not disappear with the overthrow and abolition of imperialism—indeed, they are likely to intensify as a plurality of perspectives spring forth.[142]

A communal participatory polity may be constituted in accordance with the following principles: (1) political power should flow from below, with base councils self-organized at the level of residential street, open to all members of the community, forming the foundation of the polity and a hub of everyday political life; (2) all delegates selected to council levels above that of the base are immediately accountable to and recallable by a vote of their sending council or, in the case of at-large delegates elected to higher councils, recallable by the general population; and, (3) rotation of council delegates should be mandatory, and their political duties should be integrated into polytechnic work assignments in order to inhibit the development of a bureaucracy. In contrast with the dull bureaucracy of authoritarian statecraft, we envision a lively festival of the people, a gathering of comrades and friends to engage in the political administration of our streets, neighborhoods, wards, municipalities, and beyond.

In contrast to a purely instrumental conception of politics, communism liberates politics as an activity of empowered communities. Politics becomes more than a means of legislation, implementation, and adjudication for a social system within a given territory, but also a space of place-making for

142. Stephen R. Shalom, "ParPolity: Political Vision for a Good Society" (2005/2011), *Znet*, https://zcomm.org/znetarticle/parpolity-political-vision-for-a-good-society-by-stephen1-shalom/.

the cultivation of meaningful civic life. A communal polity is dramatically different from the passive and exclusionary conceptions of "citizenship" and "democracy" characteristic of the authoritarian state.

This polity is governed within the framework established by a social charter, enumerating the territorial commune's guiding principles. A social constitution provides the regulatory framework for the administrative functioning of the social system's polity within the territory. Social charters and constitutions could be adopted at the continental and global levels, as well as in the case of a polity composed of various autonomous regions within a common geographic area.

A Communal Participatory Polity

We propose a federated, polycentric polity, in which there exist multiple centers through which the people exercise political power. This vision of a communal participatory polity is rooted in a synthesis of both direct and delegated systems of democracy, or "direct democracy with delegations."[143] The primary level of the communal polity are its base councils, or, autonomous assemblies consisting of the inhabitants of a particular residential street.[144] Each base council selects a delegate from its ranks to a second-level council—the neighborhood council. The neighborhood council then selects a delegate to a third-level council—the ward council, and so on, until councils have been established at the level of municipality, bioregion, and territory. At each level, councils should be "small enough to guarantee that people can be involved in face-to-face discussions; but yet big enough so that (1) there is adequate diversity of opinion included; and (2) the number of layers of councils needed to accommodate the entire society is minimized."[145] There is potential for a high degree of variation within a nested council system, calibrated

143. Harnecker, *A World to Build*, 74.
144. Shalom, "ParPolity."
145. Shalom, "ParPolity."

in accordance with the needs of a particular social formation, and revised on the basis of experience.

At each level, delegates are responsible for reflecting the views and perspectives of their sending council, and should conduct ongoing social investigations to ensure they maintain an intimate understanding of the past and present issues affecting their constituency.[146] However, delegates would not be told how they should vote in advance, as each level of council is a *deliberative body*, in which a variety of views and perspectives are heard, and delegates are empowered to alter their position in accordance with new information.[147] This is held in check by the sending council, who may reprimand or recall their delegate for inadequately reflecting the views and perspectives of the sending constituency.

Base councils include delegates selected by and accountable to households at the street level, as well as from various local associations and institutions, encompassing culture, education, healthcare, ecology, justice, defense, security, transportation, and so on. The autonomous participatory assemblies of the base council are a clearinghouse for all political matters, a space of comradely debate and disagreement, and a vehicle for conflict mediation and restorative justice. The assemblies are where local and translocal policies are determined and larger neighborhood, ward, municipal, bioregional, territorial, and global issues and concerns are discussed and debated. Every base council is allocated space for an autonomous social center equipped with auditoriums where assemblies are held, in addition to offices for council staff, committees, and associations.

At all levels of the polity, councils hold deliberative popular assemblies, striving for consensus whenever possible but defaulting to majority vote whenever necessary. Each council autonomously decides its preferred rules and procedures for decision-making. At higher levels of the polity, councils may agree to standardize certain decision-making rules, as well as

146. Harnecker, *A World to Build*, 77.
147. Harnecker, *A World to Build*, 75.

procedures to ensure accountability, continuity, and expediency. Furthermore, social emergencies (such as environmental disasters, infrastructural failures, public health crises, and war) require a political response within a specific timetable and demand the coordination of certain emergency procedures.

Voting at all levels is conducted openly, as citizens of a polity "should be publicly answerable for their votes, not in the sense that there will be punishments for inappropriate votes, but that they can be asked by others why they voted the way they did. This will encourage people to vote in a discursively defensible manner."[148] All council assemblies above the base will be open, recorded, broadcast, and archived to enable review by lower councils levels, specifically the base.

At levels above the base council, if consensus cannot be reached and a vote would be contentious, the council returns the decision to the base for referendum or a petition approved by a certain number of base councils could guarantee that a decision be returned to the base for a popular vote. It's important that certain decisions return to the base, as there are situations in which the decision of a higher-level council inevitably fails to reflect the priorities of the base councils. However, returning all decisions to the base for a popular vote would prove extremely inefficient and take away from more pressing everyday local concerns.

In the final analysis, political power always rests with the base councils. In addition to the recourse to referendum, the base councils maintain accountability of higher-level councils via delegate rotation, immediate recall of delegates by a vote of the sending council, and through public records. Delegates are responsible for regularly returning to their sending council, to report on their activities as a member of the higher-level council and to receive critical input from their sending council.

At the level of a territorial commune, one possible configuration for the polity is to establish a *people's assembly* for the whole country, consisting of delegates elected by two

148. Shalom, "ParPolity."

methods: (1) a majority of delegates elected directly from, accountable to, and recallable by the next lowest council level, as a logical continuation of the system of nested councils thus far elaborated; and, (2) a minority of delegates selected at large by the general population of the territory via a system of popular elections by majority vote. The reason for having this system is to ensure there are delegates who are: (1) directly accountable to the nested councils (and hence in dialogue with specific regional constituencies); and, (2) delegates selected on the basis of certain issues that affect the territorial social formation as a whole. We envision delegates selected via the nested council system sharing and advocating the perspectives of specific regional constituencies with whom they are in dialogue, whereas the delegates selected via general elections would likely be partisans of certain political platforms and programs with implications for the administration of the territorial commune as a whole, as well as its relations with other territorial social formations. The latter would run not as individual personalities, but as members of organized political tendencies, be they in the form of a revolutionary party or some other association.

A two-tiered delegation system for the people's assembly ensures a degree of reciprocal accountability that neither pure decentralism nor centralism can achieve. While authoritarian state power organized at the unitary level has more than played its role, many great inequalities and injustices have been perpetuated by reactionary forms of localism, such as racial segregation in the United States and South Africa. Recognizing these as historical realities, the people's assembly is responsible for taking measures against such forms of reactionary localism, prohibiting and breaking-up garrison communities as necessary, and fostering mutual understanding and symbiotic interdependence.[149] However, the social charter and constitution should always maintain

---

149. Symbiosis Research Collective, "'Dark Municipalism'—The Danger of Local Politics," *The Ecologist*, June 26, 2018, https://theecologist.org/2018/jun/26/dark-municipalism-dangers-local-politics

the right of self-determination and secession for historically oppressed communities.

Conflict Resolution and Restorative Justice

Inevitably, many conflicts and contradictions will persist under communism, even within the context of its consolidation and stabilization on a world scale. For example, domestic conflicts among members of a particular dwelling, conflicts among neighbors, and conflicts within and between communities will likely persist. In contrast to the punitive "justice" of imperialism, the central objective of communist adjudication should be *restorative justice*, with implementation conducted by peace and justice committees and popular courts directly attached to the polity's councils, to whom they are directly accountable. There are three primary functions of adjudication: (1) judicial review, or the determination of a law's justice; (2) criminal adjudication, or determining if a particular individual has violated the laws of the polity; and, (3) civil adjudication, or resolving disputes between individuals.[150] Judicial review is accomplished primarily by the popular courts attached to every council level, whereas criminal and civil adjudication become primarily the responsibility of peace and justice committees, before being turned over to the court system in more challenging situations.

Each council will form peace and justice committees to facilitate restorative justice in cases of civil and criminal adjudication, aiming "not to condemn one or both sides in a proceeding but to achieve consensus between conflicting parties."[151] The aim is for lasting peace with justice, achieved through consensual and feminist means. Peace and justice committees could be formed by various popular social groups to deal with specific grievances or injustices, such as a feminist peace and justice committee to handle heteropatriarchal violence, and a trans peace and justice committee to handle

150. Shalom, "ParPolity."
151. Knapp et al., *Revolution in Rojava*, 166.

transphobic discrimination and violence. When a peace and justice committee at the base cannot achieve consensus, or the severity of the violation of the social contract or constitution is so extreme, the case can be gradually moved to higher-level peace and justice committees, corresponding the appropriate council level. If a resolution cannot be achieved, then the case is turned over to the popular courts, with judges chosen and accountable to the appropriate council level.

Communal Defense and Security

The most effective defense policy for a communal polity is the construction of federated autonomous participatory institutions that produce autonomy within solidarity, ensuring social cohesiveness, strengthening our capacities of self-government, and ensuring collective survival and communal abundance. However, despite the proliferation of strong autonomous participatory institutions in all areas of social life, oppressive behavior and counter-revolutionary armed conflict may continue into the future, especially prior to successful communization on the world scale. Communal defense and security can be organized and coordinated directly by the councils of the polity. Unlike the police and military of the old repressive state apparatus, the people's defense organizations are rooted in protecting and expanding communist social relations.

Each base council forms its own defense committee responsible for the local maintenance of defensive military equipment, the education and training of people's defense organizations, and coordinating emergency preparedness and response. Defense committees can be formed at the higher-level councils of the polity—including the neighborhood, ward, municipality, bioregion, and territory—to coordinate the activities of local defense organizations and to mobilize people's defense organizations in the event of an emergency. Parallel to defense organizations, base councils form security committees, responsible for public safety, community patrols, investigations, forensics, apprehension, intelligence, and counter-intelligence, which are coordinated by the councils in tandem with peace and justice committees. Directly accountable to the will of the councils and under the jurisdiction of popular courts, security committees may establish offices to deal with specific issues and constituencies, such as gender and sexual issues (including, for example, rapid response to heteropatriarchal violence) or particular community issues (including special subcommittees composed of members chosen by a specific community acting as a liaison).

3.5: The World Commune

Our ultimate goal is the generalization of a communist praxis of liberation on a world scale, co-producing an alternative world-system built upon the institutional foundations of commons, conviviality, and councils: the realization of a world commune. Central to this strategy is a transnational federation of territorial communes that have delinked from the imperialist world-system, thus creating a global area of autonomy that exists outside and against the space dominated by imperialism: "Previous generations of communist theorists have misunderstood the transition to communism as temporal in nature, passing through the intermediate stages of socialism, when it is in fact better thought of as spatial transition: the geographical spread of an immediately social communism that is contagious for the precise reason that it is fully realized."[152]

However, as imperialism only exists as a world-system, the negation of the negation can only produce the positive content of a communist alternative through the negative process of overthrowing and abolishing imperialism on a *world* scale. By establishing counter-hegemonic geopolitical blocs and coupling circuits of an emerging communal world-economy on the basis of free association, direct social cooperation,

152. Bernes, "The Belly of the Revolution," 359–360.

and symbiotic interdependence, communism will gradually encircle imperialism, liberating humanity-in-nature from its domination, and effectively cutting it off from its life-blood of cheap labor-power and cheap nature. The goal is clear: a world without bosses or borders, which shall have finally beaten swords into plowshares, where all enjoy the fruits of the cooperative commonwealth, co-produced and reproduced through our collective social activities and those of our ancestors, where all share responsibilities for the collective stewardship of our environments.

We have witnessed what happens when revolutionary situations fail to spread beyond the territorial confines of a determinate social formation—when a revolutionary wave fails to generalize on a world scale—and communist partisans fail to prepare for situations of relative self-sufficiency. The geographic isolation of the social revolution has been the nail in the coffin of every great experiment with communism, from the Paris Commune of 1871 onward. Indeed, Marx conveyed this in assessing the mistakes of the Parisian Communards: "They should have marched at once on Versailles [the seat of the counter-revolutionary government]," but failed to do so for fear of sparking *civil war*, as if the French imperialists had not already sparked such a war by besieging the Commune![153] In the twentieth century, in reflecting upon the probable fate of the Russian Revolution, Rosa Luxemburg prophetically grasped the necessity for the diffusion and consolidation of a worldwide revolution:

> In this, the Russian Revolution has but confirmed the basic lesson of every great revolution, the law of its being, which decrees: either the revolution must advance at a rapid, stormy and resolute tempo, break down all barriers with an iron hand and place its goals ever farther ahead, or it is quite soon thrown backward behind its feeble point of departure and suppressed by counter-revolution. To stand still, to

153. Karl Marx, "Marx to Dr. Kugelmann Concerning the Paris Commune (1871)," Marxists Internet Archive, https://www.marxists.org/archive/marx/works/1871/letters/71_04_12.htm/.

mark time on one spot, to be contented with the first goal it happens to reach, is never possible in revolution.[154]

While undoubtedly one of the most complex events of the twentieth century, the geographic isolation of the Russian Revolution functioned as an incubator for counterrevolutionary tendencies, which ultimately cannibalized the meager victories of 1917. This effectively transformed an emergent revolutionary dictatorship of the proletariat into *a reactionary dictatorship over and against the proletariat*. Indeed, even a counter-hegemonic bloc of territorial communes will face great difficulties: the ultimate aim must be to break the counterrevolutionary encirclement of imperialism, and advance the construction of the world commune.

The world commune is not an unachievable utopia, it is but one possible alternative for our future. Communism will not produce social systems without conflicts and contradictions, but the conflicts and contradictions rooted in the oppressive relations of enclosure, exploitation, and dependency will have been resolved in the liberation of the proletarian and popular social groups. Even with the successful construction of world communism, the ecological rift and demands of global justice will solicit generations of mutual-aid organizations and ongoing mass struggles to assist the processes of social reconstruction throughout the former peripheries and in areas damaged by war and environmental degradation. We envision the construction of alternative global institutions, such as: a global people's assembly federating the polities of territorial communes; the extension of communal participatory planning to the level of a world commune; the sustainable stewardship of our biosphere and geosphere as elements of our planetary environmental commons; the administration of infrastructures as the basis of a global technical commons; and, the emergence of a global social commons archiving the whole

154. Rosa Luxemburg, "The Russian Revolution," in Peter Hudis and Kevin B. Anderson (eds.), *The Rosa Luxemburg Reader* (New York: Monthly Review Press, 2004), 287.

of human cultural production as an open source repository accessible to all.

What could possibly drive masses of people, in the millions and billions, to take risks and make sacrifices of the magnitude required to actualize a world revolution and build world communism? The accumulated "hatred for this world" would most certainly play its part. Yet, as Andrew Culp cautions, "the only future we have comes when we stop reproducing the conditions of the present."[155] There is another affect that will likely play a leading role:

> Love is arguably the emotion that most strongly underlies the vital force that impels many ordinary people into extraordinary acts, across time and place. Expressing hope and optimism, it provides a constructive counterpoint to those other powerful animating emotions, hatred and anger. Love of life, love of people, love of justice all play a role across revolutionary political cultures. This is something that the revolutionaries of the future will need to learn to nurture and build upon.[156]

Love is "the domain of those relational behaviors through which the other arises as a legitimate other in coexistence with oneself."[157] Through love, we develop an affectionate connection to all forms of life and the myriad struggles for liberation through an emerging consciousness of our mutual interdependence. Revolutionary love is grounded in the recognition that the freedom of each is bound to the freedom of all, for "if our imagination is to be sustained by our associating, the ways we meet and cooperate and feel towards one another must develop not from experiences of the most repressive and authoritarian encounters, but from our understandings of more loving, free ways of connecting to others

155. Andrew Culp, *Dark Deleuze* (Minneapolis: University of Minnesota Press, 2016), 13.
156. John Foran, *Taking Power: On the Origins of Third World Revolutions* (Cambridge: Cambridge University Press, 2007), 274.
157. Humberto Maturana and Gerda Verden-Zöller, *The Origins of Humanness in the Biology of Love* (Charlottesville, VA: Imprint Academic, 2008), 138.

and acting."[158] As Che said: "At the risk of seeming ridiculous, let me say that the true revolutionary is guided by a great feeling of love. It is impossible to think of a genuine revolutionary lacking this quality."[159]

158. Sheila Rowbotham, "The Women's Movement and Organizing for Socialism," in Sheila Rowbotham, Lynne Segal, and Hilary Wainwright (eds.), *Beyond the Fragments: Feminism and the Making of Socialism* (Boston: Alyson Publications, Inc., 1981), 82.

159. Che Guevara, "Socialism and Man in Cuba," in María del Carmen Ariet García (ed.), *Global Justice: Liberation and Socialism* (Melbourne: Ocean Press, 2002), 44.

4

Building the Commune

Constructing the world commune will require a social revolution within and against the imperialist world-system. This revolution can only be made "from below and to the left" by a revolutionary people arising from the multitude of proletarian and popular social groups. Consolidated within a system of counterpower that governs an increasingly expansive territory, these groups can work to initiate an insurrectionary rupture. However, building towards this insurrectionary rupture—the moment when a direct transition to a communist social system within a specific territory becomes a concrete possibility—is a protracted process that will entail the accumulation of multiple "everyday ruptures" within cycles of struggle.[1] It requires the arduous work of political combat on the terrain of everyday life, digging deep into the trenches of civil society and gradually advancing from a "war of position" to a "war of movement."[2] As Antonio Gramsci emphasized, "the decisive element in every situation is the permanently organized and long-prepared force which can be put into the field when it is judged that the situation is favorable (and it can be favorable only in so far as such a force exists, and is full of fighting spirit)."[3] Thus the communist movement aims to prepare such a force by rooting itself among the proletarian and popular social groups, building a mass base for social revolution, and deepening the people's collective consciousness, self-organization, and self-activity.

1. Teresa Kalisz, "Everyday Ruptures: Putting Basebuilding on a Revolutionary Path," *The Left Wind*, April 24, 2020, https://theleftwind.wordpress.com/2020/04/24/ everyday-rupture s-putting-basebuilding-on-a-revolutionary-path/.

2. Antonio Gramsci, *Selections from the Prison Notebooks* (New York: International Publishers, 1971), 229–239.

3. Gramsci, *Selections from the Prison Notebooks*, 185.

The central task of a revolutionary organizer is to prepare, initiate, defend, and complete a protracted revolutionary struggle. As a revolutionary people emerges and a system of counterpower proliferates, a dual-power situation arises in which the imperialist world-system and the emergent commune struggle for hegemony, ultimately contending for territorial control. Within the context of a world-systemic crisis, this will be a multidirectional fight in which we can expect multiple forces to emerge with conflicting social visions. This dual-power situation is inherently unstable, resolving itself in either a successful revolution, a successful counter-revolution, or common ruin—"a peace of the grave-yard," as Gramsci put it.[4]

How can we help unleash a continuous revolution that results in the world commune? As the partisans of the Rojava Revolution recommend: "Build a strong revolutionary movement in your own country."[5] However, this also means building solidarity among revolutionary movements across the global center/periphery divisions of imperialism.[6] Revolutionaries concentrated in the metropolitan core have a responsibility to listen to and learn from the revolutionary movements emerging from the peripheries and to provide direct material solidarity in the form of mutual aid, volunteering to participate in revolutionary defense and social reconstruction, and building international campaigns to free political prisoners and prisoners of war and to lift legal prohibitions against revolutionary organizations. Such work must not be conducted on the basis of charity, "but on the awareness that the emancipation of the proletariat in the exploited countries is a condition of the destruction of the imperialist system."[7]

4. Gramsci, *Selections from the Prison Notebooks*, 185.

5. Knapp et al., *Revolution in Rojava*, 256–257.

6. Knapp et al., *Revolution in Rojava*, 257.

7. Manifest-Kommunistisk Arbejdsgruppe (M-KA), "What Can Communists in the Imperialist Countries Do?," in Gabriel Kuhn (ed.), *Turning Money into Rebellion: The Unlikely Story of Denmark's Revolutionary Bank Robbers* (Oakland: PM Press, 2014), 206.

4.1: Organized Autonomy

During the course of a protracted revolutionary struggle, diverse organizational forms are created by liberation movements arising from the multitude of proletarian and popular social groups. These forms have historically included autonomous mass organizations, people's defense organizations, and revolutionary party organizations. The task of communists is to help build an *area of autonomy* through which these diffuse organizational forms can coalesce into an increasingly dense network of communication, cooperation, and coordination. Tracing its conceptual origins to the Italian communist movement of the 1970s, an area of autonomy can be understood as "an expression of the movement in which different currents and tendencies unite and coexist."[8] At the same time, such organizations should remain anchored to everyday grassroots social struggles through specific forms of mediation, such as autonomous workers' councils organized at the point of social production or autonomous neighborhood councils organized at the point of social reproduction.

From tactical united fronts formed to win immediate objectives to strategic united fronts formed to pursue a revolutionary program, the ultimate culmination of this organizational process is the articulation of a *system of counterpower* from within an emergent area of autonomy. As this system is consolidated, it unites a revolutionary bloc of the proletarian and popular social groups that is capable of initiating an insurrectionary rupture with the imperialist world-system, conquering political power throughout the territory, and establishing the infrastructural basis for a direct transition to communism. As protracted revolutionary struggles proliferate globally, it is our duty to assist comrades in all corners of the world with the construction of such systems of counterpower, linking together insurgent

8. Alfredo M. Bonanno, "A Few Notes on the Revolutionary Movement in Italy" (The Anarchist Library, 2017), https://theanarchistlibrary.org/library/alfredo-m-bonanno- a-fe w-notes-on-the-revolutionary-movement-in-italy/.

revolutionary movements and liberated territories to build the world commune.

While organizational forms are necessary mediations between grassroots struggles and the communist vision and program, our ultimate commitment is to the communist social revolution itself and not a specific organizational form. "An organization ought to be judged not for the results it has bequeathed over the course of its long-term historical development," Mario Tronti reminds us, "but for the political function it fulfilled in the given moment in which it emerged."[9] A specific organizational form may only emerge or take on special importance at a certain phase of the struggle. Sometimes organizational forms span several phases of the struggle. Sometimes they die out, having become superfluous. The task of the organizer is to discover, through militant social investigation, organizational configurations of political struggle that correspond to the prevailing structures of the conjuncture encountered. There are, of course, no guarantees that these emergent organizational forms will develop or retain a revolutionary character. "Any political form can be captured by the adversary and [even] the most democratic of organizations can be transformed into its opposite when it remains a prisoner of the situation it has created," notes Mimmo Porcaro.[10] All truly revolutionary struggles are effectively *guerrilla struggles,* requiring the development of our collective capacities for imagination, creativity, and versatility on a hostile terrain.[11]

Recognizing the context that informs the adoption of specific modes of struggle, centuries of an unfolding dialectic of liberation nonetheless reveal the likelihood of certain organizational forms emerging. Based on a historical analysis, we have identified the following categories of organized autonomy: (1) organs of counterpower, encompassing the autonomous

9. Mario Tronti, *Workers and Capital* (London: Verso, 2019), 312.

10. Mimmo Porcaro, "Occupy Lenin," *Socialist Register 2013: The Question of Strategy* 49, (2013): 96.

11. Carlos Marighella, *Mini-Manual of the Urban Guerrilla* (Montreal: Abraham Guillén Press & Arm The Spirit, 2002), 5.

mass organizations and alternative institutions through which proletarian and popular social groups develop collective consciousness, self-organization, and self-activity, and from which arises the possibility of advancing from partial struggles and "everyday ruptures" to a generalized antagonism and insurrectionary rupture with the imperialist world-system; (2) people's defense organizations, through which this emerging system of counterpower maintains, consolidates, and extends the area of autonomy against the armed counter-revolution; (3) parties of autonomy, through which revolutionaries unite on the basis of common political affinities, articulating the communist content implicit in grassroots social struggles and assisting the construction of a system of counterpower from within the area of autonomy; and (4) united fronts, through which alliances are formed among these disparate organizational forms for the achievement of specific tactical, operational, or strategic objectives, and from which arise networks of communication, cooperation, and coordination, ultimately coalescing into a system of counterpower articulated at the territorial level. These complementary forms of organized autonomy emerge in nearly every revolutionary situation, albeit under a variety of names. From Russia to Mexico, China to El Salvador, Catalonia to Rojava, we can observe these forms of organized autonomy articulated in a variety of historical-geographical conjunctures.

Organs of Counterpower

During Italy's "red years" of 1919–1920, Gramsci posed a question to the emerging communist movement: "How to weld the present to the future, satisfying the urgent necessities of the present and working usefully to create and 'anticipate' the future?"[12] Every communist movement faces this contradiction: mass organizations must both defend the everyday interests of the proletarian and popular social groups *and*

---

12. Antonio Gramsci, "Workers' Democracy (1919)," Marxists Internet Archive, https://www.marxists.org/archive/gramsci/1919/06/workers-democracy.htm/.

prefigure a communist alternative.[13] It is through autonomous mass organizations—simultaneously instruments of political combat and "schools of communism"—that proletarian and popular social groups are prepared for the task of social reconstruction once a revolutionary situation emerges.[14] To this end, we aim to create an area of autonomy comprised of a dense network of *organs of counterpower*. These organs of counterpower—exemplified historically in the form of autonomous action committees, assemblies, and councils—are simultaneously instruments of struggle against the imperialist world-system and embodiments of a communist alternative. To address the challenge of uniting these seemingly opposed elements, we can explore a variety of historical examples in which such autonomous mass organizations have emerged.

Rank-and-file strategy

Revolutionaries don't always need to found new organizations, but can often organize within established formations to democratize them, return power to rank-and-file members, adopt a revolutionary program, and transform them into organs of counterpower. Historically, this approach is known as the *rank-and-file strategy*, or "boring from within." In general, this approach is only effective in organizations that remain instruments of people's power to some degree, as in the case of trade unions. This is achieved through publications, educational initiatives, opposition caucuses, and the formation of independent workplace committees. For example, the Trade Union Educational League (TUEL) in North America pursued this strategy in the 1920s, seeking to promote an insurgent class-struggle unionism that united all workers on an industrial basis regardless of craft and on the basis of a communist program.[15]

13. Sojourner Truth Organization (STO), "Mass Organization in the Workplace (1972)," Sojourner Truth Organization Electronic Archive, http://sojournertruth.net/massorganization.html/.
14. V.I. Lenin, *'Left-Wing' Communism, An Infantile Disorder* (Peking: Foreign Languages Press, 1970), 41; Rudolf Rocker, *Anarcho-Syndicalism: Theory and Practice* (Oakland: AK Press, 2004), 57.
15. James R. Barrett, *William Z. Foster and the Tragedy of American Radicalism* (Urbana: University of Illinois Press, 1999), 121–122.

The TUEL and the communist nuclei it cultivated origi-
nated in political committees previously established within a
number of local unions, such as Local 25 of the International Ladies Garment Workers Union (ILGWU). While these
political committees were short-lived, looser opposition
groups lingered in several locals and came together in 1919
with the goal of transferring power from bureaucratic union leadership to rank-and-file members.[16] This opposition
movement attracted communists, socialists, and anarchists
who shared a common interest in democratizing the unions
and transforming them into weapons of proletarian class
struggle. This approach won many supporters, with militants
affiliated with the TUEL winning majority support in several
union locals of the ILGWU.

The TUEL was most successful in developing an oppositional nucleus within those locals with longstanding histories
of militant rank-and-file struggle for union democracy, proletarian autonomy, and a post-capitalist vision of liberation.
However, the strategy of "boring from within" can also inhibit class autonomy where such traditions do not exist or
where the union bureaucracy is firmly established. In such
situations, the construction of action committees, assemblies, and councils completely autonomous from and parallel
to the mainstream unions may be more appropriate. This
approach, historically known as *dual unionism,* has the goal
of creating revolutionary labor unions that compete with the
mainstream reformist labor unions for hegemony within the
mass movement.

The rank-and-file strategy is still applied today. One of
the most successful examples in the US has been the Caucus
of Rank-and-file Educators (CORE) organizing inside the
Chicago Teachers Union (CTU).[17] After years of grassroots
organizing to build a united front against school closings
in working-class communities of color, CORE won CTU

16. Barrett, *William Z. Foster,* 127.
17. David Kaplan, "The Chicago Teachers' Strike and Beyond: Strategic Considerations," *Solidarity: A Socialist, Feminist, Anti-Racist Organization,* June 21, 2013, https://
solidarity-us.org/the_ctu_strike_and_beyond/.

leadership in 2010 on a program of radical change in public education. Under CORE's leadership, the CTU built action committees in every school, convened mass assemblies open to all union members, encouraged rigorous debate among the rank and file in the formulation and implementation of union strategy, and launched major strikes in 2012 and 2019 which shook Chicago to the core.

One big union

For much of the nineteenth and twentieth centuries, "craft unionism" dominated the workers' movement in North America. This form of unionism divided the working class by skill and reproduced social hierarchies along lines of race, nation, language, gender, and employment status. It proved particularly unsuitable to organizing the mass worker produced by the technical recomposition of modern capitalist industry. In opposition to such narrowness, the Industrial Workers of the World (IWW), or "Wobblies," proposed the formation of autonomous unions that organized workers *as a class,* uniting "fellow workers" on an industrial basis regardless of skill or social group and organizing against the "differential identities" that divided craft unions.[18] In contrast to the tepid reformism of the American Federation of Labor (AFL), the IWW advanced militant class-struggle politics, declaring as ultimate objectives the "abolition of the wage system," the expropriation of the capitalist class, and the administration of society by a free association of producers. They advocated direct action in the workplace and community as a means of improving living conditions today and preparing the masses for social revolution tomorrow.[19]

At a time when racial segregation prevailed in both society and the trade union movement, the IWW built a multiracial, multinational workers' union. As a matter of principle, the IWW embraced all workers, organizing the

18. Nicholas Thoburn, "The Hobo Anomalous: Class, Minorities and Political Invention in the Industrial Workers of the World," *Social Movement Studies* 2, no. 1 (2003): 65.
19. Jeremy Brecher, *Strike!* (Cambridge, MA: South End Press, 1997), 116.

unskilled and deskilled mass workers concentrated in big factories, agriculture, and mining. Unlike the prevailing craft unions, who organized workers in a single workplace into separate unions based on craft rather than common industry or geographic area, the IWW organized precarious and unskilled itinerant workers, who were often recent immigrants or the children of immigrants; they sought to "organize the unorganized." The IWW's politics were *internationalist*, recognizing that the global mobility of capital must be matched and challenged by the global unity of the working class. For the Wobblies, the international unity of the working class on an industrial basis prefigured the world commune governed by a free association of producers, with industrial unions preparing workers to collectivize the means of production and administer society directly.[20]

One of the most successful IWW unions was the Agricultural Workers Organization (AWO). Founded in Kansas City, Missouri in 1915, the AWO aimed to organize a single industrial union around the entire wheat harvest, from Texas to Manitoba.[21] However, AWO organizers found it more difficult to organize in the fields than the factories, as they could no longer rely upon familial and ethnic ties to build class solidarity.[22] Harvest workers faced long hours, brutal heat, poor living conditions, lice infestations, low wages, and predatory job sharks.[23] After the harvest, they would take jobs as lumberjacks and on highway and railroad labor gangs. Many migrated to the cities of the Midwest, where they had access to IWW union halls and reading rooms and could keep up-to-date on the labor movement. Thus the migrant "hobo-workers" constituted "a mass informal work group as they traveled the country, job to job, via the undercarriages, grainers, and

20. Paul Buhle, "The Legacy of the IWW," *Monthly Review*, June 1, 2005, https://monthlyreview.org/2005/06/01/the-legacy-of-the-iww/.

21. Jesse Heckman, "The Agricultural Workers Organization," *Kansas City Labor History* (2004), http://cas2.umkc.edu/labor-ed/documents/AgrWorkersOrganizationIWW.pdf/.

22. Buhle, "The Legacy of the IWW."

23. Heckman, "The Agricultural Workers Organization."

boxcars of the freight train."[24] The AWO was able to overcome its initial difficulties by embedding itself within this hobo-worker counterculture, and union membership became customary for the itinerant worker riding the rails.

The AWO created a system of recruitment and education known as the "job delegate system," in which IWW organizers would obtain employment in strategic harvest regions, ride the rails, and sleep in migrant worker camps.[25] This enabled Wobblies to effectively organize the "hobo-worker" of North America. Groups of job delegates would travel the country from early spring to late fall, recruiting and building rapport among workers, distributing information, helping workers form defensive associations against muggings and assaults on the rails, and organizing mass assemblies of workers in the fields.[26]

While the IWW's existence as an autonomous organization meant a degree of separation from the broader workers' movement, its dual unionism also meant independence from the craft unionism and social chauvinism of the AFL.[27] This enabled the IWW to experiment with new forms of workplace and community organizing, much of which would later be adopted by oppositional currents within the AFL itself (such as the TUEL) and would influence the communists who helped organize the Committee for Industrial Organization (CIO) in the 1930s. The IWW embodied a form of revolutionary class organization that grasped the diffusion of capitalist social relations throughout the social formation. It anticipated the condition of the precarious, mobile, and networked migrant worker of contemporary global class struggles, and developed, through its job delegate model, an organizational instrument for intervening in the political recomposition of the class.

24. Heckman, "The Agricultural Workers Organization."

25. Heckman, "The Agricultural Workers Organization."

26. Thoburn, "The Hobo Anomalous," 76.

27. Mike Davis, "The Stop Watch and the Wooden Shoe: Scientific Management and the Industrial Workers of the World," in James Green (ed.,) *Workers' Struggles, Past and Present: A "Radical America" Reader* (Philadelphia: Temple University Press, 1983), 98.

The historical legacy of the IWW remains relevant, as the neoliberal restructuring of the imperialist world-system has created new forms of precarity and mobility, while simultaneously creating new possibilities for building workers' power. Such possibilities are apparent in the 2016 strike of Deliveroo courier workers in London, which quickly spread to other food delivery platforms across the UK, Italy, Germany, and Spain.[28] The IWW and Independent Workers' Union of Great Britain (IWGB) were both involved in organizing the striking workers, and the communist political organization Plan C produced *Rebel Roo,* a newspaper for Deliveroo workers that quickly grew to a circulation of more than 1,500 per month. Organized delivery platform workers have relied heavily upon mass strike waves, flying pickets, mobile blockades, and militant street demonstrations. Ironically, these tactics were made possible by the non-standard employment relations of neoliberalism: as legal protections were stripped to enable further exploitation of workers, legal protections for bosses were eroded as well.[29] In this context, militant wildcat strikes became the most viable tactic.

Like their train-hopping Wobbly predecessors, the workers of Deliveroo identified strategic possibilities contained within the prevailing technical composition of the class and initiated a process of political recomposition by forging community through encrypted messaging apps and mass meetings that Deliveroo could not control, since the company lacked on-the-ground supervisory capacity.[30] One cannot help but hear echoes of the AWO's mass assemblies in the fields of North America as these delivery workers assemble in the squares of European cities to rebuild proletarian counter-power against capital and the state.

---

28. Callum Cant, "Precarious Couriers are Leading the Struggle Against Platform Capitalism," *Political Critique,* (August 3, 2017), http://politicalcritique.org/world/2017/precarious-couriers-are-leading-the-struggle-against-platform-capitalism/.

29. Cant, "Precarious Couriers are Leading the Struggle."

30. Cant, "Precarious Couriers are Leading the Struggle."

Black liberation as the frontline of class struggle

The League of Revolutionary Black Workers was founded in Detroit, Michigan in 1969 as a federation of *revolutionary union movements* (RUMs) based in various workplaces and linked to an expansive network of community associations.[31] The League fused unorthodox Marxism with Black Power, focusing on the dual struggle against capital and the racism encountered by Black workers on the job, in the union, and throughout society as a whole.[32] The League was preceded by opposition caucuses formed by Black members of the United Automobile Workers (UAW) to fight against speed-ups and racism on the shop floor. These caucuses had been quickly recuperated by the union bureaucracy and the company through firings and bribery of caucus leadership.[33]

In contrast to the earlier opposition caucuses, which could only apply pressure to union leaders and company management, the League was completely autonomous from the UAW bureaucracy.[34] It operated directly from the shop floor, ready to fight both the union bureaucracy and management in the name of asserting workers' power. "The League insisted that the working class would make the revolution—with Black workers, situated at the intersection of class exploitation and racial oppression, at the pivot."[35] Black worker autonomy was a prerequisite for the reunification of the class on an explicitly antiracist basis.[36]

The League recognized that the rank and file, exhausted by their long hours, generally did not have the energy to manage organizational operations and all the tasks involved

31. Dan Georgakas and Marvin Surkin, *Detroit: I Do Mind Dying, A Study in Urban Revolution* (Boston: South End Press, 1998), 69.

32. Nicola Pizzolato, *Challenging Global Capitalism: Labor Migration, Radical Struggle, and Urban Change in Detroit and Turin* (New York: Palgrave Macmillan, 2013), 185.

33. John Watson, *To the Point... of Production: An Interview with John Watson* (Detroit, MI: Radical Education Project, 1969), 1.

34. Martin Glaberman, "Black Cats, White Cats, Wildcats: Auto Workers in De- troit, 1969," *Libcom*, July 25, 2005, https://libcom.org/library/black-cats-white-cats-wildcats-martin-glaberman.

35. Max Elbaum, *Revolution in the Air: Sixties Radicals Turn to Lenin, Mao, and Che* (London: Verso, 2006), 82.

36. Watson, *To the Point... of Production*, 4–5.

therein.[37] It was necessary to establish a labor-community alliance via the League, which could provide the necessary resources to produce and distribute publications, coordinate meetings, maintain communications between cells within and across different workplaces, mobilize community support for direct actions, build a legal defense team, and minimize the duplication of efforts. They didn't have to start each RUM from scratch; the League could place organizational infrastructure and resources at the workers' disposal. On a day-to-day basis, the League was led by a seven-person Executive Committee and an eighty-member Central Staff.[38] The League's workplace and community nuclei were relatively autonomous and were free to determine the best course of action for their area of work.

The original RUM organization was the Dodge Revolutionary Union Movement (DRUM), which sought freedom of movement and action for rank-and-file workers by circumventing the UAW to organize beyond narrow trade unionism, emphasizing the importance of winning direct representation of Black workers, and developing a revolutionary organization self-managed by workers.[39] DRUM had no stake in the UAW's corporatist labor-capital pact and, while it concentrated on organizing Black workers autonomously, it consistently upheld the unity of all workers as a class in their struggle against the boss, advancing a program that would uplift all workers, regardless of race, gender, or age.[40]

In the summer of 1973—after the League had dissolved—a wave of wildcat strikes was unleashed in three Chrysler factories, sparked by issues similar to those around which DRUM had formed. During these strikes, leaders communicated from a clear class perspective and strikers showed a high degree of multiracial class unity.[41] "Wildcat summer" was made possible by the groundwork previously

37. Watson, *To the Point... of Production*, 3.
38. Georgakas and Surkin, *Detroit: I Do Mind Dying*, 70.
39. Georgakas and Surkin, *Detroit: I Do Mind Dying*, 36.
40. Georgakas and Surkin, *Detroit: I Do Mind Dying*, 36.
41. Georgakas and Surkin, *Detroit: I Do Mind Dying*, 189.

laid by the League-affiliated RUMs. "By focusing on the workplace," Lee Sustar observes, "DRUM and its offshoots provided a model for militant whites, even those who were initially unsympathetic to the politics of Black liberation."[42] The lasting legacy of the League's praxis was to show how the autonomous liberation struggles of the Black working class served to lead the way forward for the class as a whole. As Harry Haywood once remarked, the Black liberation struggle was and remains "a spark, a catalyst pushing forward the whole working-class and people's struggle... [it is] a clarion call to all oppressed peoples throughout the world to rise up and defeat imperialism."[43]

Women's autonomy in El Salvador

In the midst of the Salvadoran Revolution and Civil War (1979–1992), the *Asociación de Mujeres de El Salvador* (Women's Association of El Salvador, or AMES) constituted an instrument of women's autonomy and organ of counterpower within the context of a broader protracted revolutionary struggle. AMES organized to liberate proletarian and peasant women from the dual oppressions of patriarchy and capital.[44] AMES emerged from the *Fuerzas Populares de Liberación Farabundo Martí* (Farabundo Martí Popular Liberation Forces, or FPL), a Marxist politico-military organization affiliated to the *Frente Farabundo Martí para la Liberación Nacional* (Farabundo Martí National Liberation Front, or FMLN), an umbrella organization of revolutionary parties leading the struggle in El Salvador. Founded by a popular assembly in 1979, AMES grew to be the largest women's organization of the Salvadoran Revolution, organizing approximately 10,000 members in the country, with

42. Lee Sustar, "Uprising of the Black Autoworkers," *Socialist Worker*, March 1, 2013, https://socialistworker.org/2013/03/01/uprising-of-the-black-autoworkers/.

43. Harry Haywood, "We Have Taken the First Step on a Long March (1977)," Marxists Internet Archive, https://www.marxists.org/history/erol/ncm-3/haywood-1st.htm/.

44. Asociación de Mujeres de El Salvador (AMES), "Reflections of Salvadoran Women: Participation of Latin American Women in Social and Political Organizations," in New Americas Press (eds.), *A Dream Compels Us: Voices of Salvadoran Women* (Boston: South End Press, 1989), 82.

many more operating in exile in Nicaragua, Costa Rica, Mexico, the United States, Canada, and France.[45]

AMES was particularly successful in the liberated zones established by FMLN guerrillas, where participatory democracy was realized through popular assemblies and councils responsible for the administration of social life and a communal economy to meet basic needs. The FMLN cultivated an area of autonomy from which communist-feminists could expand their revolutionary challenge to the sphere of kinship relations by politicizing the labors of social reproduction, deepening women's participation in revolutionary struggle, and building alternative institutions to generate feminist social relations.[46] A dialectic of liberation was unleashed, whereby the liberated zones expanded the possibilities for women's autonomy while the movement for women's autonomy challenged the vision and program of communism within these liberated zones.

The founders of AMES feared that if they did not establish their own mass organization to fight for women's autonomy—an organ of feminist counterpower—then the needs and desires of revolutionary women would be subsumed by the patriarchal tendencies of the broader national liberation movement. In challenging the forced assignment of women to domestic labor, "our aim was to break down barriers in ideas and practice, to understand the conditions of our lives," they explained.[47] The experience of AMES, whose revolutionary praxis was grounded in a critique of conventional gender relations, shows that the struggle for particular forms of autonomy deepens the communist vision of human liberation and integral development. While the FPL upheld women's liberation, it was AMES that revolutionized communist theory and practice by making it

45. Diana Carolina Sierra Becerra, "For Our Total Emancipation: The Making of Revolutionary Feminism in Insurgent El Salvador, 1977–1987," in Kevin A. Young (ed.), *Making the Revolution: Histories of the Latin American Left* (Cambridge: Cambridge University Press, 2019), 269.

46. Becerra, "For Our Total Emancipation," 266–267.

47. Malena Giron, "Breaking Down Barriers in Ideas and Practice," in New Americas Press ed., *A Dream Compels Us: Voices of Salvadoran Women* (Boston: South End Press, 1989), 94.

relevant to the lives of rural peasant women.[48] The organized autonomy of women enriched the revolutionary movement's praxis of liberation as a whole.

Autonomous social centers

Historically, a key organ of counterpower at the neighborhood and municipal level has been the *autonomous social center*. These centers have served as both focal points for the recomposition of the revolutionary movement amid repression and "red bases" for the consolidation of a revolutionary counterculture. In Spain and Latin America, these centers—called *ateneos* (or *ateneus* in Catalan)—offered a diverse range of political and cultural events and activities, such as literacy classes and study groups, aimed at building the capacity of workers to make change.[49] They also provided childcare, which allowed for all community members, including whole families, to participate, and for youth and adults to build friendships across generations.[50] In Barcelona in the years preceding the Spanish Revolution and Civil War (1936–1939), these autonomous social centers were embedded within an area of autonomy methodically constructed by the grassroots fighting organizations of the *Confederación Nacional del Trabajo* (National Confederation of Labor, or CNT), complementing an expansive network of workplace assemblies, shop stewards, neighborhood committees, tenant unions, and defense groups. CNT *ateneos* offered services like reduced-price food cooperatives, affordable music and arts performances (usually leftist and radical in nature, as entertainment and social events were always combined with agitation, education, organization), sporting activities and outdoor excursions, camping, hiking, libraries, coastal and countryside retreats, reading rooms, debate and lecture venues, theaters, cafés, and auditoriums for public forums.[51]

48. Becerra, "For Our Total Emancipation," 292.

49. Tom Wetzel, "Why Revolutionary Syndicalism?" *Ideas and Action* (October 31, 2012), http://ideasandaction.info/2012/10/why-revolutionary-syndicalism-2/.

50. Chris Ealham, *Anarchism and the City: Revolution and Counter-Revolution in Barcelona, 1898–1937* (Oakland: AK Press, 2010), 47.

51. Ealham, *Anarchism and the City*, 45.

In El Cerro district of Montevideo, Uruguay in the 1950s and '60s, following a restructuring of class relations and repression against the Meatworkers' Federation (a particularly advanced sector of the Uruguayan working class), the Ateneo Cerro was established as a hub for reconstructing the revolutionary workers' movement. This social center provided a space for meetings of union organizers and antifascists, political forums and debates, movie screenings and discussions, musical and theatrical performances, and dances.[52] The Ateneo Cerro sought "to rally scattered forces so as to rebuild the fabric of social solidarity"; in other words, to regenerate networks of communication, cooperation, and coordination among all proletarian social institutions in the barrio.[53]

In Italy, the *centri sociali ocupati* (occupied social centers) and *centri sociali autogestiti* (self-managed social centers) began to form in Milan and Rome in the mid-seventies in response to the crisis of social reproduction caused by deindustrialization and austerity policies that eroded social welfare programs. Like the *ateneos* in Spain and Latin America, these social centers aimed to create spaces for proletarian youth to develop their capacities to autonomously organize social reproduction.[54] The buildings that housed social centers were frequently appropriated from their owners by communist militants, immigrants from Africa and Asia, and antifascist football clubs to be used as meeting spaces and centers for social provisioning.[55] Autonomous social centers thus served as focal points around which the proletarian and popular social groups could resist gentrification of their neighborhoods and mobilize around demands for self-managed childcare facilities, schools, libraries, women's health clinics, cafeterias, gyms, and cultural institutions.

52. Paul Sharkey, *The Federacion Anarquista Uruguaya (FAU): Crisis, Armed Struggle and Dicatorship 1967–1985* (London: Kate Sharpley Library, 2009), 10.

53. Sharkey, *The Federacion Anarquista Uruguaya*, 10.

54. Patrick Cunninghame, "Mapping the Terrain of Struggle: Autonomous Movements in 1970s Italy," *Viewpoint*, (November 1, 2015), https://www.viewpointmag.com/2015/11/01/feminism-autonomism-1970s-italy/.

55. Cunninghame, "Mapping the Terrain of Struggle."

In the 1970s, the Sojourner Truth Organization (STO), a communist political organization based primarily in Chicago, established the South Chicago Workers' Rights Center, which operated primarily as a legal clinic, offering free advice to workers from lawyers and paralegals who were STO members.[56] At the time, Black, Mexican, Puerto Rican, and white workers in South Chicago were living in the same neighborhoods and working in the same factories, but waging separate struggles. Through this workers' center, STO cadre were able to establish a hub around which proletarian autonomy could be developed, creating an organizational center for the coordination of these local struggles.

The Center's staff represented workers at unemployment compensation hearings, challenging companies' bogus claims, winning workers their benefits, and ensuring that benefits were actually distributed by the companies.[57] They took direct action and, in one instance, mobilized local media against employers who failed to follow through, occupying the local unemployment office to demand that all workers waiting in line receive their checks within one week. The action was successful and helped the Workers' Rights Center set a precedent for autonomous class struggle within the local community. Word got around, and soon after the action, Black workers from a local steel mill approached the Center about forming an autonomous Black caucus to wage class struggle against the boss *and* antiracist struggle within the union.[58]

From Spain to Uruguay, Italy to South Chicago, autonomous social centers can serve as hubs for autonomous mass organizations to rally and cohere. This organizational form may prove particularly effective in zones where neighborhood residents are geographically dispersed or internally fragmented along cultural lines, or where workplaces and

---

56. Michael Staudenmaier, *Truth and Revolution: A History of the Sojourner Truth Organization, 1969–1986* (Oakland: AK Press, 2012), 57.

57. David Ranney, *Living and Dying on the Factory Floor: From the Outside In and the Inside Out* (Oakland: PM Press, 2019), 2–3.

58. Ranney, *Living and Dying on the Factory Floor*, 12–13.

industries are organized in such a way that shop-floor direct action is difficult without a broader mass base.

Defending the Area of Autonomy

The ruling class and the forces of fascism will never allow the revolutionary movement to peacefully dismantle the imperialist world-system. As organs of counterpower proliferate and an area of autonomy begins to coalesce, the emerging revolutionary movement will need to develop defensive capacities to resist the armed counter-revolution and to prepare for an insurrectionary rupture with imperialism. Only a direct confrontation between the imperialist ruling class and the accumulated forces of communist social revolution—including a significant section of the armed forces—can liberate the emergent area of autonomy from the yoke of imperialism. Alongside the formation of revolutionary organizations among the personnel of the repressive state apparatus itself, a general arming of the people through the formation of *people's defense organizations* will be a necessary means of protecting, consolidating, and advancing the construction of a system of counterpower. Armed struggle will likely play a decisive role in securing the ultimate victory of the social revolution. However, we agree with communist revolutionary Torkil Lauesen, who asserts that "armed struggle is not a revolutionary principle. Armed struggle is a means that people, under certain circumstances, deem necessary; usually, when all other means have failed."[59]

Historically, people's defense organizations were often linked to specific workplace and neighborhood organizations and were used as instruments for enforcing the decisions of the movement's organs of counterpower by stopping evictions, defending picket lines, and generalizing strike actions. In the nineteenth century, groups such as the *Lehr und Wehr Verein* (Education and Defense Association) were formed

59. Torkil Lauesen, *The Global Perspective: Reflections on Imperialism and Resistance* (Montreal: Kersplebedeb, 2018), 408.

by revolutionary immigrant workers in Chicago to defend the movement against armed thugs hired by the bosses, who would break up workers' meetings, attack strikers and their supporters, and arrest socialist leaders.[60] Individual companies of the *Lehr und Wehr Verein* were typically linked to a specific community hall or social center, where they held weekly drills and instruction, as well as cultural events and fundraisers. Each month, defense organizations from across the city would meet for collective drills.[61]

Communists should not wait until after the revolution to organize self-defense. As the Italian militant organization *Potere Operaio* (Workers' Power) declared, "democracy is the rifle on the worker's shoulder." Past movements have suffered too many tragic defeats from failing to adequately prepare the defense of territorial counterpower. Gradualist illusions of a slow, peaceful accumulation of progressive forces have frequently disarmed the movement, diverting the proletarian and popular social groups from the real task at hand: settling matters with "our" ruling class.[62] The fall of Red Vienna to fascism, the overthrow of Salvador Allende's Popular Unity government in Chile, and the genocidal slaughter of Indonesian communists by Suharto all reveal the bloody costs of such naivety.[63]

While people's defense organizations frequently emerge organically in response to concrete local conditions, it is important that such organizations remain accountable to the revolutionary movement as a whole, that their social composition should reflect their base among the proletarian and popular social groups, and that their fighting units should be organically embedded within the cycle of struggle from which they emerge. In addition to the fighting formations

60. Paul Avrich, *The Haymarket Tragedy* (Princeton: Princeton University Press, 1984), 45.

61. Avrich, *The Haymarket Tragedy*, 161.

62. Marx and Engels, *The Communist Manifesto*, 20.

63. Kuhn, *Antifascism, Sports, Sobriety*, 15–25; James Petras, *Critical Perspectives on Imperialism and Social Class in the Third World* (New York: Monthly Review Press, 1978), 217–218; Nathaniel Mehr, "Reaction and Slaughter: Indonesia 1965–66," in Mike Gonzalez and Houman Barekat (eds.), *Arms and the People: Popular Movements and the Military from the Paris Commune to the Arab Spring* (London: Pluto Press, 2013), 232–247.

of the people's defense organizations, *autonomous defense organizations* may be established by social groups facing specific forms of oppression, as in the community self-defense units of the Black Panther Party (BPP) and Black Liberation Army (BLA), or the *Yekîneyên Parastina Jin* (Women's Protection Units, or YPJ) formed by the Kurdish Freedom Movement during the Rojava Revolution.[64] When called upon, the people's defense organizations and autonomous defense organizations must be capable of engaging in sustained defensive combat with enemy forces, containing and suppressing the counter-revolution in order to stabilize a system of counterpower. However, it should be emphasized that the revolution must always command the armed forces: *the armed forces must never be allowed to command the revolution.* Defensive military work must always and everywhere be completely subordinated to the constructive political tasks of the communist social revolution.

The specific organizational structures adopted by the people's defense organizations will vary in accordance with the conditions within a given territory. However, historical experience teaches several important lessons: (1) a network of defense organizations should be built on a voluntary and internally democratic basis; (2) defense organizations serve an important educational function by generalizing knowledge of community self-defense; and (3) the people's defense organizations must have the capacity to effectively engage their adversaries. Defense networks should be organized on a federative basis, with assemblies of local defense groups electing delegates to militia councils, militia councils electing delegates to columns, and columns electing delegates to a central council of defense organizations. Within such a politico-military structure, the cadre of officers, commanders, and political advisers should be subject to recall by a vote of the sending council, and politico-military policy should be widely discussed among the defense network and broader movement as a whole.

64. Jalil A. Muntaqim, *We Are Our Own Liberators: Selected Prison Writings* (Portland: Arissa Media Group, 2010), 27–40; Knapp et al., *Revolution in Rojava*, 133–140.

Create Two, Three, Many Parties of Autonomy!

From strike committees to workers' councils, tenant unions to neighborhood assemblies, the disparate forms of organized autonomy that arise during a protracted revolutionary struggle will not automatically fuse with communist politics to create a cohesive system of counterpower. Nor will a majority of the proletarian and popular social groups automatically unite with the communist movement. The imperialist world-system exerts tremendous pressure against the organic emergence of a communist worldview on a mass scale. Reformism, authoritarianism, bureaucratism, and social chauvinism within the movement can divert grassroots struggles away from a revolutionary path. What organizational form can facilitate the political development of the mass movement in a communist direction? What form can foster communication, cooperation, and coordination across multiple fronts of struggle and movement sectors? We believe the answer is found in the construction of an independent communist political organization, or *party of autonomy.*

This is not a call for a party of the bourgeois type. Social revolutions are made by the autonomous initiative of a revolutionary people, not by counting votes or *coup d'état.* We reject parties that aim to take control of the existing state machinery.[65] Rosa Luxemburg identified a revolutionary party of autonomy as the "most conscious, purposeful part of the proletariat, which points the entire broad mass of the working class toward its historical tasks at every step," always linking its grassroots political work to the ultimate goal of communism.[66] It is a *connective party,* establishing linkages between different fronts of struggle through social investigations and organizational networks, connecting local and national concerns with an analysis of the world situation and

65. Peter Nettl, "The German Social Democratic Party 1890–1914 as a Political Model," *Past and Present,* no. 30 (1965): 67.

66. Rosa Luxemburg, "What Does the Spartacus League Want?," in Peter Hudis and Kevin B. Anderson (eds.), *The Rosa Luxemburg Reader* (New York: Monthly Review Press, 2004), 356.

the tasks of the world revolution.[67] Such a party strengthens the organized autonomy of the proletarian and popular social groups at the base, recognizing that the people come to act as a collective revolutionary subject only through the self-management of the revolutionary struggle itself. This fighting revolutionary party is nothing less than a *partisan war machine*: an instrument for laying siege to imperialism.[68]

A party of autonomy does not stand outside or above the revolutionary process. Rather, such a party is internal to this process, as an integral and complementary part of an emerging system of counterpower. Thus, a party of autonomy is a dialectical product of, and active factor in, the development of revolutionary consciousness, self-organization, and self-activity among the proletarian and popular social groups.[69] A party is simply the self-organization of revolutionaries. As Agustín Guillamón has emphasized, multiple revolutionary organizations, groups, and tendencies will emerge in a revolutionary situation. In their totality, these groups constitute the historical party of communism, which is locked in antagonistic struggle against the historical party of imperialism (which is also constituted by multiple organizations, groups, and tendencies).[70] The anarchist Errico Malatesta described the historical party of communism as including "all who are *on the same side* … [who] struggle for the same ends against common adversaries and enemies. But this does not mean it is possible—or even desirable—for all of us to be gathered into one specific association."[71] Given diverse political situations and the prevailing fragmentation of proletarian and popular social groups, a high degree of

67. Mimmo Porcaro, "A Number of Possible Developments of the Idea of Connective Party," *Transform!* (2011), https://www.transform-network.net/uploads/tx_news/Porcaro_Sviluppi_final.pdf/; Porcaro, "Occupy Lenin."

68. J. Moufawad-Paul, "The Austerity Apparatus: Some Preliminary Notes," *Arsenal: Theoretical Journal of the PCR-RCP*, no. 9 (September 2017): 196.

69. Agustín Guillamón, "The Theorization of Historical Experiences," *Libcom*, November 28, 2013, https://libcom.org/history/theorization-historical-experiences-agustín-guillamón/.

70. Guillamón, "The Theorization of Historical Experiences."

71. Errico Malatesta, "A Project of Anarchist Organization (1927)," Marxists Internet Archive, https://marxists.architexturez.net/archive/malatesta/1927/10/project.htm/.

organizational flexibility is required. We believe room must be made not only for multiple factions and caucuses within a singular party of autonomy, but also for multiple parties within the broader communist movement: "Let a hundred flowers blossom, let a hundred schools of thought contend."[72]

The formation and development of a party of autonomy is a process that embodies both micropolitical and macropolitical dimensions.[73] The ability to mediate between the two has been a distinguishing feature of successful revolutionary parties. In the Russian Revolution of 1917, clusters of Bolshevik party activists concentrated in workplaces recognized that the grassroots councils (*soviets*) emerging from the struggles of workers embodied the nuclei of an alternative social system.[74] Thus, the party's organization at the point of production enabled revolutionaries to link workplace struggles against exploitation with the struggle against imperialism and to link the emergent councils with the insurrectionary struggle to establish a system of territorial counterpower.[75]

A party of autonomy fuses with organs of counterpower and people's defense organizations. It organizes tactical and strategic united fronts, with the aim of articulating a system of counterpower that can contend with the authoritarian state for territorial control. It wages struggle on the terrain of everyday life—the workplace, neighborhood, school, prison, or barracks—and moves within the flow of emergent networks, structures, and processes. This requires coordination, discipline, planning, and unity in action.[76] At all scales of operation, a party of autonomy presents the most advanced demands and deploys its most capable militants to the

72. Mao Zedong, "On the Correct Handling of Contradictions Among the People (1957)," Marxists Internet Archive, https://www.marxists.org/reference/archive/mao/selected-works/volume-5/mswv5_58.htm/.

73. Gilles Deleuze and Félix Guattari, *A Thousand Plateaus*, trans. Brian Massumi (Minneapolis: University of Minnesota Press, 1991), 105–106.

74. Donny Gluckstein, "The Missing Party (1984)," Marxists Internet Archive, https://www.marxists.org/history/etol/writers/gluckstein/1984/xx/missing.html/.

75. Charles Bettelheim, *Class Struggles in the USSR, First Period: 1917–1923* (New York: Monthly Review Press, 1976), 73.

76. Bookchin, *Post-Scarcity Anarchism*, 139.

frontlines of the revolutionary struggle and within emergent organs of counterpower.[77]

A party is a part of an emergent system of counterpower. Far from seeking to dominate the autonomous liberation struggles of the proletarian and popular social groups, "the party must be built in the fire of struggles, step by step, under the control of the mass political movement."[78] Such a party aims to root itself among the oppressed masses, participate in their struggles, "and thus organize while being organized by the masses."[79] If the social revolution is indeed "a process of assemblage" that links multiple fronts of struggle into a united front, then the party functions as the key instrument of linkage.[80]

Articulation and fusion: the functions of a party organization

What are the functions of a party of autonomy? Revolutionary parties operate as *articulators* of a communist praxis. Concretely, such organizations help to articulate: (1) the communist content implicit in grassroots social struggles via militant social investigation that combines a practice of inquiry with relentless agitation, education, and organization; and (2) an area of autonomy composed of heterogeneous—and at times contradictory—social forces, reaching an organizational apex first with the formation of a system of counterpower, and later with the establishment of a territorial commune. As Salar Mohandesi puts it, the work of articulation performed by a party of autonomy is twofold: "On the one hand, to articulate is to communicate, formulate, or express a given content by moving it to a different register. On the other hand, to articulate is to join separate elements together, and the articulator, in this sense, can be

77. Bookchin, *Post-Scarcity Anarchism*, 140.

78. L'Union des Communistes de France marxiste-léniniste (UCFML), "l'UCFML: une organisation révolutionnaire marxiste-léniniste-maoïste," Le Marxiste-Léniniste: Journal Central de l'UCFML, no. 18/19 (July-August 1977): 4.

79. J. Moufawad-Paul, *Continuity and Rupture: Philosophy in the Maoist Terrain* (Winchester, UK: Zero Books, 2016), 198.

80. Biel, *The Entropy of Capitalism*, 328.

understood as the joint itself."[81] A few historical examples may serve to elucidate the role and function of a party of autonomy as an articulator of a communist praxis.

Throughout the Great Depression, the Alabama Communist Party fused Marxist theory with local cultures, articulating the communist content implicit in Southern Black resistance to racial oppression and class exploitation and building an area of autonomy consisting of Black rural sharecroppers, industrial workers, the unemployed, women, poor whites, and radical youth. It achieved this through organizations such as the Trade Union Unity League, Sharecroppers' Union, National Committee of Unemployed Councils, Young Communist League, and Alabama Farmers' Relief Fund. In addition to campaigns for Black self-determination, antiracist class unity, unemployment and underemployment relief, eviction and foreclosure defense, rank-and-file unionism, wage increases, public education, and voter rights, the local units of the Communist Party published *Southern Worker,* a regional communist newspaper with a focus on Black liberation and proletarian class struggle. In the words of Robin D.G. Kelley:

> The Party offered more than a vehicle for social contestation; it offered a framework for understanding the roots of poverty and racism, linked local struggles to world politics, challenged not only the hegemonic ideology of white supremacy but the petite bourgeois racial politics of the Black middle class, and created an atmosphere in which ordinary people could analyze, discuss, and criticize the society in which they lived.[82]

Another historical example is the *Federación Anarquista Ibérica* (Iberian Anarchist Federation, or FAI).[83] The FAI formed in 1927 with the aim of establishing a symbiotic

81. Salar Mohandesi, "All Tomorrow's Parties: A Reply to Critics," *Viewpoint*, May 23, 2012, https://www.viewpointmag.com/2012/05/23/all-tomorrows-parties-a-reply-to-critics/.

82. Robin D.G. Kelley, *Hammer and Hoe: Alabama Communists During the Great Depression* (Chapel Hill: University of North Carolina Press, 1990), 93.

83. Roberto Bordiga, "Per la storia degli anarchici spagnoli," *Primo Maggio*, no. 6 (1976): 83.

relationship with *Confederación Nacional del Trabajo* (the National Confederation of Labor, or CNT). It worked to unite anarcho-communist forces throughout the Iberian peninsula and diaspora in order to struggle against reactionary currents in the CNT, articulate the communist content implicit in class struggle, and accelerate the development of a revolutionary situation.[84] All FAI cadre were expected to agree with anarcho-communist principles and join a local CNT union.[85] Within those unions, FAI cadre established a *trabazón* or "organic link" between the two organizations, effectively fusing anarcho-communist vision (embodied in the FAI) with the anarcho-syndicalist strategy of rank-and-file class struggle unionism (embodied in the CNT).[86] Joint councils operated as a hub or point of convergence for both the CNT rank and file and FAI cadre.[87] This *trabazón* did not aim to subordinate the CNT to the FAI. It was a pedagogical relationship, whereby the FAI sought to unleash the emancipatory currents within the CNT and to push back against conservative elements within the workers' movement. The aim was to cultivate a symbiotic interdependency within a broader system of counterpower, in which each organization retained a relative degree of autonomy in pursuit of a common objective: social revolution for the establishment of libertarian communism on a world scale.

The FAI created a revolutionary party of autonomy of a specifically anarchist character. The radical achievements of the proletariat and peasantry in Spain during this period are partially attributable to the immense effort and sacrifice of FAI cadres to rebuild the CNT in the face of reformism and state repression and to advance a specifically anarcho-communist vision. FAI cadres within the CNT

84. Stuart Christie, *We, the Anarchists! A Study of the Iberian Anarchist Federation* (FAI), 1927–1937 (Oakland: AK Press, 2008), 39.

85. Murray Bookchin, *The Spanish Anarchists: The Heroic Years 1868–1936* (Oakland: AK Press, 1998), 198.

86. Jason Garner, *Goals and Means: Anarchism, Syndicalism, and Internationalism in the Origins of the Federación Anarquista Ibérica* (Oakland: AK Press, 2016), 214.

87. Garner, *Goals and Means*, 222.

ceaselessly worked to initiate an insurrectionary rupture with the old society, emphasizing that the counter-hegemonic communal governance of the working class could only be established via grassroots participatory democracy in federations of unions, assemblies, committees, councils, and collectives. However, while the FAI embodied a party of autonomy in its historical functioning, its lack of political cohesion around a sufficiently developed platform and program, combined with a propensity to engage in reckless armed actions, limited its effectiveness as an articulator of communist content, especially as the Spanish proletariat and peasantry stepped onto the battlefield of civil war.

In Chile, *Movimiento de Izquierda Revolucionaria* (Revolutionary Left Movement, or MIR) exemplified a party of autonomy, operating as a catalyst in the construction of autonomous popular power, which included grassroots fighting organizations, alternative institutions, defense groups, united fronts, and a nuanced relationship with electoral politics. A diverse group of militants founded the MIR in 1965 at the University of Concepción. By 1973, the MIR would have more than ten thousand members engaged in organizing students, staff, and faculty on university campuses, the urban poor in shantytowns, peasants in the countryside, rank-and-file industrial workers in the unions, and soldiers in the armed forces. During the presidency of Salvador Allende, the MIR radicalized the grassroots base of the *Unidad Popular* (Popular Unity) coalition, and subsequently led the antifascist resistance against the dictatorship of Augusto Pinochet. In their grassroots political work, MIR cadre emphasized popular self-organization through expropriations (*tomas*), the formation of communal workers' councils, and the construction of a revolutionary people's army.

The MIR nucleus emerged from the *Movimiento Universitario de Izquierda* (Left University Movement, or MUI),which was based on popular assemblies. Like their New Left contemporaries in other countries, MUI demanded that the university be opened to all and democratically governed by a community of students, staff, and faculty.[88] MUI revolutionaries would go on to form the core leadership of the MIR, which combined participatory democracy in popular assemblies and communal councils with militant direct action via occupations and expropriations. The MIR later replicated the assembly-based model initially developed by the MUI, extending it beyond the city of Concepción to Chile as a whole, encompassing a multitude of grassroots social struggles.

One of the MIR's most important projects was *Campamento Lenin,* an encampment in Concepción that served as a home for 3,000 *pobladores* [houseless urban poor]. While many organizations fought for housing justice, the MIR was unique in emphasizing direct action and the prefiguration of communism. According to historian Marian Schlotterbeck, the MIR "promoted direct actions in the form of *tomas de terrenos urbanos,* literally taking unoccupied urban lands, as a means to create territorial expressions of popular power."[89] Following expropriation and occupation, the MIR helped create communal forms of governance based on autonomous popular assemblies, thereby developing a minor communist politics understood "as participation, as liberation, and as a means to equality."[90] Through Campamento Lenin, the MIR articulated communist politics and a counter-hegemonic alliance. It organized the mass expropriation of land for housing, bringing together *pobladores,* students, labor unions, and communist political organizations into a solidarity committee, which reflected MIR strategy to forge a revolutionary people by uniting multiple sectors of struggle.[91] The origins of Campamento Lenin can be traced to the MIR's militant social investigations. Local *miristas,* primarily students, surveyed the everyday problems faced by *pobladores* in

88. Marian E. Schlotterbeck, "Everyday Revolutions: Grassroots Movements, the Revolutionary Left (MIR), and the Making of Socialism in Concepción, Chile, 1964–1973," PhD diss., Yale University (2013), 19.

89. Schlotterbeck, "Everyday Revolutions," 71.

90. Schlotterbeck, "Everyday Revolutions," 67.

91. Schlotterbeck, "Everyday Revolutions," 83.

the shantytowns in order to build a network of contacts and identify prospective plots of land for expropriation. Upon the completion of an initial survey, *miristas* would synthesize the information collected to formulate a programmatic orientation for popular mobilization.[92]

From its initial base among students in the MUI to organizing *pobladores* and Campamento Lenin, the MIR laid the groundwork to expand its infrastructure. It built organs of counterpower among industrial workers in the coal mining and textile industries through the *Frente de Trabajadores Revolucionarios* (Revolutionary Workers Front, or FTR), and among rural workers through the *Movimiento Campesino Revolucionario* (Revolutionary Peasant Movement, or MCR). Its ultimate aim was to link these diverse fronts of struggle as system of counterpower, culminating with the formation of a Popular Assembly to express the will of an emergent revolutionary people.[93]

The MIR took cadre development extremely seriously. According to *mirista* Carlos Robles, "It wasn't just show up and do some activity—like pass out pamphlets or sell *El Rebelde*—no, there was a space for reflection. A space for everything because it wasn't just politics that we had, there was also personal growth (*formación humana*)—this is important—the development of the individual as such."[94] The base organizations of the MIR advanced a communist praxis that prioritized full human development and the politicization of everyday life, pushing the boundaries of what constituted the political.[95] The MIR's holistic praxis of liberation enabled them to overcome class differences internally, despite the organization's initial base among students and faculty at a single university: "The investment the MIR made in forming militants was also an investment in forming people—instilling a sense that each voice mattered and each person had

92. Schlotterbeck, "Everyday Revolutions," 73.
93. Schlotterbeck, "Everyday Revolutions," 242.
94. Schlotterbeck, "Everyday Revolutions," 143.
95. Schlotterbeck, "Everyday Revolutions," 143.

something to contribute to the revolutionary struggle in Chile."[96] It was this dialogic pedagogy practiced by MIR base organizations that enabled them to win the trust of the urban and rural poor, peasants, and industrial workers who went on to join the MIR and make it their own.

A cadre party

These case studies provide inspiring examples of the concrete operations of a party of autonomy. With minimal personnel and resources, initially concentrated in limited geographic areas and among particular sectors of the proletarian and popular social groups, these revolutionary parties patiently organized an area of autonomy. Informed by a revolutionary vision of communism and a strategy of protracted struggle, they inspired masses of people to fight for radical change. In all of the above examples, the conscious recruitment, development, and coordination of *cadre* made victories possible. The word cadre is of French origin, meaning "framework." Cadre are "active worker-organizers," or "a multilayered stratum of activists committed to the movement's continuity through the ups and downs of its daily routine."[97]

Parties of autonomy can be understood as *cadre organizations,* assembling frameworks that inform the everyday praxis of communist partisans operating in a variety of contexts. Such a framework should include: (1) a *platform* articulating an analysis of the imperialist world-system from the standpoint of the proletarian and popular social groups, a vision of a communist alternative, and a strategy of protracted revolutionary struggle; (2) a *program* that emerges from militant social investigations and which articulates the concrete tasks of cadre in symbiotic relationship with emerging grassroots social struggles; and (3) an *organizational culture and style of doing politics* that is collective, creative, humble, patient,

96. Schlotterbeck, "Everyday Revolutions," 147.

97. Wobblyist Working Group, "Wobblyism: Revolutionary Unionsim for Today," *Libcom,* December 11, 2013, http://libcom.org/library/wobblyism-revolutionary-unionism-today; Wright, *Storming Heaven,* 75.

militant, and open to refinement and transformation. Reflecting upon the legacy of the New Communist Movement of the 1970s and 1980s in North America, movement veteran Max Elbaum emphasizes the importance of cadre organization:

> Revolutionary spirit, hard work, personal sacrifice, and the willingness to subordinate individual interests to the political tasks at hand are all crucial qualities for a successful radical movement. So too is the commitment to sink roots among the exploited and oppressed and to struggle within the movement over inequalities of class, race, and gender. And—whether or not they are now in fashion—so are organizations capable of functioning on the basis of well-worked out strategies, unity in action, and a measure of collective discipline.[98]

Cadre *organize* to help others develop their own potential.[99] However, what distinguishes a party of autonomy's cadre from other types of organizers is that they have a common political platform and program to orient their work and an organizational center to which they are accountable.[100] Specifically, a party of autonomy should focus on producing and circulating the knowledge and skills needed to build organized autonomy, including organs of counterpower, people's defense organizations, and united fronts. Cadre build conscious forms of *collective leadership*, which for Ella Baker meant "leadership that helped people to help themselves and allowed ordinary people to feel that they could determine their own future."[101] The forms of organized autonomy that allow masses of people to exercise self-management, self-government, and self-determination do not emerge spontaneously. Cadre intentionally exercise

98. Elbaum, *Revolution in the Air*, 180.
99. Charles M. Payne, *I've Got the Light of Freedom: The Organizing Tradition and the Mississippi Freedom Struggle* (Berkeley: University of California Press, 1996), 84.
100. Mann, *Playbook for Progressives*, 71.
101. Barbara Ransby, *Ella Baker and the Black Freedom Movement: A Radical Democratic Vision* (Chapel Hill: University of North Carolina Press, 2003), 167.

collective leadership to assist their initial formation and guide their development towards revolutionary objectives in symbiotic relation with the masses.[102]

The basic organizational unit of a party of autonomy at the level of a municipality or neighborhood could be the *local branch*, which functions as a hub for the organization's activities. The local branch could convene meetings of members on a regular basis, collect dues, organize political education workshops and technical trainings, and conduct militant social investigations to inform the initial selection of sites of struggle where the party organization focuses its time, energies, and resources. At the territorial level, a party could convene organizational congresses consisting of delegates from each local branch, which could in turn elect a coordinating committee to maintain the day-to-day operations of the party, encompassing communications, publications, finances, and the intentional cultivation of comradely relations and alliances with other revolutionary organizations and sectors of the movement.

As a local branch grows in size and capacity, it could create *clusters*, or smaller fractions of comrades formed on the basis of common affinities and concentration in a common front of struggle. Each cluster could function as an intimate space for political education, mutual aid, and the forging of a shared political praxis. This is a *cellular* organization, as advocated by Ella Baker, who "envisioned small groups of people working together but also retaining contact in some form with other such groups, so that coordinated action would be possible whenever large numbers really were necessary."[103] The political cohesion and strategic unity of these forces can enable effective operational and tactical convergence or dispersion, in accordance with the situation encountered. However, the communicative burden for such organizational forms is high, as each cluster must have the capacity not only to send and receive information, but to process it quickly.

102. Bookchin, *The Next Revolution*, 181.
103. Payne, *I've Got the Light of Freedom*, 369.

As a member of the Alabama Communist Party from Birmingham once remarked: "There ain't one of us here who was born a communist; we learned it and it ain't easy to learn."[104] A party of autonomy functions simultaneously as a school, workshop, and laboratory for learning, testing, and refining the craft of revolutionary organizing. A party organization is thus an instrument for aggregating, collectivizing, and circulating knowledge co-produced through past and present cycles of struggle in order to strengthen the possibilities for future victories. It is an organization of *revolutionaries by trade* and, as with any trade, the grassroots political work conducted by party cadre requires time, patience, commitment, openness, and reflexivity.[105]

The party organization should develop political education programs to foster collective leadership. It cannot effectively agitate, educate, and organize for communism if it lacks a sufficient base of trained cadre who are transformed with time and experience into battle-hardened veterans of protracted revolutionary struggle. During the initial process of formation, a party organization will need to focus on *internal programs.* Such internal programs could include: (1) political education to strengthen the knowledge, skills, and capacities of individual cadre; (2) the production of agitational and educational materials (such as literature, podcasts, films, and posters) to popularize the politics of the organization and to hone the skills of cadre in disseminating these materials; (3) recruitment, since future projects depend upon a sizable and growing core of cadre to enable an effective division of tasks, a rotation of responsibilities, and a capacity for increasingly complex projects. To ensure that the party organization maintains a responsive and symbiotic relationship with the masses, each project should be subject to a critical assessment of its effectiveness. The combination of organizational discipline, unity around a common political platform and

104. Kelley, *Hammer and Hoe*, 93.
105. Lars T. Lih, *Lenin Rediscovered: 'What is to be Done?' in Context* (Chicago: Haymarket Books, 2008), 459.

program, and autonomy of local branches and clusters, along with the development of an organizational culture and style of work synchronized with local conditions and customs, makes for an organization with a greater capacity to organize an area of autonomy, build a system of counterpower, resist counter-revolutionary repression, and prefigure the social relations of communism.

The area of the party

In order to consolidate the communist movement, we are faced with the question of *unity*, or the task of forging bonds of solidarity among multiple revolutionary parties, grounded in mutual respect for the independence of each organization and a recognition that no one organization or tendency can or will have all the answers. As Jose Carlos Mariátegui emphasized, "the existence of defined and precise tendencies and groups is not an evil. On the contrary, it is the sign of an advanced period of the revolutionary process. What matters is that these groups and tendencies know how to understand themselves when facing the concrete reality of the day."[106] The task is to unify the communist movement on the basis of "contingent, *concrete,* and practical action."[107]

To achieve this unity in diversity—to create a "neighborhood of a thousand flags"[108]—we propose building a network of interorganizational communication, cooperation, and coordination among multiple revolutionary parties. We call this the *area of the party*, or "a party of a networked type."[109] Instead of sects competing with each other for dominance, each organization could operate as a complementary part of a more complex whole. Within this organizational ecology,

106. José Carlos Mariátegui, "The United Front," *Cosmonaut*, November 23, 2019, https://cosmonaut.blog/2019/11/23/the-united-front-by-jose-carlos-mariategui/.

107. Mariátegui, "The United Front."

108. Manju Rajendran, "Revolutionary Work in Our Time: Can't Keep Quiet, This Time Gon' Be More Than a Riot," *Left Turn*, June 1, 2010), http://www.leftturn.org/revolutionary-work-our-time-gonna-be-more-riot/.

109. Nick Dyer-Witheford and Svitlana Matviyenko, *Cyberwar and Revolution: Digital Subterfuge in Global Capitalism* (Minneapolis: University of Minnesota Press, 2019), 148.

the whole is greater than the sum of its parts, while the associated parties are defined by their practical initiatives.[110] The crucial aspect is that the relative autonomy of each affiliate organization is respected and leadership functions are distributed throughout the network, where "each member can play, from time to time, a hegemonic role," with room for divergent perspectives on certain issues within an overall context of unity in action.[111] Whether this area of the party ultimately coalesces into a unitary party organization we leave open to contingency.

The area of the party, in our conception, is *segmentary, polycentric,* and *networked*.[112] It is *segmentary* because it is composed of multiple party organizations or "segments," each with their own political platform, program, and style of work. This segmentary character enables the area of the party to permeate different sectors of society and fronts of struggle simultaneously, reflecting the various standpoints and forms of life articulated by the proletarian and popular social groups.[113] With multiple party organizations, a division of labor can be established with varying degrees of specialization at certain nodes and with failsafe measures distributed throughout the network. A measure of redundancy, duplication, and overlap contributes to overall system reliability, while the capacity to propose "many different solutions to a problem [is] the institutional equivalent to biodiversity in the ecosystem."[114] Within this pluralist organizational ecology, a culture of *emulation* among the affiliated organizations can amplify and accelerate dynamics of experimentation, adaptive learning, and militancy. Instead of a singular and

---

110. Rodrigo Nunes, "Notes Toward a Rethinking of the Militant," in Shannon Brincat (ed.), *Communism in the 21st Century, Volume 3: The Future of Communism: Social Movements, Economic Crises, and the Re-imagination of Communism* (Santa Barbara, CA: Praeger, 2014), 177.

111. Porcaro, "A Number of Possible Developments of the Idea of Connective Party."

112. Luther P. Gerlach, "The Structure of Social Movements: Environmental Activism and its Opponents," in John Arquilla and David Ronfeldt (eds.), *Networks and Netwars: The Future of Terror, Crime, and Militancy* (Santa Monica, CA: RAND, 2001).

113. Gerlach, "The Structure of Social Movements," 293.

114. Biel, *The Entropy of Capitalism*, 340.

undifferentiated political line for all times and places, different strategic, operational, and tactical approaches can be tested in a range of situations, with area-wide learning facilitated through an integrated information and communications infrastructure.

The area of the party is *polycentric* because it does not consist of a single central leadership, instead opting for collective leadership distributed at various scales through multiple leadership centers.[115] Horizontality and verticality, centralism and decentralism, are not absolute principles, but contingent possibilities whose effective applications rest upon acknowledging the dialectical relation between these polarities along with analyses of concrete situations.[116] We must determine "what *balances* to strike between openness and closure, dispersion and unity, strategic action and process, and so forth."[117] Formal leadership positions should be rotated and held directly accountable to the rank-and-file membership of the affiliated organizations through regular areawide assemblies. The area of the party reintroduces a dialectical method of analysis into the science of revolutionary organization, recognizing both the *situational* and *strategic* dimensions of leadership. Against "leader*less*" resistance, we posit a "leader*ful*" revolutionary movement.[118]

Finally, the area of the party is *networked*, which enables the associated parties "to exchange information and ideas and to coordinate participation in joint action."[119] As the imperialist world-system has already adopted a networked approach to counter-revolution through forms of inter-agency cooperation, revolutionaries would be wise to recognize that "*it takes a network to fight a network.*"[120] This integrated network

115. Gerlach, "The Structure of Social Movements," 294.

116. Lauesen, *The Global Perspective*, 446–447.

117. Rodrigo Nunes, *Organisation of the Organisationless: Collective Action After Networks* (Post-Media Lab and Mute Books, 2014), 13.

118. Nunes, *Organisation of the Organisationless*, 33.

119. Gerlach, "The Structure of Social Movements," 295.

120. Michael Hardt and Antonio Negri, *Multitude: War and Democracy in the Age of Empire* (New York: Penguin Books, 2004), 58. See also David Ronfeldt et al., *The Zapatista Social Netwar in Mexico* (Santa Monica, CA: RAND, 1998).

could be maintained through traveling educators, agitators, and organizers; overlapping membership across affiliate party organizations; integrated information and communications infrastructure; joint initiatives, projects, and campaigns; and recognition of a common struggle, a common enemy, and a common objective, even if the particularities of each affiliate party's analysis, vision, and strategy diverge on specific points. At the level of a neighborhood or municipality, the area of the party could emerge through joint councils or "fusion centers" to coordinate the activities of various party branches and collectives concentrated in a common zone. Indeed, the construction of this integrated network could itself function as the scaffolding for articulating a system of counterpower from within the area of autonomy, constituting the institutional basis of a communal social system.

A segmentary, polycentric, and networked area of the party may prove to be resilient in the face of counter-revolutionary repression and adaptive in the face of a rapidly changing terrain of struggle. There are several potential sources of this resiliency. As Luther P. Gerlach argues, "To the extent that local groups are autonomous and self-sufficient, some are likely to survive the destruction of others. This is also true of leaders; some will survive and even become more active and radical when others are removed, retired, or coopted."[121] Furthermore, distributing and rotating leadership functions throughout the area of the party can help mitigate the consequences of burnout, as another group can pick up the banner of revolution and carry it forward into battle.

The area of the party has several historical precedents. During the Salvadoran Revolution and Civil War (1979–1992), there emerged a united front of revolutionary anti-imperialist forces, encompassing an alliance of the *Frente Farabundo Martí para la Liberación Nacional* (Farabundo Martí National Liberation Front, or FMLN) and *Frente Democrático Revolucionario* (Revolutionary Democratic Front, or FDR), which fought together under the banner

121. Gerlach, "The Structure of Social Movements," 303.

of the "FMLN-FDR."[122] While the FDR united a network of mass organizations, such as labor unions, peasant associations, barrio committees, and student groups, the FMLN united five revolutionary parties to coordinate a common politico-military struggle. The FMLN thus constituted an area of the party embedded within a broader area of autonomy encompassing the liberated zones within the guerrilla territories, the base organizations affiliated with the FDR, and the more diffuse organizations and militants outside FMLN-FDR networks. What made the FMLN unique was that it established a mechanism of communication, coordination, and cooperation among the various politico-military organizations—El Salvador's area of the party—in a common revolutionary struggle with a common program. The five parties affiliated to the FMLN each maintained their own organizational autonomy, while five commanders, one representing each party, collectively made decisions for the FMLN as a whole.[123] As one FMLN guerrilla put it: "There's a real danger of each group going its own way, but it's also difficult to decree unity. We have genuine differences of approach, and the answer is not for every organization to renounce its beliefs in the name of unity. That smells of Stalinism to me."[124]

The Guatemalan Revolution and Civil War (1960–1996) displayed many features similar to those in El Salvador. After years of sectarianism, rivalry, non-cooperation, and "zonalization" (where each revolutionary organization controlled a territory that was not to be encroached upon by others), four revolutionary parties came together under the umbrella of the *Unidad Revolucionaria Nacional Guatemalteca* (Guatemalan National Revolutionary Unity, or URNG) in January 1982. During the course of the revolutionary struggle, leadership functions within the URNG were rotated among

122. Yvon Grenier, "Understanding the FMLN: A Glossary of Five Words," *Conflict Quarterly* 11, no. 2, Spring 1991: 52.

123. Cynthia McClintock, *Revolutionary Movements in Latin America* (Washington, DC: United States Institute of Peace, 1998), 48.

124. McClintock, *Revolutionary Movements in Latin America*, 56.

affiliate parties. The URNG stated that it was "fighting for space, not for itself as a political party, but for the formulation of alternative, popularly based solutions to the country's crises."[125] The URNG did not see itself as the future holder of state power, but as a revolutionary catalyst working to deepen, defend, and expand the broader mass movement.[126] What emerged from the experience of the URNG by the end of the 1980s was a clear distinction between the area of the party (embodied in the URNG and its affiliate party organizations) and the area of autonomy (embodied in the popular organizations of the mass movement). The ultimate aim was to achieve "a popular/revolutionary convergence," or the articulation of a system of counterpower from among these disparate elements:

> The formulations [of the URNG] concerning alliances reflected new thinking about the relationship of revolutionary forces to the popular movement as the latter reemerged. On the one hand, all parties had learned the painful lessons of the late 1970s and early 1980s, when some popular organizations were more exposed to repression because of their open identification with the guerrilla movement. On the other hand, it was also important to overcome the disarticulation that existed in the 1980s between the revolutionary left and (nonclandestine) popular movements. The challenge was to define a new relationship, taking into account a necessary degree of autonomy of the popular organizations.[127]

Judging from the accumulated historical experience of revolutionary struggles against imperialism, it appears unlikely that a monolithic mass party will prove useful (or even possible) for today's communist movement. The forging of a revolutionary movement for communism will likely result from the converging efforts of multiple revolutionary parties

125. Susanna Jonas, *The Battle for Guatemala: Rebels, Death Squads, and U.S. Power* (Boulder, CO: Westview Press, 1991), 237.
126. Jonas, *The Battle for Guatemala*, 192.
127. Jonas, *The Battle for Guatemala*, 192.

(the area of the party) with a more expansive network of autonomous mass organizations and defense groups (the area of autonomy).

From United Front to System of Counterpower

How can we shift from defending the immediate interests of the oppressed to actualizing our collective historical interests as a sovereign revolutionary people? How can multiple fronts of struggle be assembled into a cohesive movement of movements with a coherent communist program? The area of the party may uphold, defend, and advance the general interests and unity of the proletarian and popular social groups at a programmatic level, and party organizations play a central role in articulating and connecting disparate social forces as a social bloc of the oppressed. But a singular party organization, or area of the party, is not a substitute for the collective consciousness, self-organization, and self-activity of a revolutionary people in arms.[128]

The ultimate aim of the communist movement is to assemble the aforementioned forms of organized autonomy—organs of counterpower, people's defense organizations, and parties of autonomy—into a coherent *system of counterpower* that can disarticulate and smash the authoritarian state, delink from the imperialist world-system, and build territorial communes on the way to the world commune. The task is to achieve a degree of *organic centralism from below,* establishing networks of communication, cooperation, and coordination among the movement's many parts and integrating these elements into a cohesive, articulated whole. It is at this point that we can speak of the emergence of a *historical party of communism* as the motive force of the social revolution against imperialism.

United fronts enable revolutionaries to win the wavering elements of the people to a communist program. The Fourth

128. Leon Trotsky, "Our Political Tasks (1904)," Marxists Internet Archive, https://www.marxists.org/archive/trotsky/1904/tasks/.

World Congress of the Communist International defined the united front as "an initiative whereby the communists propose to join with all workers belonging to other parties and groups and all unaligned workers in a common struggle to defend the immediate, basic interests of the working class against the bourgeoisie. Every action, for even the most trivial everyday demand, can lead to revolutionary awareness and revolutionary education."[129] Through the experience of common struggle via united fronts, proletarian and popular social groups can be won to the program of communist social revolution. Communists can win the trust and respect of the base, as reformist bureaucrats will often prove to be both incompetent fighters for reforms and inadequate defenders of the people in the face of repression.

The geographies of the metropolitan core and urbanized peripheries of the imperialist world-system today offer a distinct series of challenges for articulating a system of counterpower.[130] Here, the construction of a system of counterpower will take place not in an isolated jungle or mountain range, but in the heart of enemy territory. Organs of counterpower, people's defense organizations, and parties of autonomy will be constructed and linked within and across workplaces, neighborhoods, prisons, barracks, and schools in the midst of struggle. Prior to an insurrectionary rupture with the imperialist world-system, a system of counterpower may initially emerge in clandestine fashion, with open revolutionary base areas only emerging later from the disarticulation of the authoritarian state's apparatuses and the destruction of imperialist state power.

---

129. Communist International (Comintern), "Theses on Comintern Tactics (1922)," Marxists Internet Archive, https://www.marxists.org/history/international/comintern/4th-congress/tactics.htm/.

130. Collective of Communist Prisoners, "The Twenty Theses of the Collective of Communist Prisoners of the Red Brigades (1980)," *Urban Guerilla*, September 21, 2017, http://urbanguerilla.org/the-twenty-theses-of-the-collective-of-communist-prisoners-of-the-red-brigades-december-1980/.

A system of counterpower in Oaxaca

The potential for a rapid evolution from united front to system of counterpower was illustrated during the Oaxaca Uprising of 2006 in Mexico, where a strike of education workers quickly transformed into an insurrectionary social strike. The uprising began in May of that year, when Section 22 of the *Coordinadora Nacional de Trabajadores de la Educación* (National Coordinator of Education Workers, or CNTE)—a rank-and-file opposition movement within the mainstream teachers' union, the *Sindicato Nacional de Trabajadores de la Educación* (National Union of Education Workers, or SNTE)—organized their annual *plantón* (occupation) of the central square of Oaxaca City. Strategically positioned, the teachers were primarily Indigenous, working with the children and families of the poor in both the classroom and community.[131] Raising demands that extended far beyond their immediate concerns as education workers (e.g., wages and working conditions), the strikers focused on the social reproduction of the class as a whole, including demanding free school supplies, clothing, and healthcare for students.[132]

After the corrupt governor Ulises Ruiz Ortíz deployed police forces to repress the teachers' movement, the strike mushroomed from 80,000 to 120,000 demonstrators, who seized the streets of Oaxaca.[133] Students occupied the university radio station, seizing the airwaves. "Long lines formed outside the radio station, where people patiently waited their turn to denounce the government's abusive practices, corruption, and arrogance," explain two historians of the uprising.[134] These guerrilla radio stations did more than knit together the emerging movement—they functioned "as a means of autonomous cultural expression and popular education, taking up issues such as the struggle

131. David McNally, *Global Slump: The Economics and Politics of Crisis and Resistance* (Oakland: PM Press, 2011), 164.

132. McNally, *Global Slump*, 164.

133. McNally, *Global Slump*, 164.

134. Gerardo Rénique and Deborah Poole, "The Oaxaca Commune: Struggling for Autonomy and Dignity," North American Congress on Latin America (NACLA), May 1, 2008, https://nacla.org/article/oaxaca-commune-struggling-autonomy-and-dignity/.

of the Palestinian people for self-determination."[135] From the outset, the Oaxaca Uprising adopted a revolutionary internationalist and anti-imperialist perspective.

It was only a few days before the police were deployed to contain and suppress the *plantón*. But the teachers fought back, and thousands more residents ultimately joined them to reclaim the city. Barricades were erected, street fighting erupted, the police and death squads were momentarily defeated, and a general strike of more than 800,000 workers shut down the city. It was in this context that the *Asamblea Popular de los Pueblos de Oaxaca* (Popular Assembly of the Peoples of Oaxaca, or APPO) was born. This participatory democratic assembly brought together delegates from 365 groups, uniting workers' unions and Indigenous organizations, feminists and environmentalists, Marxists and anarchists, in a common front of struggle. "APPO emerged as an expression of insurgent assembly-style democracy. More than that, it burst forth as a site of dual power—a forum for vibrant popular democracy through which the oppressed of Oaxaca began to manage large parts of everyday social life," explains David McNally.[136]

Grounding itself in an Indigenous praxis of liberation, the APPO organized autonomous assemblies, councils, and action committees as the central organs of counterpower. It developed collective leadership by applying the Zapatista principle *mandar obedeciendo*, or "lead by obeying." It rejected the practice of a singular leader or group occupying a permanent hegemonic position while recognizing the need for an organizational center to coordinate the movement's many moving parts.[137] The APPO came to be a center of convergence for struggles over water access, alternative media, Indigenous culture, and a new constitution for Mexico. From autonomous mass organizations emerged alternative institutions in all spheres of social life, constituting the infrastructure of a system of counterpower:

135. McNally, *Global Slump*, 167.
136. McNally, *Global Slump*, 165.
137. Rénique and Poole, "The Oaxaca Commune."

The barricades were a key site of popular power; neighborhood committees effectively used them as spaces of resistance, democratic discussion, and self-organization. The insurgent people also seized key government buildings, in the process paralyzing the traditional institutions of power. Meanwhile, APPO provided a framework for these grassroots neighborhood collectives to converge with unions, student groups, and Indigenous and women's organizations. Every morning, people awoke to new stenciled art, woodblock prints, and spray-painted images and slogans across the city. Huge marches brought people together in their tens and hundreds of thousands. But absolutely crucial to the Oaxaca Commune was citizens' radio, where the voices of the oppressed burst forth from the darkness to reclaim the airwaves, rename their circumstances, and coordinate resistance.[138]

The APPO rapidly pivoted from a united front in defense of the teachers' strike to a localized system of counterpower. Having provisionally expelled the authorities, the APPO assumed the role of a revolutionary communal government, establishing itself in opposition to the reactionary central government. However, as with the Paris Commune of 1871, the Oaxaca Commune of 2006 faced the problem of "a commune in one city," since, as McNally observes, "a working class government confined to one city is a very precarious thing."[139] On the brink of civil war, the federal police were deployed to repress the Oaxaca Uprising, during which they brutalized, tortured, imprisoned, and assassinated many leading APPO militants. Without the *territorial generalization* of a system of counterpower, it will be impossible for the communist social revolution to break the chains of imperialist domination and advance the construction of the world commune.

138. McNally, *Global Slump*, 166.
139. McNally, *Global Slump*, 167.

4.2: Protracted Revolutionary Struggle

A Path to Liberation

The revolutionary struggle is *protracted*. It will likely span multiple historical eras and integrate asymmetrical and non-linear processes of building the organized autonomy of the people. A successful protracted revolutionary struggle must combine three levels of political praxis: strategic, operational, and tactical. A *strategy* is a plan of action for the achievement of political objectives, within a specified historical time and geographical space, utilizing limited resources and personnel, in the context of uncertain, changing, and potentially hostile conditions. The *strategic level* encompasses the articulation and implementation of a *grand strategy* for the overthrow of imperialism and construction of the world commune as well as a *programmatic strategy,* or an immediate plan of action to advance the movement in the direction of the grand strategy within a particular territory.

With the general framework established by a grand strategy and program, the *operational level* of political praxis is concerned with the planning and conduct of *campaigns* for the immediate phase of struggle and deals with the planned cooperation among revolutionary forces within one or more fronts of struggle.[140] A *campaign* is a series of operations undertaken to achieve specific objectives within a determinate time-space, whereas an *operation* consists of the selective deployment of a set of tactics to achieve one or more campaign objectives. According to T. Derbent, "the operation is the means of strategy, operational art is the material of strategy; the battle is the means of the operation, the tactics are the material of the operational art."[141] Operational plans should therefore correspond to the goals and projects selected at the strategic level through militant social investigation. Based on further inquiries conducted

140. T. Derbent, *Categories of Revolutionary Military Policy* (Montreal: Kersplebedeb, 2006), 31.
141. Derbent, *Categories of Revolutionary Military Policy*, 31.

locally, specific objectives that correspond to a given operational area can be selected and synchronized with the local conditions encountered. Each operational plan should be developed with specific, actionable goals and timetables. It should anticipate the availability of personnel and resources and include contingency plans based on an assessment of the balance of forces and possible outcomes.

Operational plans are developed to manage the use of organizational resources in pursuit of campaign objectives. Operational plans can be revised or abandoned as the struggle advances or retreats and as the operational context changes. For revolutionaries, operational plans clarify our tasks and responsibilities. Following the completion of an operational plan, it is our responsibility to assess its effectiveness in achieving strategic objectives and to summarize lessons accordingly. As plans are completed, the initial results should be recorded and summarized, becoming part of the organization's memory and serving as material for future political education. Evaluations of the plan's successes and drawbacks should also be made available to the broader movement. This can serve the movement by clarifying our position within the overall development of the revolutionary struggle. It can also aid the process of making adjustments when confronted with new developments.

Finally, the *tactical level* of political praxis is concerned with the planning and conduct of *engagements* or *battles*. This level is characterized by the application of concentrated force, consisting of *offensive actions* to gain objectives and *defensive actions* to hold objectives or create space for regroupment and counteroffensive. From protests and pickets to strikes and occupations, *tactics* are devices for accomplishing operational objectives. Parameters for the deployment of specific tactics should be determined by the engagement in question and by the overall political objectives and ethical criteria set at the strategic and operational levels.

Social revolutions advance through a series of overlapping phases, with certain core characteristics corresponding to each phase. The framework of *protracted revolutionary struggle* consists of four phases: (1) *laying the groundwork,* or building a proletarian and popular base for communism through militant social investigations that identify strategic sites of struggle and scaffold an infrastructure of dissent, encompassing the emergent forms of organized autonomy and revolutionary countercultures; (2) *the emergence of territorial counterpower,* or the construction of a dual-power situation through the proliferation and consolidation of areas of autonomy, coalescing as a system of counterpower that can contend with the ruling class for social hegemony and territorial control; (3) *insurrectionary rupture,* or the smashing of imperialism's territorial domination and the overthrow of the authoritarian state through a mass revolutionary uprising or social strike; and (4) *direct transition to communism,* or the establishment, consolidation, and defense of territorial communes and their eventual federation into a world commune.

Phase One: Laying the Groundwork

At the outset of a protracted revolutionary struggle, the key task of communists is to get rooted and build counterpower at key strategic points throughout society. Through social investigations and a range of projects, campaigns, and programs, we can assist the articulation, construction, and consolidation of an area of autonomy. Alan Sears refers to this process as building the *infrastructure of dissent,* or an "amalgam of spaces, networks, and institutions" that develop the collective capacities of the movement to fight back against imperialism while reappropriating time, space, and resources for communal forms of life.[142] This is a phase of militant social investigation and grassroots base-building that opens the path to subsequent phases, leading towards the emergence of a system of counterpower at the territorial and eventually world level. With this infrastructure of dissent

---

142. Alan Sears, *The Next New Left: A History of the Future* (Winnipeg: Fernwood Publishing, 2014), 100.

constructed, our aim should be to accelerate the emergence of a dual-power situation in which the hegemonic power of imperialism is directly challenged and subsequently broken by the revolutionary movement, and the emergent system of counterpower is increasingly accepted as a legitimate alternative to the imperialist system by the masses of people throughout the territory.

In this first phase, the revolutionary movement must sink deep roots among workers concentrated in *essential industries,* defined as those necessary for continued social (re)production during an insurrectionary rupture and capable of providing the necessities for the survival and defense of the social revolution.[143] By seizing and reappropriating the industrial base inherited from the old society, the social revolution will be able to sustain and generalize an insurrectionary rupture—*a social strike*—throughout the territory. Essential industries will likely include agriculture; food processing and production; water supply and treatment, waste management, and general cleaning; energy production; transportation; logistics, warehousing, and retail; information and communications; care work, including healthcare, childcare, and adult care; construction and maintenance; engineering and manufacturing; print, broadcast, and digital media; the postal service; governmental administration and the public sector; and the military.[144] With a militant workers' movement rooted in these essential industries, the social revolution will be in a strategic position to both halt the capitalist economy *and* lead a direct transition to a new mode of social (re)production.

In addition to these essential industries, the movement will need to build a base among workers in *advanced industries,* which often encompass irrelevant or harmful sectors of production—such as armaments and automobiles—but which include both workers with essential forms of knowledge and

---

143. Angry Workers of the World, "Insurrection and Production," August 29, 2016, https://angryworkersworld.wordpress.com/2016/08/29/insurrection-and-production/.
144. Angry Workers of the World, "Insurrection and Production."

technological systems that will need to be transferred to other production sectors and reconfigured to ensure the survival and defense of the social revolution. Advanced industries may also include those forms of production considered essential within a context of revolutionary civil war (as arms and transportation will be necessary to defend the territorial commune from the armed counter-revolution), or whose infrastructure poses a threat to public health and safety in the event of neglect or attack (as in the case of nuclear energy facilities).

Simultaneous to organizing proletarian counterpower at the point of social production, the movement must organize feminist counterpower at the point of social reproduction. The movement could work to build clusters of communal habitations to serve as centers for neighborhood decision-making, the collectivization of domestic work, and the provisioning of essential goods and services. According to M.E. O'Brien, these communal habitations could collectivize social reproduction, "including childcare and education; collective laundry, apartment cleaning, canteen food cooking and serving; repair and maintenance of household goods; mental health and regular care; and group entertainment activities."[145] The formation of communal habitations is as crucial to the communist social revolution as building working-class counterpower in the essential industries, "mainly in order to break the isolation of domestic work and gender hierarchies, but also to create a counter-dynamic to the centralization in the essential industries: a decentralization of certain social tasks and decision-making."[146] Initially formed through the initiatives of tenant unions, community organizations, neighborhood councils, and clusters of party cadre, these communal habitations could later be linked with workers' councils organized at the point of production to establish the initial basis for a system of participatory planning of economic activity.

145. M.E. O'Brien, "Communizing Care," *Pinko*, October 15, 2019, https://pinko.online/pinko-1/communizing-care.
146. Angry Workers of the World, "Insurrection and Production."

Where to begin with building these forms of organized autonomy at key strategic points and throughout the whole fabric of society? It is from reform struggles that the autonomous mass organizations of the proletariat initially emerge, and through which an emerging revolutionary people gains its first experiences with organized political combat against the class enemy. Through reform struggles, the proletarian and popular social groups develop consciousness of their power in society, articulate organizational forms that contain the nuclei of a communist alternative, win material improvements, and learn that through solidarity and direct action, the imperialist ruling class can be overthrown. Furthermore, certain reforms can shift the balance of forces in favor of the revolutionary movement, if only in a limited fashion. While reforms cannot be gradually added up to produce a qualitatively revolutionary situation, they can provide important experiences of "everyday ruptures" through which revolutionary forces can gain the initiative and build offensive capacities. When assessing the strategic relevance of a particular reform struggle, we should ask ourselves: How is the reform struggle being waged? Which sections of the masses are engaged? What organizational forms are created? Is the struggle applying pressure to strategic chokepoints of the imperialist world-system, specifically the apparatuses of the authoritarian state?[147]

To propel the social revolution forward, the proliferation of militant reform struggles must be complemented by a radical change in proletarian and popular sensibilities. This is the role of counterculture. Social revolutions happen not because the masses of people are oppressed, but because oppression is resisted—"because the old forms of human social existence can no longer contain or give meaning to the new substance of human potential," as Greg Calvert and Carol Neiman explain.[148] Revolutionary countercultures bind lib-

147. Teresa Kalisz, "Rethinking Reforms," *Regeneration Magazine*, April 19, 2019, https://regenerationmag.org/rethinking-reforms/.

148. Greg Calvert and Carol Neiman, *A Disrupted History: The New Left and the New Capitalism* (New York: Random House, 1971), 171.

eration movements together and are a direct expression of an emergent communist society. The Russian revolutionary Alexander Bogdanov envisioned the intentional construction of such "an autonomous proletarian culture."[149] To this end, Bogdanov cofounded the organization Proletkult (for *Proletarskaia Kultura*, or "proletarian culture"), whose three-fold mission was to: (1) *change labor* by overcoming the division between manual and conceptual categories of work, fusing artistic and scientific activity; (2) *change everyday life* by abolishing gender hierarchies and constructing communal forms of social reproduction; and (3) *change affect* by creating new structures of feeling.[150] At its peak, Proletkult had thousands of members and hundreds of local studios, clubs, and factory organizations throughout the Soviet Union.

An autonomous revolutionary counterculture emerges initially from the interstices of bourgeois society. It generates new forms of cultural expression, recovers long-repressed cultural forms from past cycles of struggle, and reappropriates and repurposes cultural forms inherited from the old society. Comradely cooperation is the cultural basis of a society that prioritizes the full and free development of humanity.. The deeper this revolutionary counterculture permeates the fabric of everyday life, the more complete will be the insurrectionary rupture with the old society, and the more solid will be the material foundation for the construction of the territorial commune. Indeed, Bogdanov argued that the conscious development of comradely cooperation was a necessary prerequisite to the collectivization of the means of social (re)production and the establishment of a stateless, classless society.[151]

The proliferation of organized autonomy at strategic points throughout society alongside the creation of revolutionary countercultures on the terrain of everyday life results in the emergence of diffuse areas of autonomy. The task of

149. White, *Red Hamlet*, 397.
150. Wark, *Molecular Red*, 35.
151. Bogdanov, "Socialism in the Present Day."

revolutionaries is to consolidate and expand these areas into a compact system of counterpower. When building counterpower, we are confronted with both temporal and spatial difficulties. If counterpower fails to proliferate throughout the territory quickly enough, then the forces of repression will be able to contain and coopt these revolutionary developments. Similarly, if a system of counterpower is geographically isolated or too widely dispersed, it will be susceptible to containment and suppression by the forces of reaction.

We have seen this tragedy unfold repeatedly in the past, as with the Paris Commune of 1871, the Bavarian Council Republic of 1919, the Shanghai Commune of 1967, or the Gwangju Commune of 1980. To successfully establish a revolutionary base, proletarian and popular counterpower must generalize throughout the territory with decisive speed. Argentine revolutionary Mario Roberto Santucho reminds us:

> The creation of open organs of local power cannot be an isolated nor spontaneous act. As soon as the enemy becomes aware that, in a barrio, locality, or in a city, the people have organized themselves and have begun to solve their problems of production, health, education, public safety, justice, etc., in their own way, they will unleash with fury all the armed forces at their disposal, with the savage intention of drowning that attempt at sovereignty in blood. That is why the use of local power should be the result of a general national process, where, here and there, in the north and in the south, in the east and in the west, organs of popular power begin to be formed, the masses begin to take on the responsibility of governing their zones.[152]

The greater the territorial extension of a system of counterpower, the better the chances of defeating the counter-revolution. As diffuse areas of autonomy are consolidated and a system of counterpower is extended throughout

152. Mario Roberto Santucho, *Argentina: Bourgeois Power, Revolutionary Power* (Oakland: Resistance Publications, 1976), 24.

the territory, imperialism's centers of power will be gradually eroded and encircled by the forces of social revolution. Transitioning from a strategic defensive to strategic equilibrium, the revolutionary movement will be tasked with building the system of counterpower's capacity to contend directly for territorial sovereignty.

Phase Two: The Emergence of Territorial Counterpower

This phase marks the leap from diffuse areas of autonomy to a consolidated system of territorial counterpower. The previous phase can force an unstable period in which the nucleus of a communist alternative contends with a decaying imperialism for hegemony. The task of the social revolution at this conjuncture is to accelerate and coordinate the consolidation of areas of autonomy, with the goal of extending liberated zones throughout the territory and linking together organs of counterpower, people's defense organizations, and parties of autonomy. This is the phase of *dual power,* a revolutionary crisis that arises from the irreconcilable conflict between a revolutionary people and a counter-revolutionary ruling class. In this phase, a communist alternative emerges, establishing the material foundation for a direct transfer of power from the imperialist ruling class to the proletarian and popular social groups. While official power continues to rest with the imperialist ruling class, *real power* increasingly resides with the emergent forms of organized autonomy. As Trotsky reminds us: "The splitting of sovereignty foretells nothing less than a civil war."[153]

Through autonomous mass organizations and revolutionary countercultures, the movement builds the people's collective capacities to liberate the territory from imperialist domination. These actions are necessary prerequisites in building towards an insurrectionary rupture capable of smashing the authoritarian state and delinking from the

153. Leon Trotsky, *History of the Russian Revolution* (Chicago: Haymarket Books, 2008), 150.

imperialist world-system. This dual power situation is a *strategic equilibrium* in which the state is unable to reclaim the territory liberated by the emerging system of counterpower, but this counterpower has not yet succeeded in conquering the strategic positions required to completely overthrow the territorial control of imperialism.

As support for the revolution grows, the movement must establish a proletarian and popular mandate for the territorial extension of this embryonic commune. As the forms of counterpower assume functional control of social life within an increasingly expansive territory, imperialism will be severed from its bases of support. Increasingly deprived of the necessary soldiers, workers, resources, and territory, imperialism's solutions to the contradictions of the dual-power crisis will become increasingly fascistic. Only by winning the overwhelming support of the people to the communist project, consolidating a system of territorial counterpower, and fracturing the state's repressive apparatuses will the social revolution be able to break the stalemate and advance to the next phase of launching a strategic counter-offensive.

Phase Three: Insurrectionary Rupture

With the emergence of a system of territorial counterpower, the revolutionary movement will be put to the ultimate test. The social revolution must break the strategic equilibrium by launching a *strategic offensive* that smashes the authoritarian state machinery and delinks the territory from the imperialist world-system. Doing so requires an *insurrectionary rupture* in which proletarian and popular social groups, organized as a revolutionary people, consciously seize control of the means of social (re)production, enabling the movement to generalize and sustain the uprising. In this social strike, workers consciously withdraw their labor-power from capital at the point of social production, rebel soldiers break ranks to join the revolutionary uprising, and the masses of people seize power in all areas of social life, establishing a material basis for a direct transition to a communal social system.

A social strike is a "general strike" in the sense that it *generalizes* or spreads the refusal of imperialist domination throughout the fabric of society, transforming resistance in different spheres of social life into a singular demand for power.[154] At this point, autonomous assemblies, councils, and action committees of workers and neighbors will begin to assume direct control of social (re)production. Throughout the territory, these organs of counterpower must assess the bare minimum required for society to materially reproduce itself within the context of a revolutionary uprising. In particular, they will be tasked with evaluating: (1) available foodstuffs for immediate redistribution; (2) anticipated effects of being cut off from the world-market and external energy supplies; (3) the class composition of essential and advanced industries; (4) geographic concentrations of essential and advanced industries; (5) the composition and anticipated behaviors of non-proletarian classes, such as the coordinator class and petite bourgeoisie; (6) the social, technological, and ecological composition of agriculture; and (7) the means by which the repressive state apparatuses—specifically the police and military—are materially reproduced.[155] It will be at this moment that the communist movement's work in previous phases to build a base in essential and advanced industries, as well as to construct alternative systems of social reproduction, will be tested.

This insurrectionary rupture is not the end of the revolutionary process, but its real beginning. "The act of revolution," one comrade reminds us, "brings an immediate transformation in the sense that the foundations of society are radically changed, but a progressive transformation in the sense that communism is a constant development."[156] It is the ultimate

154. Michael Hardt and Antonio Negri, *Assembly* (New York: Oxford University Press, 2017), 240.
155. Angry Workers of the World, "Insurrection and Production."
156. Fontenis, "Manifesto of Libertarian Communism," 20.

trial by fire for the communist social revolution, as the territory is delinked from the imperialist world-system; the institutions of oppression are rendered inoperable; and a situation arises in which a direct transition to communism is enabled based on the forms of organized autonomy established in the preceding phases. This is the phase of the movement's strategic counter-offensive against the imperialist world-system, the generalization of counter-systemic antagonism to the point of rupturing imperialist domination, and the establishment of a territorial commune. During previous phases, the repressive capacity of the state is gradually worn down; through the insurrectionary rupture, it is decisively broken.

Phase Four: Direct Transition to Communism

Having successfully overthrown the state and delinked the territory from the imperialist world-system, the social revolution is tasked with initiating, in conjunction with a global revolutionary process, a direct transition to communism. Immense organizational work is required in the years preceding this moment of transition:

> It remains a tragic irony that insurrections not defeated outright by superior military forces often froze into immobility once they took power from their class enemies and rarely took the organizational steps necessary to retain their power. Without a theoretically trained and militant organization that had developed a broad social vision of its tasks and could offer workers practical programs for completing the revolution that they had initiated, revolutions quickly fell apart for lack of further action.[157]

Oftentimes, tendencies towards indecision or atrophy are compounded by the global character of the struggle against imperialism, for "the revolution which breaks out and triumphs in one country thus finds itself immediately

157. Bookchin, *The Next Revolution*, 182.

confronted by an alliance of all the neighboring states in which the old system still survives."[158] With a successful insurrectionary rupture, it will be the duty of revolutionaries to defend the emergent territorial commune from the forces of internal and external counter-revolution, to push forward a continuous revolution that radically transforms all spheres of social activity, and to proceed without delay towards the consolidation of a communist social system.

If successful in delinking from imperialism and consolidating a territorial commune, the insurrectionary rupture will position the revolution at a crossroads: either take the road back to the old society or pursue the road that opens a phase of direct transition to communism, building upon the forms of organized autonomy constructed in the preceding phases.[159] Far from putting off the task of constructing and consolidating more "advanced" communist institutions until a later date, a direct transition is a necessity for our collective survival and liberation. During this transition, the system of counterpower constructed in previous phases must be consolidated throughout the territory as a *revolutionary counterstate*. This proletarian and popular counterstate—a revolutionary people's government—functions as a shield for defending the emergent commune from the armed counter-revolution, a rampart with which to break the stubborn resistance of the former ruling class, and an instrument for continuing the struggle for the total transformation of social relations. This counterstate institutionalizes the gains of the preceding phases, establishing the autonomous mass organizations and people's defense organizations as instruments of a counter-hegemonic social power.

Only a federated communal council system can combine elements of centralization and decentralization to establish an effective administrative framework based on grassroots

158. Victor Serge, *Revolution in Danger: Writings from Russia 1919–1921* (Chicago: Haymarket Books, 2011), 131.
159. Louis Althusser (attributed), "On the Cultural Revolution," *Décalages* 1, no. 1 (2010), https://scholar.oxy.edu/decalages/vol1/iss1/9/.

participatory democracy for our hyper-complex world.[160] To the extent that the relations inherited from imperialism survive, we will need to construct means of resolving contradictions in all areas of social life, from the level of a workers' council within a collective enterprise to the communal planning that governs the economy as a whole, from the base councils of the polity up to their federations at the neighborhood, ward, municipal, bioregional, and territorial levels. However, if the means for resolving such contradictions destroy the very core characteristics of communism that we aim to develop—either reinforcing the residual characteristics inherited from imperialism or creating new oppressive relations—it will be unnecessary to speak of a transitional phase from the present to a future communism, because communism will cease to exist and we will transition to something entirely different.[161] Rather than a mechanical process of moving from "lower" to "higher" stages, we must recognize the intrinsically communist character of the process of liberation, for *"it is not the transition that reveals itself (and eliminates itself) in the form of communism, but rather it is communism that takes the form of the transition."*[162]

A Continuous Revolution

Frederick Douglass proclaimed: "If there is no struggle, there is no progress."[163] Following insurrection, emergent communes will face an ongoing struggle. Geographical isolation, hostility from what remains of the imperialist world-system, and a battle against the forces of counter-revolution will render their position tenuous. Resource scarcity, internal social instability, and the counter-revolution's attempts at containment and suppression are all likely hurdles. Such obstacles

---

160. Kuhn, "Don't Mourn, Organize!"

161. Albert and Hahnel, *Unorthodox Marxism*, 275.

162. Antonio Negri, *Marx Beyond Marx: Lessons on the Grundrisse* (Brooklyn: Autonomedia, 1991), 152–153.

163. Frederick Douglass, "West India Emancipation (1857)," Frederick Douglass Project, University of Rochester, https://rbscp.lib.rochester.edu/4398/.

can only be overcome through ongoing experimentation in all spheres of social activity, the continuing creative participation of the masses of proletarian and popular social groups in the processes of revolutionary defense and social reconstruction, and lending material support to the global proliferation of revolutionary struggles.

If the social revolution atrophies, failing to establish the foundations of an alternative social system throughout the territory, it will be undermined by the forces of *internal* counter-revolution. If the revolution within a particular country fails to generalize beyond its borders, it will be contained and suppressed by forces of *external* counter-revolution. The external counter-revolution will likely include direct military intervention, covert infiltration and disruption, terrorism, disinformation, media blackouts, and economic blockades. To prevent either outcome, communist social reconstruction must take the path of *continuous revolution*, both within the emergent territorial commune and on a global scale through the counter-encirclement of imperialism. Within a given territory, this process ensures that an emerging communist social system maintains autonomy within solidarity through anti-authoritarian, anti-bureaucratic campaigns unleashed from below. On a global scale, this process enables the extension of communist social revolution to both the imperialist centers and peripheries, undermining the global hegemony and territorial control of the metropolitan states.

Within a particular territory, the social revolution will create a society in which many contradictions persist.[164] The basic function of continuous revolution is to advance the struggle to resolve these contradictions, to prevent the ossification and bureaucratization of the new social system, and to challenge the forms of internalized oppression inherited from imperialism. "Without a conscious and protracted effort to combat these tendencies they can grow into an important social force," noted William Hinton in his study of

164. Michael Albert, *What Is To Be Undone? A Modern Revolutionary Discussion of Classical Left Ideologies* (Boston: Porter Sargent Publisher, 1974), 242.

the Cultural Revolution in China. "They can and do create new bourgeois individuals who gather as a new privileged elite and ultimately as a new exploiting class."[165] Therefore, the creative spontaneity of the revolutionary people must be continuously mobilized and exercised. We should always remain aware that many times in the past, the forms of organized autonomy that emerged from revolutionary struggles were turned into their opposite by a new ruling elite. The people must continuously mobilize to seize power from below in every aspect of life, unleashing microrevolutions within the revolution to overthrow and abolish all forms of oppression, construct communist relations in all spheres of social activity, and defend the revolution against tendencies towards dogmatism and conformity.

In addition to the task of overthrowing and abolishing imperialist social relations *within* a territory, the continuous revolution is integral to the process of *communization on a world scale*, or the relatively rapid proliferation and federation of territorial communes globally. Revolutionary upsurges must initially consolidate themselves within limited geographic areas, creating regional blocs that enable the co-production and circulation of knowledge and resources, integrating local, territorial, and regional social systems, establishing a sustainable socioecological metabolism, and fortifying territorial communes as base areas from which the communist social revolution can be consolidated and extended. Without such processes of communization on a world scale, the limited advances made by the social revolution will be reversed, as the imperialist world-system cannot permit the continued existence of authentic communist alternatives. It will likely require multiple revolutionary upsurges for the hegemony of imperialism to be broken and for communism to take root on a world scale. Furthermore, many problems inherited from imperialism, such as the economic dependency of the peripheries upon the center,

165. William Hinton, *Turning Point in China: An Essay on the Cultural Revolution* (New York: Monthly Review Press, 1972), 21.

ecological disequilibrium created by extractive industries, and climate change, will require global solutions.

While we must work to establish communist social relations to the greatest degree possible within emergent areas of autonomy prior to the consolidation of a system of territorial counterpower, the struggle between revolution and counter-revolution will continue long after the communist institutions have reached a degree of stabilization, self-regulation, and self-sufficiency. Many relations inherited from imperialism—including reactionary ideas, behaviors, institutions, technologies, and ecologies—will continue to exist throughout the phase of transition. Within the context of the territorial commune, the struggle to overcome the old ways of thinking and acting will continue, and so long as imperialism exists as both a hegemonic global force and articulated social system, it will pose a continual threat to the emergent realm of freedom unleashed by the communist social revolution.

The consolidation of the territorial commune functions as a shield for the defense of autonomy against the counter-revolution, a base area for the articulation and development of a communist social system, and a beacon of hope for the world revolution. As the ethical and educational functions of communist society are expanded and deepened, and territorial communes are constructed, stabilized, and networked on a world scale, defensive politico-military functions will be made increasingly superfluous and gradually dissolved as mass movements advance a continuous revolution in all spheres of social activity. At last the grand visions of all great revolutionary struggles of the past shall be realized:

A revolt that never ends.
A world in which many worlds fit.
Long live the world commune of communes!

Conclusion

Summation

The purpose of this book has been to synthesize the initial results of an ongoing co-production of communist politics, emerging from our direct participation with and within grassroots social struggles against the imperialist world-system. To summarize the key points of our platform:

1. The Weapon of Theory: We propose for communist theory to ground its analysis in a multiplicity of sciences, conducting militant social investigations rooted in the onto-epistemological worldview of historical-geographical materialism. We recognize being human as a praxis, the multiple partisan standpoints implicit in scientific research, and the complex intra-actions among multiple spheres of social activity that co-produce our material realities.

2. Imperialism and Revolution: A macro-analysis of the imperialist world-system should at minimum recognize the enmeshing and intra-action of the world-producing social forces of heteropatriarchy, capital, colonialism, and the state within and through the web of life. By adopting multiple analytical standpoints, we recognize the multiplicity of forms of proletarian and popular resistance that manifest immanent communist counter-tendencies. Paying attention to world-systemic crises can enable communist partisans to hasten the emergence of a revolutionary situation and thwart the rise of fascism.

3. Envisioning the Commune: Our praxis of liberation should be inspired by a revolutionary vision of communism rooted in the abolition of all forms of oppression, the revolutionary transformation of social relations at the point of reproduction, the construction of systems of commons, and the establishment of systems of social administrtion and coordination by means of federated councils. The emergence of liberated territories—territorial communes delinked from the imperialist world-system—can lay the foundation for transitioning to the world commune.

4. Building the Commune: A strategic orientation towards communist social revolution should at minimum address certain forms of organized autonomy (organs of counterpower, people's defense organizations, and parties of autonomy), with the aim of uniting these forms as a system of counterpower, and outline a path of protracted revolutionary struggle that lays the groundwork for the emergence of a dual-power situation, culminating in an insurrectionary rupture and the establishment of a territorial commune on the road to the world commune.

As we have emphasized throughout this text, a new beginning for communist politics means resisting dogmatism and remaining permanently open to future contingencies. If successful, we anticipate that this platform of revolutionary struggle will be continuously transformed and modified by communist partisans in order to meet the challenges posed by the new situations that will inevitably emerge.

The Question of Program

We have emphasized that our political platform aims to stimulate a communist political imaginary, not impose itself upon the future course of events. Therefore, we now turn our attention to the question of *program*. What is a program?

According to anti-authoritarian communist, trade unionist, and educator Georges Fontenis, a program is "an ensemble of analyses and proposals which set out purposes and tasks" for the communist movement, "determined by the study, the testing, and the tradition of what is constantly sought by the masses." This program can "be modified as analysis of the situation and the tendencies of the masses progresses, and can be reformulated in clearer and more accurate terms."[1] For Asad Haider, a program is a political prescription that reveals the possibilities of a conjuncture, "that is, it shows us *people's capacity*, a capacity which cannot be captured or understood from above by a party or state. The prescription opens up what is possible within the specific situation."[2] The process of assembling and formulating a program necessarily begins with militant social investigation within a rising cycle of struggle, and the self-critical assessment and summation of lessons drawn from experience. Such a process places the emphasis on learning with and through struggles.

There are many promising sectors in which to begin such social investigations, and around which we can immediately begin to construct militant research networks from which more developed grassroots organizational infrastructure can arise. From illuminating the power of workers in the global supply chains and logistical clusters of cybernetic capitalism to assisting the disruption and blockading of the flows of capital by mapping and identifying strategic chokepoints, to circulating the lessons of clandestine prisoner organizing against the neo-slave regime of mass incarceration and prison labor, there are immense possibilities for communist partisans to play a useful role in the co-production of revolutionary strategies, operations, and tactics against imperialism. Through the militant social investigations conducted by parties of autonomy, we can make visible the "invisible organizations" formed by the proletarian and popular social

1. Fontenis, "Manifesto of Libertarian Communism."
2. Asad Haider, "Socialists Think," *Viewpoint Magazine*, September 24, 2018, https://www.viewpointmag.com/2018/09/24/socialists-think/.

groups to resist oppression and win liberation.[3] We can help make connections and build networks, linking multiple fronts of struggle into a united front for revolution.

We don't know what the future holds. We keep our attention focused on the possibilities of our historical-geographical conjuncture, and the emancipatory possibilities contained within it. We can make no promises of eternal peace and harmony. Rather, we orient our praxis of liberation towards organizing and deepening social antagonisms against the imperialist world-system, with the aim of abolishing empire and delinking our territories from this death-world, liberating time, space, and resources for the emergence and stabilization of the world commune.

3. Evan Calder Williams, "Invisible Organization: Reading Romano Alquati." *Viewpoint Magazine*, September 26, 2013, https://www.viewpointmag.com/2013/09/26/invisible-organization-reading-romano-alquati/.

References

Adam, David. "Marx's Critique of Socialist Labor-Money Schemes and the Myth of Council Communism's Proudhonism." *With Sober Senses* (blog), January 21, 2013. https://www.marxisthumanistinitiative. org/alternatives-to-capital/marxs-critique-of-socialist-labor-money -schemes-and-the-myth-of-council-communisms-proudhonism.html.

Ajl, Max. "A Socialist Southern Strategy in Jackson." *Viewpoint Magazine*, June 5, 2018. https://www.viewpointmag.com/2018/06/05/a-socialist-s outhern-strategy-in-jackson/.

Albert, Michael. *Parecon: Life After Capitalism.* London: Verso, 2003.

———. *What Is To Be Undone? A Modern Revolutionary Discussion of Classical Left Ideologies.* Boston: Porter Sargent Publisher, 1974.

Albert, Michael, and Robin Hahnel. *Marxism and Socialist Theory.* Boston: South End Press, 1981.

———. *Socialism Today and Tomorrow.* Boston: South End Press, 1981.

———. *The Political Economy of Participatory Economics.* Princeton: Princeton University Press, 1991.

———. *Unorthodox Marxism.* Boston: South End Press, 1978.

Albert, Michael, Holly Sklar, Leslie Cagan, Noam Chomsky, Robin Hahnel, Mel King, and Lydia Sargent. *Liberating Theory.* Boston: South End Press, 1986.

Althusser, Louis. "On the Cultural Revolution." *Décalages* 1, no. 1 (2010). https://scholar.oxy.edu/decalages/vol1/iss1/9.

———. *On the Reproduction of Capitalism: Ideology and Ideological State Apparatuses.* London: Verso, 2014.

Amil K. "After #IdleNoMore: How Can We Unite the Struggle for Communism with the Indigenous National Liberation Struggles?" *Revolutionary Initiative* (blog), February 28, 2013. https:// revolutionary-initiative.com/2013/02/28/after-idlenomore-how-ca n-we-unite-the-struggle-for-communism-with-the-indigenous-nation al-liberation-struggles/.

Angry Workers of the World. "Insurrection and Production." *Angry Workers of the World* (blog), August 29, 2016. https://angryworkersworld.wordpress.com/2016/08/29/ insurrection-and-production/.

Angus, Ian. "Vladimir Vernadsky and the Disruption of the Biosphere." *Climate and Capitalism* (blog), June 5, 2018. https:// climateandcapitalism.com/2018/06/05/vladimir-vernadsky-and-th e-disruption-of-the-biosphere/.

Asociación de Mujeres de El Salvador. "Reflections of Salvadoran Women: Participation of Latin American Women in Social and Political Organizations." In *A Dream Compels Us: Voices of Salvadoran Women*, edited by New Americas Press, 81–88. Boston: South End Press, 1989.

Avrich, Paul. *The Haymarket Tragedy*. Princeton: Princeton University Press, 1984.

Azzellini, Dario. *Communes and Workers' Control in Venezuela: Building 21st Century Socialism from Below*. Leiden: Brill, 2017.

Barad, Karen. *Meeting the Universe Halfway: Quantum Physics and the Entanglement of Matter and Meaning*. Durham, NC: Duke University Press, 2007.

Baronov, David. "The Analytical-Holistic Divide Within World-System Analysis." In *The World-System as Unit of Analysis: Past Contributions and Future Advances*, edited by Roberto Patricio Korzeniewicz, 6–16. New York: Routledge, 2017.

Barreto, Juan. "Multitud en movimiento." *Aporrea* (blog), October 30, 2014. https://www.aporrea.org/actualidad/a197491.html

Barrett, James R. *William Z. Foster and the Tragedy of American Radicalism*. Urbana: University of Illinois Press, 1999.

Becerra, Diana Carolina Sierra. "For Our Total Emancipation: The Making of Revolutionary Feminism in Insurgent El Salvador, 1977-1987." In *Making the Revolution: Histories of the Latin American Left*, edited by Kevin A. Young, 266–93. Cambridge: Cambridge University Press, 2019.

Benjamin, Walter. *Reflections: Essays, Aphorisms, Autobiographical Writings*. New York: Schocken Books, 2007.

Berger, Dan. "The Malcolm X Doctrine: The Republic of New Afrika and National Liberation on U.S. Soil." In *New World Coming: The Sixties and the Shaping of Global Consciousness*, edited by Karen Dubinsky, Catherine Krull, Susan Lord, Sean Mills, and Scott Rutherford, 46–55. Toronto: Between the Lines, 2009.

Bernes, Jasper. "Logistics, Counterlogistics and the Communist Prospect." In *Endnotes #3: Gender, Race, Class and Other Misfortunes*. London: Endnotes, 2013.

———. "The Belly of the Revolution: Agriculture, Energy, and the Future of Communism." In *Materialism and the Critique of Energy*, edited by Brent Ryan Bellamy and Jeff Diamanti, 331–375. Chicago: MCM' Publishing, 2018.

Bettelheim, Charles. *Class Struggles in the USSR, First Period: 1917-1923*. New York: Monthly Review Press, 1976.

Biel, Robert. *Eurocentrism and the Communist Movement*. Montreal: Kersplebedeb, 2015.

———. *The Entropy of Capitalism*. Chicago: Haymarket Books, 2013.

———. *The New Imperialism: Crisis and Contradictions in North/South Relations*. London: Zed Books, 2000.

Bogdanov, Alexander. "Socialism in the Present Day." 1911. Reprint, Libcom, 2015. https://libcom.org/library/socialism-present-day-alexander-bogdanov.

Bohrer, Ashley J. *Marxism and Intersectionality: Race, Gender, Class and Sexuality under Contemporary Capitalism*. New York: Columbia University Press, 2020.

Bonanno, Alfredo M. "A Few Notes on the Revolutionary Movement in Italy." The Anarchist Library, 2017. https://theanarchistlibrary.org/library/alfredo-m-bonanno-a-few-notes-on-the-revolutionary-movem ent-in-italy.

Bookchin, Murray. *Post-Scarcity Anarchism*. Oakland: AK Press, 2004.

———. *The Next Revolution: Popular Assemblies and the Promise of Direct Democracy*. London: Verso, 2015.

———. *The Spanish Anarchists: The Heroic Years 1868-1936*. Oakland: AK Press, 1998.

Bordiga, Roberto. "Per la storia degli anarchici spagnoli." *Primo Maggio*, no. 6 (1976): 79–88.

Brecher, Jeremy. *Strike!* Cambridge, MA: South End Press, 1997.

Buhle, Paul. "The Legacy of the IWW." *Monthly Review* (blog), June 1, 2005. https://monthlyreview.org/2005/06/01/the-legacy-of-the-iww/.

C17. "11 Theses on Possible Communism." *Viewpoint Magazine*, January 31, 2018. https://www.viewpointmag.com/2018/01/31/11-these s-possible-communism/.

Calvert, Greg. *Democracy from the Heart: Spiritual Values, Decentralism, and Democratic Idealism in the Movement of the 1960s*. Eugene, OR: Communitas Press, 1991.

Calvert, Greg, and Carol Neiman. *A Disrupted History: The New Left and the New Capitalism*. New York: Random House, 1971.

Capra, Fritjof, and Pier Luigi Luisi. *The Systems View of Life: A Unifying Vision*. Cambridge: Cambridge University Press, 2018.

Cant, Callum. "Precarious Couriers Are Leading the Struggle Against Platform Capitalism." *Political Critique* (blog), August 3, 2017. http://politicalcritique.org/world/2017/precarious-couriers-are-leadin g-the-struggle-against-platform-capitalism/.

Christie, Stuart. *We, the Anarchists!: A Study of the Iberian Anarchist Federation (FAI) 1927-1937*. Oakland: AK Press, 2008.

Churchill, Ward. *Struggle for the Land: Indigenous Resistance to Genocide, Ecocide and Expropriation in Contemporary North America*. Monroe: Common Courage Press, 1993.

Ciccariello-Maher, George. *Decolonizing Dialectics*. Durham: Duke University Press, 2017.

Cleaver, Harry. *Reading Capital Politically*. Oakland: AK Press, 2000.

Communist International (Comintern). "Theses on Comintern Tactics (1922)." Marxists Internet Archive. https://www.marxists.org/history/international/comintern/4th-congress/tactics.htm.

Communist Prisoners Collective. "The Twenty Theses of the Collective of Communist Prisoners of the Red Brigades." *Urban Guerilla* (blog), September 21, 2017. http://urbanguerilla.org/the-twent y-theses-of-the-collective-of-communist-prisoners-of-the-red-br igades-december-1980/.

Cope, Zak. *Divided World, Divided Class: Global Political Economy and the Stratification of Labour Under Capitalism.* Montreal: Kersplebedeb, 2012.

Costa, Mariarosa Dalla. "The Door to the Flower and the Vegetable Garden (2002)." *Viewpoint Magazine*, June 20, 2017. https://www.viewpointmag.com/2017/06/20/the-door-to-the-flower-and-the-vegetable-garden-2002/.

Cozzarelli, Tatiana. "Class Reductionism is Real, and It's Coming from the Jacobin Wing of the DSA." *Left Voice*, June 16, 2020. https://www.leftvoice.org/class-reductionism-is-real-and-its-coming-from-the-jacobin-wing-of-the-dsa/.

Culp, Andrew. *Dark Deleuze.* Minneapolis: University of Minnesota Press, 2016.

Cunninghame, Patrick. "Mapping the Terrain of Struggle: Autonomous Movements in 1970s Italy," November 1, 2015. https://www.viewpointmag.com/2015/11/01/feminism-autonomism-1970s-italy/.

Davis, Mike. "The Stop Watch and the Wooden Shoe: Scientific Management and the Industrial Workers of the World." In *Workers' Struggles, Past and Present: A "Radical America" Reader*, edited by James Green, 83–100. Philadelphia: Temple University Press, 1983.

De Angelis, Massimo. *The Beginning of History: Value Struggles and Global Capital.* London: Pluto Press, 2007.

Debord, Guy. "Definitions." Translated by Ken Knabb. *Internationale Situationniste* 1 (1958). https://www.cddc.vt.edu/sionline/si/definitions.html.

Deleuze, Gilles, and Félix Guattari. *A Thousand Plateaus.* Minneapolis: University of Minnesota Press, 1991.

Derbent, T. *Categories of Revolutionary Military Policy.* Montreal: Kersplebedeb, 2006.

Douglass, Frederick. "West India Emancipation." Frederick Douglass Project, University of Rochester, 1857. https://rbscp.lib.rochester.edu/4398.

Dunbar-Ortiz, Roxanne. *An Indigenous Peoples' History of the United States.* Boston: Beacon Press, 2014.

Dussel, Enrique. *Twenty Theses on Politics.* Durham, NC: Duke University Press, 2008.

Dyer-Witheford, Nick. *Cyber-Proletariat: Global Labour in the Digital Vortex.* London: Pluto Press, 2015.

———. "Commonism." In *What Would It Mean to Win?*, edited by Turbulence Collective, 106:105–12. Oakland: PM Press, 2010.

Dyer-Witheford, Nick, and Svitlana Matviyenko. *Cyberwar and Revolution: Digital Subterfuge in Global Capitalism.* Minneapolis: University of Minnesota Press, 2019.

Ealham, Chris. *Anarchism and the City: Revolution and Counter-Revolution in Barcelona, 1898–1937.* Oakland: AK Press, 2010.

Eaubonne, Françoise d'. "What Could an Ecofeminist Society Be?" *Ethics and the Environment* 4, no. 2 (2000): 179–84.

Edu-Factory Collective (ed.). *Toward a Global Autonomous University: Cognitive Labor, The Production of Knowledge, and Exodus from the Education Factory.* New York: Autonomedia, 2009.

Elbaum, Max. *Revolution in the Air: Sixties Radicals Turn to Lenin, Mao, and Che.* London: Verso, 2006.

Engels, Frederick. "Engels to August Bebel in Zwickau (1875)." Marxists Internet Archive. https://www.marxists.org/archive/marx/works/1875/letters/75_03_18.htm.

———. *The Condition of the Working Class in England.* Chicago: Academy Chicago Publishers, 1994.

Escobar, Arturo. *Designs for the Pluriverse: Radical Interdependence, Autonomy, and the Making of Worlds.* Durham, North Carolina: Duke University Press, 2017.

Fanon, Frantz. *The Wretched of the Earth.* New York: Grove Weidenfeld, 1991.

Federação Anarquista de Rio de Janeiro. *Social Anarchism and Organisation.* Johannesburg: Zabalaza Books, 2012.

Federici, Silvia. *Caliban and the Witch: Women, the Body and Primitive Accumulation.* Brooklyn: Autonomedia, 2004.

———. *Revolution at Point Zero: Housework, Reproduction, and Feminist Struggle.* Oakland: PM Press/Common Notions, 2010.

Fisher, Mark. *Capitalist Realism: Is There No Alternative?* Winchester, UK: O Books, 2009.

Fontenis, Georges. "Manifesto of Libertarian Communism." The Anarchist Library, 1953. https://theanarchistlibrary.org/library/georges-fontenis-manifesto-of-libertarian-communism.pdf.

Foran, John. *Taking Power: On the Origins of Third World Revolutions.* Cambridge: Cambridge University Press, 2007.

Foster, John Bellamy. "The Anthropocene Crisis." *Monthly Review* (blog), September 1, 2016. https://monthlyreview.org/2016/09/01/the-anthropocene-crisis/.

Freire, Paulo. *Pedagogy of the Oppressed.* New York: Continuum, 2000.

Garner, Jason. *Goals and Means: Anarchism, Syndicalism, and Internationalism in the Origins of the Federación Anarquista Ibérica.* Oakland: AK Press, 2016.

Georgakas, Dan, and Marvin Surkin. *Detroit: I Do Mind Dying, A Study in Urban Revolution.* Boston: South End Press, 1998.

Gerlach, Luther P. "The Structure of Social Movements: Environmental Activism and Its Opponents." In *Networks and Netwars: The Future of Terror, Crime, and Militancy,* edited by John Arquilla and David Ronfeldt, 289–310. Santa Monica, CA: RAND, 2001.

Gilbert, David. *Love and Struggle: My Life in SDS, the Weather Underground, and Beyond.* Oakland: PM Press, 2012.

Gilbert, Jeremy. "Psychedelic Socialism: The Politics of Consciousness, the Legacy of the Counterculture and the Future of the Left," 2017. https://jeremygilbertwriting.files.wordpress.com/2017/09/psychedelic-socialism2.pdf.

Gilmore, Ruth Wilson. "Abolition Geography and the Problem of Innocence." In *Futures of Black Radicalism*, edited by Gaye Theresa Johnson and Alex Lubin, 225–40. London: Verso, 2017.

Giron, Malena. "Breaking Down Barriers in Ideas and Practice." In *A Dream Compels Us: Voices of Salvadoran Women*, edited by New Americas Press, 93–96. Boston: South End Press, 1989.

Glaberman, Martin. "Black Cats, White Cats, Wildcats: Auto Workers in Detroit, 1969." Libcom, July 25, 2005. https://libcom.org/library/black-cats-white-cats-wildcats-martin-glaberman.

Gluckstein, Donny. "The Missing Party (1984)." Marxists Internet Archive. https://www.marxists.org/history/etol/writers/gluckstein/1984/xx/missing.html.

Goff, Stan. *Full Spectrum Disorder: The Military in the New American Century*. Brooklyn: Soft Skull Press, 2004.

Goldstein, Jesse. *Planetary Improvement: Cleantech Entrepreneurship and the Contradictions of Green Capitalism*. Cambridge: MIT Press, 2018.

Gorz, André. *Ecology as Politics*. Boston: South End Press, 1980.

———. *Socialism and Revolution*. London: Allen Lane, 1975.

Gramsci, Antonio. *Selections from the Prison Notebooks*. New York: International Publishers, 1971.

———. "Workers' Democracy (1919)." Marxists Internet Archive. https://www.marxists.org/archive/gramsci/1919/06/workers-democracy.htm.

Grenier, Yvon. "Understanding the FMLN: A Glossary of Five Words." *Conflict Quarterly* 11, no. 2 (1991).

Griffiths, K.D., and J.J. Gleeson. "Kinderkommunismus: A Feminist Analysis of the Twenty-First Century Family and a Communist Proposal for Its Abolition." *Ritual*, June 21, 2015. http://www.ritual-mag.com/kinderkommunismus/.

Gruppe Internationaler Kommunisten (GIK). "Fundamental Principles of Communist Production and Distribution." 1930. Reprint, Libcom, July 25, 2005. https://libcom.org/library/fundamental-principles-communist-production-gik.

Guevara, Che. "Socialism and Man in Cuba." In *Global Justice: Liberation and Socialism*, edited by María del Carmen Ariet García, 29–46. Melbourne: Ocean Press, 2002.

Guillamón, Agustín. "The Theorization of Historical Experiences." Libcom, November 28, 2013. https://libcom.org/history/theorization-historical-experiences-agust.

Hahnel, Robin. *Of The People, By The People: The Case for a Participatory Economy*. London: Soapbox Press, 2012.

———. *The ABCs of Political Economy: A Modern Approach*. London: Pluto Press, 2002.

Haider, Asad. *Mistaken Identity: Race and Class in the Age of Trump*. London: Verso, 2018.

———. "Socialists Think." *Viewpoint Magazine*, September 24, 2018. https://www.viewpointmag.com/2018/09/24/socialists-think/.

Hansen, Bue Rübner. "Surplus Population, Social Reproduction, and the Problem of Class Formation." *Viewpoint Magazine*, October 31, 2015. https://www.viewpointmag.com/2015/10/31/surplus-populatio n-social-reproduction-and-the-problem-of-class-formation/.

Haraway, Donna. *Manifestly Haraway*. Minneapolis: University of Minnesota Press, 2016.

———. *Simians, Cyborgs, and Women: The Reinvention of Nature*. New York: Routledge, 1991.

———. "Anthropocene, Capitalocene, Plantationocene, Cthulucene: Making Kin." *Environmental Humanities* 6, (2015): 159–165.

Harding, Sandra. *Objectivity and Diversity: Another Logic of Scientific Research*. Chicago: University of Chicago Press, 2015.

Hardt, Michael. "The Common in Communism." In *The Idea of Communism*, edited by Costas Douzinas and Slavoj Žižek, 131–44. New York: Verso, 2010.

Hardt, Michael, and Antonio Negri. *Assembly*. New York: Oxford University Press, 2017.

———. *Empire*. Cambridge: Harvard University Press, 2000.

———. *Multitude: War and Democracy in the Age of Empire*. New York: Penguin Books, 2004.

Harnecker, Marta. *Rebuilding the Left*. London: Zed Books, 2007.

———. *A World to Build: New Paths Toward Twenty-First Century Socialism*. New York: Monthly Review Press, 2015.

Harney, Stefano, and Fred Moten. *The Undercommons: Fugitive Planning and Black Study*. New York: Minor Compositions, 2013.

Harrison, Scott. *The Mass Line and the American Revolutionary Movement*. Massline.info, 2010. http://massline.info/mlms/mlms.htm.

Harvey, David. *Spaces of Hope*. Berkeley: University of California Press, 2000.

———. *The Enigma of Capital and the Crises of Capitalism*. Oxford: Oxford University Press, 2011.

Haywood, Harry. "We Have Taken the First Step on a Long March (1977)." *Marxists Internet Archive*. https://www.marxists.org/history/erol/ncm-3/haywood-1st.html/.

Heckman, Jesse. "The Agricultural Workers Organization." *Kansas City Labor History*, 2004. http://cas2.umkc.edu/labor-ed/documents/AgrWorkersOrganizationIWW.pdf.

Hinton, William. *Turning Point in China: An Essay on the Cultural*

Revolution. New York: Monthly Review Press, 1972.

Hoffman, Marcelo. *Militant Acts: The Role of Investigations in Radical Political Struggles*. Albany: State University of New York Press, 2019.

Holman, Christopher. "The Councils as Ontological Form: Cornelius Castoriadis and the Autonomous Potential of Council Democracy." In *Council Democracy: Towards a Democratic Socialist Politics*, edited by James Muldoon, 131–49. New York: Routledge, 2018.

Hudis, Peter. "Rethinking the Idea of Revolution." Herramienta, 2003. https://www.herramienta.com.ar/articulo.php?id=78.

———. "The Vision of the New Society in Marx's *Capital*." *Logos Journal*, 2018. http://logosjournal.com/2018/the-vision-of-the-new-societ y-in-marxs-capital/.

Illich, Ivan. *Tools for Conviviality*. London: Marion Boyars, 2009.

Jackson, George. *Soledad Brother: The Prison Letters of George Jackson*. Chicago: Lawrence Hill Books, 1994.

Johnson, Elizabeth R, and Jesse Goldstein. "Biomimetic Futures: Life, Death, and the Enclosure of a More-than-Human Intellect." *Annals of the Association of American Geographers* 105, no. 2 (2015): 387–96.

Jonas, Susanna. *The Battle for Guatemala: Rebels, Death Squads, and U.S.* Boulder, CO: Westview Press, 1991.

Kalisz, Teresa. "Rethinking Reforms." *Regeneration Magazine*, April 19, 2019. https://regenerationmag.org/rethinking-reforms/.

———. "Everyday Ruptures: Putting Basebuilding on a Revolutionary Path." *The Left Wind*, April 24, 2020. https://theleftwind.wordpress. com/2020/04/24/everyday-ruptures-putting-basebuilding-on-a-revolutio nary-path/.

Kaplan, David. "The Chicago Teachers' Strike and Beyond: Strategic Considerations." Solidarity: A Socialist, Feminist, Anti-Racist Organization, June 21, 2013. https://solidarity-us.org/ the_ctu_strike_and_beyond/.

Karatzogianni, Athina, and Andrew Robinson. *Power, Resistance and Conflict in the Contemporary World: Social Movements, Networks and Hierarchies*. London: Routledge, 2012.

Karni, Annie. "Facebook Removes Trump Ads Displaying Symbol Used by Nazis." *The New York Times*, June 18, 2020. https://www.nytimes. com/2020/06/18/us/politics/facebook-trump-ads-antifa-red-triangle. html.

Katsiaficas, George. *The Imagination of the New Left: A Global Analysis of 1968*. Boston: South End Press, 1987.

Katsiaficas, Georgy. *The Subversion of Politics: European Autonomous Social Movements and the Decolonization of Everyday Life*. Oakland: AK Press, 2006.

Kelley, Robin D.G. "The People in Me." *Utne Reader* September–October (1999).

———. "The People in Me." *Colorlines* September-October (1999).

Knapp, Michael, Anja Flach, and Ercan Ayboga. *Revolution in Rojava: Democratic Autonomy and Women's Liberation in Syrian Kurdistan.* Translated by Janet Biehl. London: Pluto Press, 2016.

Kollontai, Alexandra. *Selected Writings of Alexandra Kollontai.* New York: W. W. Norton & Company, 1977.

Korsch, Karl. "Ten Theses on Marxism Today (1950)" Marxists Internet Archive. https://www.marxists.org/archive/korsch/1950/ten-theses.htm.

Kropotkin, Peter. *The Conquest of Bread.* Oakland: AK Press, 2007.

Kuhn, Gabriel. *Antifascism, Sports, Sobriety: Forgin a Militant Woking-Class Culture, Selected Writings by Julius Deutsch.* Oakland: PM Press, 2017.

———. "Oppressor and Oppressed Nations: Sketching a Taxonomy of Imperialism." Kersplebedeb (blog), June 15, 2017. http://kersplebedeb. com/posts/oppressor-and-oppressed-nations/.

———. "Don't Mourn, Organize! Is Communism a Pipe Dream—or a Viable Future?" *Brooklyn Rail* (blog), March 2018. https://brooklynrail. org/2018/03/field-notes/Dont-Morn-Organize-Is-Commun ism-a-Pipe-Dreamor-a-Viable-Future.

Landauer, Gustav. "Weak Statesmen, Weaker People!" In *Revolution and Other Writings: A Political Reader*, edited by Gabriel Kuhn, 213–14. Oakland: PM Press, 2010.

Lauesen, Torkil. *The Global Perspective: Reflections on Imperialism and Resistance.* Translated by Gabriel Kuhn. English translation edition. Montreal, Quebec: Kersplebedeb, 2018.

Lenin, V.I. *'Left-Wing' Communism, An Infantile Disorder.* Peking: Foreign Languages Press, 1970.

———. "Lessons of the Crisis (1917." Marxists Internet Archive. https:// www.marxists.org/archive/lenin/works/1917/apr/22b.htm.

Lih, Lars T. *Lenin Rediscovered: 'What Is to Be Done?' In Context.* Chicago: Haymarket Books, 2008.

Löwy, Michael. *Ecosocialism: A Radical Alternative to Capitalist Catastrophe.* Chicago: Haymarket Books, 2015.

———. *Morning Star: Surrealism, Marxism, Anarchism, Situationism, Utopia.* Austin: University of Texas Press, 2009.

Luxemburg, Rosa. "The Russian Revolution." In *The Rosa Luxemburg Reader*, edited by Peter Hudis and Kevin B. Anderson, 281–310. New York: Monthly Review Press, 2004.

———. "What Does the Spartacus League Want?" In *The Rosa Luxemburg Reader*, edited by Peter Hudis and Kevin B. Anderson, 349–56. New York: Monthly Review Press, 2004.

Lyons, Matthew. "Is the Bush Administration Fascist?" *New Politics* 11, no. 2 (2007). http://newpol.org/content/bush-administration-fascist.

———. "Two Ways of Looking at Fascism." *Socialism and Democracy*, March 8, 2011. http://sdonline.org/47/two-ways-of-looking-at-fascism/.

Maccani, R.J. "Enter the Intergalactic: The Zapatistas' Sixth Declaration in the U.S. and the World." *Upping the Anti* 3 (October 26, 2009). http://uppingtheanti.org/journal/article/03-enter-the-intergalactic.

Malatesta, Errico. "A Project of Anarchist Organization (1927)." Marxists Internet Archive. https://marxists.architexturez.net/archive/malatesta/1927/10/project.htm.

Malcolm X. *Malcolm X Speaks*. New York: Grove Press, 1965.

Manifest-Kommunistisk Arbejdsgruppe (M-KA). "What Can Communists in the Imperialist Countries Do?" In *Turning Money into Rebellion: The Unlikely Story of Denmark's Revolutionary Bank Robbers*, edited by Gabriel Kuhn, 203–7. Oakland: PM Press, 2014.

Mann, Eric. *Playbook for Progressives: 16 Qualities of the Successful Organizer*. Boston: Beacon Press, 2011.

Mao Zedong. "On Contradiction (1937)." Marxists Internet Archive. https://www.marxists.org/reference/archive/mao/selected-works/volume-1/mswv1_17.htm.

———. "On the Correct Handling of Contradictions Among the People (1957)." Marxists Internet Archive. https://www.marxists.org/reference/archive/mao/selected-works/volume-5/mswv5_58.htm.

———. "Report on an Investigation of the Peasant Movement in Hunan (1927)." Marxists Internet Archive. https://www.marxists.org/reference/archive/mao/selected-works/volume-1/mswv1_2.htm.

Marcuse, Herbert. *An Essay on Liberation*. Boston: Beacon Press, 1969.

———. *Counterrevolution and Revolt*. Boston: Beacon Press, 1972.

———. *Eros and Civilization: A Philosophical Inquiry into Freud*. New York: Vintage Books, 1962.

Mariátegui, José Carlos. "Peru's Principal Problem." In *José Carlos Mariátegui: An Anthology*, edited by Harry E. Vanden and Marc Becker, 139–43. New York: Monthly Review Press, 2011.

———. "The United Front." *Cosmonaut* (blog), November 23, 2019. https://cosmonaut.blog/2019/11/23/the-united-front-by-jose-carlos-mariategui/.

Marighella, Carlos. *Mini-Manual of the Urban Guerrilla*. Montreal: Abraham Guillén Press & Arm The Spirit, 2002.

Marx, Karl. "A Contribution to the Critique of Hegel's Philosophy of Right (1843)." Marxists Internet Archive. https://www.marxists.org/archive/marx/works/1843/critique-hpr/intro.htm.

———. "A Worker's Inquiry (1880)." Marxists Internet Archive. https://www.marxists.org/archive/marx/works/1880/04/20.htm.

———. *Capital: A Critique of Political Economy, Volume I*. New York: Vintage Books, 1977.

———. *Capital: A Critique of Political Economy, Volume III*. New York: Penguin Books, 1991.

———. *Grundrisse: Foundations of the Critique of Political Economy*. London: Penguin Books, 2005.

———. "Marx to Dr. Kugelmann Concerning the Paris Commune (1871)." Marxists Internet Archive. https://www.marxists.org/archive/marx/works/1871/letters/71_04_12.htm.

———. *The First International and After*. London: Verso, 2010.

Marx, Karl, and Frederick Engels. *The Communist Manifesto*. New York: International Publishers, 1948.

———. *The German Ideology*. New York: International Publishers, 2007.

Maturana, Humberto, and Francisco Varela. *The Tree of Knowledge: The Biological Roots of Human Understanding*. Boston: New Science Library, 1988.

Maturana, Humberto, and Gerda Verden-Zöller. *The Origins of Humanness in the Biology of Love*. Charlottesville, Virginia: Imprint Academic, 2008.

McClintock, Cynthia. *Revolutionary Movements in Latin America*. Washington, DC: United States Institute of Peace, 1998.

McNally, David. *Global Slump: The Economics and Politics of Crisis and Resistance*. Oakland: PM Press, 2011.

Mehr, Nathaniel. "Reaction and Slaughter: Indonesia 1965-66." In *Arms and the People: Popular Movements and the Military from the Paris Commune to the Arab Spring*, edited by Mike Gonzalez and Houman Barekat, 232–50. London: Pluto Press, 2013.

Midnight Notes. *Midnight Oil: Work, Energy, War, 1973–1992*. Brooklyn: Autonomedia, 1992.

Mies, Maria. *Patriarchy and Accumulation on a World Scale: Women in the International Division of Labor*. London: Zed Books, 1998.

Mignolo, Walter. "On Pluriversality," 2013. http://waltermignolo.com/on-pluriversality/.

Miller, Ron. *What Are Schools For? Holistic Education in American Culture*. Brandon, Vermont: Holistic Education Press, 1990.

Mills, C. Wright. *The Power Elite*. Oxford: Oxford University Press, 2000.

Mohandesi, Salar. "All Tomorrow's Parties: A Reply to Critics," May 23, 2012. https://www.viewpointmag.com/2012/05/23/all-tomorrows-parties-a-reply-to-critics/.

Molina, Marta Malo. "Common Notions, Part 1: Workers' Inquiry, Co-Research, Consciousness-Raising." European Institute for Progressive Cultural Policies, 2004. https://eipcp.net/transversal/0406/malo/en.html.

———. "Common Notions, Part 2: Institutional Analysis, Participatory Action-Research, Militant Research." European Institute for Progressive Cultural Policies, 2004. http://eipcp.net/transversal/0707/malo/en.

Moore, Jason W. *Capitalism in the Web of Life: Ecology and the Accumulation of Capital*. London: Verso, 2015.

———. "Name the System! Anthropocenes and the Capitalocene Alternative," October 9, 2016. https://jasonwmoore.wordpress.com/2016/10/09/name-the-system-anthropocene

s-the-capitalocene-alternative/.

Moufawad-Paul, J. *Continuity and Rupture: Philosophy in the Maoist Terrain*. Winchester, UK: Zero Books, 2016.

———. "The Austerity Apparatus: Some Preliminary Notes." *Arsenal: Theoretical Journal of the PCR-RCP*, no. 9 (September 2017): 163–88.

Moulier, Yann. "Introduction." In *The Politics of Subversion: A Manifesto for the Twenty-First Century*, edited by Antonio Negri, 1–44. Cambridge: Polity Press, 1989.

Muntaqim, Jalil A. *We Are Our Own Liberators: Selected Prison Writings*. Portland: Arissa Media Group, 2010.

Neel, Phil A. *Hinterland: America's New Landscape of Class and Conflict*. London: Reaktion Books, 2018.

Negri, Antonio. *Factory of Strategy: 33 Lessons on Lenin*. New York: Columbia University Press, 2014.

———. *Marx Beyond Marx: Lessons on the Grundrisse*. Brooklyn: Autonomedia, 1991.

Neill, A.S. *Summerhill: A Radical Approach to Child Rearing*. New York: Wallaby, 1977.

Nettl, Peter. "The German Social Democratic Party 1890-1914 as a Political Model." *Past and Present*, no. 30 (1965): 65–95.

Newton, Huey P. "Intercommunalism (1974)." *Viewpoint Magazine*, June 11, 2018. https://www.viewpointmag.com/2018/06/11/intercommunalism-1974/.

———. "Speech Delivered at Bothon College: November 18, 1970." In *The Huey P. Newton Reader*, edited by David Hilliard and Donald Weise, 160–75. New York: Seven Stories Press, 2002.

———. "Uniting Against a Common Enemy: October 23, 1971." In *The Huey P. Newton Reader*, edited by David Hilliard and Donald Weise, 234–40. New York: Seven Stories Press, 2002.

Nicholson, Simon. "Children as Planners." In *The Children's Rights Movement: Overcoming the Oppression of Young People*, edited by Beatrice Gross and Ronald Gross, 287–95. Garden City, New York: Anchor Books, 1977.

Nunes, Rodrigo. "Notes Toward a Rethinking of the Militant." In *Communism in the 21st Century*, edited by Shannon Brincat, 3:163–87. Santa Barbara, California: Praeger, 2014.

———. *Organisation of the Organisationless: Collective Action After Networks*. Post-Media Lab and Mute Books, 2014.

O'Brien, M.E. "Communizing Care." *Pinko*, October 15, 2019. https://pinko.online/pinko-1/communizing-care.

Out of the Woods Collective. *Hope Against Hope: Writings on Ecological Crisis*. Brooklyn: Common Notions, 2020.

Pannekoek, Anton. *Workers' Councils*. Oakland: AK Press, 2003.

Paolucci, Paul. *Marx's Scientific Dialectics: A Methodological Treatise for a New Century*. Chicago: Haymarket Books, 2009.

Parenti, Christian. *Tropic of Chaos: Climate Change and the New Geography of Violence*. New York: Nation Books, 2011.

Payne, Charles M. *I've Got the Light of Freedom: The Organizing Tradition and the Mississippi Freedom Struggle*. Berkeley: University of California Press, 1996.

Petras, James F. *Critical Perspectives on Imperialism and Social Class in the Third World*. New York: Monthly Review Press, 1978.

Pizzolato, Nicola. *Challenging Global Capitalism: Labor Migration, Radical Struggle, and Urban Change in Detroit and Turin*. New York: Palgrave Macmillan, 2013.

Podur, Justin. "Polyculturalism and Self-Determination." *Znet* (blog), July 15, 2009. https://zcomm.org/znetarticle/polyculturalism-and-self-determination-by-justin-podur/.

Porcaro, Mimmo. "A Number of Possible Developments of the Idea of Connective Party." *Transform!*, 2011. https://www.transform-network.net/uploads/tx_news/Porcaro_Sviluppi_final.pdf.

———. "Occupy Lenin." *Socialist Register 2013: The Question of Strategy* 49 (2013).

Postone, Moishe. "Anti-Semitism and National Socialism." *New German Critique* 19, no. 1 (1980): 97–115.

———. *Time, Labor, and Social Domination: A Reinterpretation of Marx's Critical Theory*. Cambridge: Cambridge University Press, 1996.

Poulantzas, Nikos. *State, Power, Socialism*. London: Verso, 2014.

Rajendran, Manju. "Revolutionary Work in Our Time: Can't Keep Quiet, This Time Gon' Be More Than a Riot." *Left Turn* (blog), June 1, 2010. http://www.leftturn.org/revolutionary-work-our-time-gonna-be-more-riot.

Ranney, David. *Living and Dying on the Factory Floor: From the Outside In and the Inside Out*. Oakland: PM Press, 2019.

Ransby, Barbara. *Ella Baker and the Black Freedom Movement: A Radical Democratic Vision*. Chapel Hill: The University of North Carolina Press, 2003.

Reich, Wilhelm. *The Mass Psychology of Fascism*. New York: Orgone Institute Press, 1946.

Rénique, Gerardo, and Deborah Poole. "The Oaxaca Commune: Struggling for Autonomy and Dignity," 2008. https://nacla.org/article/oaxaca-commune-struggling-autonomy-and-dignity.

Rocker, Rudolf. *Anarcho-Syndicalism: Theory and Practice*. Oxford: AK Press, 2004.

Roggero, Gigi. "Notes on Framing and Re-Inventing Co-Research." *Ephemera* 14, no. 3 (2014): 511–19.

Ronfeldt, David. *The Zapatista Social Netwar in Mexico*. Santa Monica, CA: RAND, 1998.

Rosales, Jose. "What Would It Mean to Love as a Communist? To Love as a Comrade?" *The Tragic Community* (blog), October 6, 2017. https://

thetragiccommunity.wordpress.com/2017/10/06/what-would-it-mea
n-to-love-as-a-communist-to-love-as-a-comrade/.

Ross, Kristin. *May '68 and Its Afterlives*. Chicago: University of Chicago
Press, 2002.

Rowbotham, Sheila. "The Women's Movement and Organizing for
Socialism." In *Beyond the Fragments: Feminism and the Making of
Socialism*, edited by Sheila Rowbotham, Lynne Segal, and Hilary
Wainwright, 21–155. Boston: Alyson Publications, Inc, 1981.

———. *Women, Resistance and Revolution*. Middlesex: Penguin Books,
1974.

Sadler, Simon. "The Dome and the Shack: The Dialectics of Hippie
Enlightenment." In *West of Eden: Communes and Utopia in Northern
California*, edited by Iain Boal, Janferie Stone, Michael Watts, and Cal
Winslow, 72–81. Oakland: PM Press, 2012.

Sakai, J. "The Shock of Recognition: Looking at Hamerquist's Fascism
and Anti-Fascism." In *Confronting Fascism: Discussion Documents for a
Militant Movement*, edited by Don Hamerquist, J. Sakai, Anti-Racist
Action Chicago, and Mark Salotte, 71–155. Chicago Anti-Racist
Action, Arsenal Magazine, and Kersplebedeb, 2002.

Santucho, Mario Roberto. *Argentina: Bourgeois Power, Revolutionary
Power*. Oakland: Resistance Publications, 1976.

Sayles, James Yaki. *Meditations on Frantz Fanon's Wretched of the Earth:
New Afrikan Revolutionary Writings*. Montreal: Kersplebedeb, 2010.

Schlotterbeck, Marian E. "Everyday Revolutions: Grassroots Movements,
the Revolutionary Left (MIR), and the Making of Socialism in
Concepción, Chile, 1964-1973." Yale University, Faculty of the
Graduate School, 2013.

Scott, James C. *Domination and the Arts of Resistance: Hidden Transcripts*.
New Haven: Yale University Press, 1990.

Sears, Alan. *The Next New Left: A History of the Future*. Winnipeg:
Fernwood Publishing, 2014.

Serge, Victor. *Revolution in Danger: Writings from Russia 1919-1921*.
Chicago: Haymarket Books, 2011.

Shalom, Stephen R. "ParPolity: Political Vision for a Good Society," *Znet*.
2005/2011.

Sharkey, Paul. *The Federacion Anarquista Uruguaya (FAU): Crisis, Armed
Struggle and Dictatorship, 1967–1985*. London: Kate Sharpley Library,
2009.

Simpson, Leanne Betasamosake. *As We Have Always Done: Indigenous
Freedom Through Radical Resistance*. Minneapolis: University of
Minnesota Press, 2017.

———. *Dancing On Our Turtle's Back: Stories of Nishnaabeg Re-Creation,
Resurgence, and a New Emergence*. Winnipeg: Arbeiter Ring, 2011.

Sojourner Truth Organization (STO). "Mass Organization in the
Workplace." Sojourner Truth Organization Electronic Archive, 1972.

http://sojournertruth.net/massorganization.html.

Stackelberg, Roderick. *Hitler's Germany: Origins, Interpretations, Legacies.* London: Routledge, 2009.

Staudenmaier, Michael. *Truth and Revolution: A History of the Sojourner Truth Organization, 1969-1986.* Oakland: AK Press, 2012.

Subcomandante Insurgente Marcos. "Fourth Declaration of the Lacandon Jungle." In *Our Word Is Our Weapon: Selected Writings,* edited by Juana Ponce León, 78–81. New York: Seven Stories Press, 2002.

Sustar, Lee. "Uprising of the Black Autoworkers." *Socialist Worker* (blog), March 1, 2013. https://socialistworker.org/2013/03/01/uprising-of-the-black-autoworkers.

Swyngedouw, Erik. "The Marxian Alternative: Historical-Geographical Materialism and the Political Economy of Capitalism." In *A Companion to Economic Geography,* edited by Eric Sheppard and Trevor J. Barnes, 41–59. Malden, MA: Blackwell Publishing, 2000.

Symbiosis Research Collective. "'Dark Municipalism'—The Danger of Local Politics." *The Ecologist* (blog), June 26, 2018. https://theecologist.org/2018/jun/26/dark-municipalism-dangers-local-politics.

Thoburn, Nicholas. "The Hobo Anomalous: Class, Minorities and Political Invention in the Industrial Workers of the World." *Social Movement Studies* 2, no. 1 (2003): 61–84.

Tomba, Massimiliano. *Insurgent Universality: An Alternative Legacy of Modernity.* New York: Oxford University Press, 2019.

———. "The Open Secret of Real Abstraction." *Rethinking Marxism* 20, no. 2 (2008): 273–87.

Trenkle, Norbert. "Value and Crisis: Basic Questions." In *Marxism and the Critique of Value,* edited by Neil Larsen, Mathias Nilges, Josh Robinson, and Nicholas Brown, 1–15. Chicago: M-C-M' Publishing, 2014.

Tronti, Mario. *Workers and Capital.* London: Verso, 2019.

Trotsky, Leon. *History of the Russian Revolution.* Chicago: Haymarket Books, 2008.

———. "Our Political Tasks (1904)." Marxists Internet Archive. https://www.marxists.org/archive/trotsky/1904/tasks/.

L'Union des communistes de France marxiste-léniniste. *Le livre des paysans pauvres: 5 années de travail maoïste dans une campagne française.* Paris: François Maspero, 1976.

L'Union des Communistes de France marxiste-léniniste. "l'UCFML: une organisation révolutionnaire marxiste-léniniste-maoïste." In *Le Marxiste-Léniniste: Journal Central de l'UCFML,* no. 18/19, July-August 1977.

Unity and Struggle. "The Communist Theory of Marx." *Unity and Struggle* (blog), November 2, 2012. http://unityandstruggle.org/2012/11/02/the-communist-theory-of-marx/.

Vansintjan, Aaron. "The Anthropocene Debate." *Uneven Earth*

(blog), June 16, 2015. http://unevenearth.org/2015/06/
the-anthropocene-debate/.

Vasquez, Delio. "Intercommunalism: The Late Theorizations of Huey
P. Newton, 'Chief Theoretician' of the Black Panther Party." *Viewpoint
Magazine*, June 11, 2018. https://www.viewpointmag.com/2018/06/11/
intercommunalism-the-late-theorizations-of-huey-p-newton-
chief-theoretician-of-the-black-panther-party/.

Vergès, Françoise. "Racial Capitalocene." In *Futures of Black Radicalism*, edited
by Gaye Theresa Johnson and Alex Lubin, 72–82. London: Verso, 2017.

Vernadsky, Vladimir I. "The Biosphere and the Noösphere." *American
Scientist* 33, no. 1 (January 1945): 1-12.

———. *The Biosphere*. New York: Copernicus Books, 1998.

Virno, Paolo. *A Grammar of the Multitude*. Los Angeles: Semiotext(e), 2004.

Wallerstein, Immanuel. *World-Systems Analysis: An Introduction*. Durham:
Duke University Press, 2004.

Wark, McKenzie. *Molecular Red: Theory for the Anthropocene*. London:
Verso, 2016.

Watson, John. *To the Point... of Production: An Interview with John Watson*.
Detroit, MI: Radical Education Project, 1969.

Wetzel, Tom. "Why Revolutionary Syndicalism?" *Ideas and Action*
(blog), October 31, 2012. http://ideasandaction.info/2012/10/
why-revolutionary-syndicalism-2/.

White, James D. *Red Hamlet: The Life and Ideas of Alexander Bogdanov*.
Leiden: Brill, 2019.

Williams, Evan Calder. "Invisible Organization: Reading Romano
Alquati." *Viewpoint Magazine*, 2013. https://www.viewpointmag.
com/2013/09/26/invisible-organization-reading-romano-alquati/.

Wilson, Alex, and Praba Pilar. "Grounding the Currents of Indigenous
Resistance." *ROAR Magazine*, January 16, 2018. https://roarmag.org/
essays/indigenous-peoples-resistance-americas/.

Wobblyist Writing Group. "Wobblyism: Revolutionary
Unionism for Today." Libcom, 2013. http://libcom.org/library/
wobblyism-revolutionary-unionism-today.

Wright, Steve. *Storming Heaven: Class Composition and Struggle in Italian
Autonomist Marxism*. London: Pluto Press, 2002.

Wynter, Sylvia, and Katherine McKittrick. "Unparalleled Catastrophe
for Our Species? Or, to Give Humanness a Different Future:
Conversations." In *Sylvia Wynter: On Being Human as Praxis*, edited by
Katherine McKittrick, 9–89. Durham: Duke University Press, 2015.

Zibechi, Raúl. *Territories in Resistance: A Cartography of Latin American
Social Movements*. Oakland: AK Press, 2012.

———. "Counter-Power and Self-Defense in Latin America."
ROAR Magazine, January 29, 2018. https://roarmag.org/essays/
raul-zibechi-counterpower-self-defense/.

Index

popular social groups, 12
Porcaro, Mimmo, 144
Portugal, 54
Potere Operaio, 160
proletariat, 9–12, 24, 43
  internal stratification, 9–10
  standpoint of, 9–10
Proletkult, 192
protracted revolutionary struggle,
  141–142, 186–203
  phases of, 188–199
Puerto Rico, 55

R
reductionism, 23–25, 30, 42
  economism, 24–25, 74
Reich, Wilhelm, 33–34
revolutionary people, 11–12, 18,
  21, 109, 141–142, 170, 181,
  191, 194, 196, 198, 201
  social bloc of the oppressed,
  11–12
revolutionary situations, 67–70
revolutionary subject, 9–12
Robles, Carlos, 170
Rojava. *See* Kurdish Freedom
  Movement
Russia, 68, 145,
Russian Revolution of 1917, 68,
  138, 164,

S
Salvadoran Revolution and Civil
  War, 154–155, 179
Santucho, Mario Roberto, 193
Schlotterbeck, Marian, 169
science, 12–45
  Marx and, 12–14
  and objectivity, 17–18, 22
  partisan social science, 12–14
  radical social science, 12–13
  science for the people, 14
  world of sciences, 13, 21–22, 23–24
  See also standpoint
Scott, James C., 18
Sears, Alan, 188

Shanghai Commune of 1967, 193
Simpson, Leanne Betasamosake, 75
Sindicato Nacional de Trabajadores
  de la Educación (SNTE), 183
social investigation, 13, 14–21, 43,
  48, 81, 144, 188–189, 205, 207
  in communist society, 131
  as dialogic process, 18–19, 21, 171
  historical background, 15–16
  as "hot investigation," 17–18
  and "infrapolitics," 18
  methods of, 18–21
  and operational planning, 187
  and parties of autonomy, 163,
  165, 170, 172, 173
socialism, 6, 53, 136
  See also communism
social reproduction, 35–36
Sojourner Truth Organization
  (STO), 158
South Africa, 55, 133
South Chicago Workers' Rights
  Center, 158
Soviet Union, 44, 192
Spain, 54, 156, 157, 159, 167
  Barcelona, 156
Spanish Revolution and Civil War,
  156, 168
spheres of social activity. *See*
  complementary holism
standpoint, 9–12, 21–22
Sudan, 69
Suharto, 160
Sun Ra, 90
surrealism, 89–90
Sustar, Lee, 154
Swyngedouw, Erik, 27
system of counterpower, 21, 143–
  145, 159, 161, 162, 163, 165,
  167, 170, 175, 180, 181–186
  in Oaxaca (Mexico), 183–186

T
tektology, 4–5
Texas, 149
Tomba, Massimiliano, 5

About Common Notions

Common Notions is a publishing house and programming platform that advances new formulations of liberation and living autonomy. Our books provide timely reflections, clear critiques, and inspiring strategies that amplify movements for social justice.

By any media necessary, we seek to nourish the imagination and generalize common notions about the creation of other worlds beyond state and capital. Our publications trace a constellation of critical and visionary meditations on the organization of freedom. Inspired by various traditions of autonomism and liberation—in the United States and internationally, historically and emerging from contemporary movements—our publications provide resources for a collective reading of struggles past, present, and to come.

Common Notions regularly collaborates with editorial houses, political collectives, militant authors, and visionary designers around the world. Our political and aesthetic interventions are dreamt and realized in collaboration with Antumbra Designs.

commonnotions.org | info@commonnotions.org

Become a Sustainer

These are decisive times, ripe with challenges and possibility, heartache and beautiful inspiration. More than ever, we are in need of timely reflections, clear critiques, and inspiring strategies that can help movements for social justice grow and transform society. Help us amplify those necessary words, deeds, and dreams that our liberation movements and our worlds so need.

Movements are sustained by people like you, whose fugitive words, deeds, and dreams bend against the world of domination and exploitation.

For collective imagination, dedicated practices of love and study, and organized acts of freedom.

By any media necessary.
With your love and support.

Monthly sustainers start at $10 and $25.

Join us at commonnotions.org/sustain.